THE ULTIMATE NEW EMPLOYEE SURVIVAL GUIDE

ED HOLTON

PETERSON'S
Princeton, New Jersey

About Peterson's

Peterson's is the country's largest educational information/communications company, providing the academic, consumer, and professional communities with books, software, and online services in support of lifelong education access and career choice. Well-known references include Peterson's annual guides to private schools, summer programs, colleges and universities, graduate and professional programs, financial aid, international study, adult learning, and career guidance. Peterson's Web site at petersons.com is the only comprehensive—and most heavily traveled—education resource on the Internet. The site carries all of Peterson's fully searchable major databases and includes financial aid sources, test-prep help, job postings, direct inquiry and application features, and specially created Virtual Campuses for every accredited academic institution and summer program in the U.S. and Canada that offers in-depth narratives, announcements, and multimedia features.

Visit Peterson's Education Center on the Internet (World Wide Web) at www.petersons.com

Library of Congress Cataloging-in-Publication Data

Holton, Ed, 1957–
    The ultimate new employee survival guide / Ed Holton.
        p.   cm.
    Includes index.
    ISBN 1-56079-979-X
    1. Vocational guidance. 2. College graduates—Employment.
3. Employee orientation. I. Title.
HF5381.A2H65 1998
650.1—dc21
                                         98-11400
                                           CIP

Composition and design by Peterson's

Printed in the United States of America

10 9 8 7 6 5 4 3 2 1

CONTENTS

· ·

PREFACE

The colleges and universities of this country award bachelor's and master's degrees each year to hundreds of thousands of students, many of whom go on to make one of the biggest transitions of their adult life: going to work. Often this is an extremely difficult process for which they have little preparation and about which they have little information. It is a time of dramatic change in their personal life and the beginning of a whole new chapter, the development of a professional career. It is a time of great excitement, anxiety, challenge, and accomplishment. As with any major transition in life, it is important that a person negotiate this transition successfully to continue with a happy and growing life. Yet very little is done to prepare students for the transition.

Employers say that the success with which graduates negotiate the transition is critical to their success within the company, as well as their satisfaction with their new career. They also say that they wish students knew more about the "real world" before they came to work. Employers who recognize the importance of a good transition are devoting considerable effort to their employee orientation programs. Most significantly, they are devoting a lot of time to non-task-related training to help employees make a smooth transition to professional life and a strong start. Why? Because these employers know that the first year is when new employees must establish their credibility as professionals. They know that the new employee's actions and performance can shape his or her entire career. They know that by teaching newly hired employees some basic breaking-in skills they can significantly improve career satisfaction, increase productivity, and, of course, reduce new employee turnover.

Yet there is little information available to help recent graduates, and what is available is restricted to bits and pieces. There are lots of books and materials to help students make a career choice and find a job. Similarly, there are lots of books and materials on climbing the professional ladder and managing a career. Many career books (including my own) have a chapter at the end with a few afterthoughts about going to work. Some of the "climbing the ladder" books begin with a little information on the employee's first year. Most, however, just seem to assume a successful transition and focus on those people who have already made a good start and are ready to climb. There is probably more treatment of the transition new employees go through from the employer's perspective, since it is an important and potentially costly organizational issue. However, this material is of little use to the individual experiencing the transition.

The impact of this problem on employers is significant, since the costs of turnover in the early years of an employee's career are very high due to the tremendous amount of time devoted to training in those years. It is estimated that between 50 and 80 percent of new college graduates leave their first job within the first three years. While a significant part of this is due to poor career planning and/or a bad job choice on the graduate's part, indications are that an equally significant part is due to problems associated with making the transition from school to work. Any effort to reduce those problems will have a direct bottom-line impact, because the evidence indicates that helping new employees make a smooth transition significantly reduces turnover.

In addition, there is the "hidden" cost of low productivity and/or low morale among new employees. While not so easy to quantify as turnover is, there is little doubt that new employees who are unhappy, disappointed, and frustrated in their job will not be as productive as they could be. In addition, unhappy employees affect the morale of everyone in the organization. Both cost money.

ABOUT THIS BOOK

It is to everyone's benefit that new employees get a fast and productive start in their new career. Yet how can we expect them to do that if we don't teach them? That is what this book is for. It is written for people who are starting their first full-time professional job; most readers will be recent college graduates. It is a handbook to help new professionals develop the foundations for career success and personal well-being as they go from student to professional and from college to work. Any undergraduate-degree holder with any major going to work in any type of organization will find it enormously

helpful. Graduate students who are starting their first job or have limited work experience will find it equally helpful. Other people who are just entering the professional workforce, no matter what their age or background, will find it valuable, too.

There are several things I hope to accomplish with this book. First, I believe that if you at least know what challenges to expect when you go to work, you will be much better prepared to deal with them. What I hear repeatedly from new college graduates is the shock they experience in their first job because they don't anticipate the changes—certainly not the hard ones. Experience has shown that a significant part of the difficulty is attributable solely to the shock of the unexpected changes, not the scope of the adjustments such changes require. Shock leads to confusion, bewilderment, and sometimes panic. A sense of aloneness often follows during these first few months on the job, as people keep their problems to themselves, thinking they are the only ones experiencing them. They begin to doubt themselves and are unable to focus on learning how to be a professional and adapt to their new organization.

Unfortunately, I cannot prevent you from having to face all the challenges. You are just going to have to live through them as with so many other things in life. But from this book you will learn that the difficulties and challenges are a normal part of a very normal transition in life. So that you can fully appreciate this and understand that others have been in this boat before, I interviewed more than 100 new hires and their managers for this book. As you read the new hires' words, you will learn firsthand what to expect, how bewildering these first-year changes seem, and what difficulties and challenges await you. Knowing what to expect, you can skip the bewilderment stage and move directly to meeting the challenges of the first year. With preparation, you will know that nothing is wrong with you or your skills, and you can relax and focus on getting a fast and successful start in your career.

Second, I want to help you do more than just react to the difficulties that come along. I want to motivate you to be proactive and take advantage of the tremendous opportunity that the first year at work offers. With a little coaching, you will be in a position to take control of your own career and plan a successful entry into your new organization. You can make a great transition that will get you on the success track early.

Third, I want to empower you to help yourself as you move into your career. I can't begin to provide precise answers to all the many dilemmas and situations you will encounter. There are so many different types of companies, careers, cultures, people, etc., that no one book can address each specifically. What this book will do is identify all the critical issues to which you should pay attention to ensure a successful transition. And it will teach you the resources to look for and the techniques you can use to find the right solution for you. You should consider this book a sort of compass to point you in the right direction to help you help yourself.

Finally, this book will help you avoid making some major mistakes that can create more problems for you. You will have enough challenges to deal with at your new job, so you don't need to make more of your own!

My recommendation is that you read this book as soon as you've accepted a job or at least two months before you graduate. Then I suggest that you review it every three months, starting the week before you go to work. You don't have to reread it completely but just scan it to remind yourself of the key points. Much happens in the first week and month, and a timely review can change the way you approach that very hectic and critical period. You may also want to make a copy of the Ultimate Survival Tips at the end of each chapter to keep as a quick reference and daily reminder.

In sum, the odds are very good that *The Ultimate New Employee Survival Guide* can help you enter an organization in a manner that allows you to stay calm and cope with challenges as they arise, know what the most critical elements of the transition are, take charge of starting your career, and avoid making major mistakes. That is a formula that means a fast start to your career!

Ed Holton

Acknowledgments

An author of a book of this type is indebted to many people; a project of this magnitude cannot be done alone. I am especially indebted because this book started with literally hundreds of hours of interviews and conversations with new hires, managers, and executives. NCNB Corporation (now Nations Bank), RJR-Nabisco, Andersen Consulting, DuPont, and C&P Telephone (a division of Bell Atlantic), in particular, provided extensive support for this project by arranging for me to spend time with many of their employees. They cannot be thanked enough. In addition, individuals from other companies, such as Meridian Bank, Texas Instruments, Corning Glass, Exxon, Secor Bank, Circuit City Stores, Hewlett-Packard, and J. P. Morgan, provided invaluable information and support over the years. Many thanks to the thousands of employers and graduates who have attended my training programs and workshops over the last ten years for the affirmation and for helping me refine my ideas. I have also been fortunate in having a core group of colleagues who have served as a sort of an "inner circle," patiently advising, reviewing manuscripts, counseling, and freely offering their time and creativity for little reward beyond a thank-you. They include Dr. Susan Taylor of the College of Business at the University of Maryland College Park; Rick Sanders of RJR-Nabisco; Barry O'Donnell, formerly with NCNB; Ed McGarrell of Corning Glass; and Richard A. Swanson at the University of Minnesota.

My other thank-yous may be traditional ones, but that does not mean they are felt any less deeply or sincerely. My loving wife, Karen, gave up many hours of our life together for this project; I am deeply grateful for her patience and encouragement. Above and beyond the call of duty, she also analyzed every hour of interview tape to obtain the quotes for this book. A special thanks, too, to Sharon Naquin, my trusted assistant who helped me make this book much better than the first!

Introduction

....

Each year, more than a million college students receive a bachelor's degree and begin their first full-time professional job. For most, it's a dream realized, the culmination of years of going to school; sweating over books, papers, and grades; and struggling to develop marketable skills. It's a true milestone!

At the same time, it's a major transition to an unfamiliar world filled with uncertainties, adjustments, and challenges. Breaking into a new career and company and becoming a professional is not easy, yet the success with which you negotiate your first year is crucial to getting a fast start in your career. This book teaches you how.

A UNIQUE CAREER STAGE

The first year in your career is critical—a unique time that requires special approaches and strategies to ensure success. Currently, the first year is a sort of no-man's-land, located somewhere between finding a job and climbing the career ladder. That makes it difficult to understand and negotiate successfully. What typically occurs is that new hires face a period of uncertainty and frustration until they get to the point where they can finally move ahead with their career.

What's needed is a recognition by employers and graduates that the first year on the job is a separate and distinct rung of the career ladder.

During the first year, you're not a college student anymore, but (this may surprise you) you haven't fully begun your career as a professional either. You are in a transitional stage that begins to make sense only if you understand that, contrary to popular belief, you don't "graduate from college and then go to work." What actually happens is that you graduate from college, go through a transition period, and only then do you really go to work.

New hires need to understand that a special game with its own rules is being played during this stage. People will respond to you, work with you, and judge you differently during your first year. You, in turn, will have to approach them differently. Only by learning special rules can you make a strong start toward the career that you want.

What typically happens, however, is that new hires play by one of the two sets of rules they know about: those for a college student or those for a full-fledged professional. They're familiar, of course, with the role of college student because they've been one. And they think they have a basic understanding of the full-fledged professional from the role models they've observed and their learning in school. (Later we'll see that their understanding of the professional role is usually inaccurate.) Thus, during the first year the following scenario typically plays itself out. The new hire either plays by the college rules for too long after starting work or begins behaving like a full-fledged professional too soon. Both are wrong strategies. You'll probably agree that college behavior is inappropriate for the new hire; but so is acting like a full-fledged professional. That's a little like getting your learner's permit before your driver's license; you may be behind the wheel and on the road, but you can't really drive yet. Until you're fully licensed, you have some special rules by which to live.

That's what this book is all about: getting your license to be a full-fledged professional. Think of it as a handbook for your first year. You'll learn why the first year is unique, what your major challenges are, how to use your rookie "license" to start your career, and how you can earn your "professional" license. It doesn't matter whether you want to get on the fast track or to proceed at a more moderate pace toward achieving your career goals. During your first year, the critical task is to build a foundation that will enable you to make this choice later on.

THE BIG CHANGE

I never really gave it much thought before I graduated. Going to work seemed like one of those natural things that just comes next in life. You know, you go to high school, graduate, fall in love, go to work, get married, and so on. It just seemed like something that was "supposed" to happen, so I always figured it would be pretty easy and pretty natural. Boy, was I wrong!

One thing is certain about the going-to-work process. It's a big change. You may not realize it, but leaving college and starting to work is one of the biggest and most important transitions you will make in your adult life. Many students overlook this and then suffer for it in their personal and professional lives.

Think back for a moment to the big changes you have made in your life. For example, do you remember going off to college? It was probably a great step for you, wasn't it? Do you remember the tremendous excitement and sense of anticipation you felt? It was great that you were now becoming an adult, maybe leaving home, finally to be "on your own." But do you also remember the adjustments you had to make? How different college was from high school? Think back to how strange you felt at first—maybe a little disoriented, confused, and puzzled by a new system and new ways of doing things. Remember how different the teachers were, how different their expectations of you were, how differently they approached classes, and how much work you had to do. Think of the many new people you had around you and how many new relationships you had to develop. If you traveled to a different city to go to school, do you remember how disoriented you felt just trying to order a pizza or shop for clothes? If you are like most people, this required a big adjustment. Sure it was great, fun, and exciting, but it was a big change in your life.

So, too, will be going to work. In fact, it will probably be a bigger change than you have ever experienced. The move to full-time employment will mean entering a world of professional work that is fundamentally different from the one in which you have been living up to now. Until now, your world has probably consisted largely of family life, education, and perhaps some part-time work. When you go to full-time work as a professional, you will be in an entirely different part of society. It will all be new and strange. People will talk and act differently and have different expectations, and you will experience new stresses, find new challenges and rewards. It will be unlike anything you have experienced before.

For the first time, you will be a professional and expected to act and perform accordingly at work. In only a few weeks you may have to magically transform yourself from a college senior to a professional. Have you thought about what that means? What is a professional anyway? How does a professional act, talk, socialize, and get along at work? How does this differ from the role of a student? Just as the world of work is totally different from anything you have experienced before, so, too, will be your role as a professional.

WHY WORRY ABOUT IT?

"Why should I worry about it?" you may ask. Well, for starters, the manner in which you enter a new organization and begin a new job has a major impact on your success within that organization. Much of your early career opportunity and success will be charted by the impressions you make and the perceptions people have of you in the early months on the job. Everyone will be watching, trying to answer questions like "Did we make a good decision?" "Does this person have potential?" "Is he or she smart, capable, etc.?"

Your challenge in these early months will be to establish yourself as a bright, capable, and valuable employee and to earn the respect of your colleagues. This is the time when you will

develop much of the professional credibility needed to carry you through the early years of your career. If you are successful in this, you will quickly be given opportunities to make a real contribution to the company and become visible to upper management. If you then take advantage of those opportunities by demonstrating what an outstanding performer you are, even more opportunities will follow, and your career will be off to a strong start.

The key is to come into an organization bringing enough real-world savvy to have appropriate expectations and attitudes, to know how to establish yourself, and to know what you need to do to impress people early. Mess up, and you may find yourself labeled "immature" and relegated to lesser assignments while your colleagues—and competitors for promotions, I might add—are busy impressing the boss with their success on juicy assignments. Do you really want to give your competitors a head start? That's not to say that an entire thirty-year career is made or broken in a few months' performance. However, the simple fact is that it can take years to recover from a poor start.

A poor start can also often mean changing jobs to get a fresh start. It is estimated that 50 percent of the new college graduates will change jobs in the first three years after graduation. That is alot of people who have to write résumés, hunt for jobs again, start over in a new organization (perhaps relocate), get to know new bosses, etc. Job hunting is not fun, nor is being unhappy at work and being forced to make a change. Sure, many people need to change because they made a bad job choice. Others just want to experiment more. But many people are forced to change because they didn't know how to break into a new organization and have to make a fresh start to get their career back on track.

If the professional reasons alone aren't enough to persuade you to read this book, then you should also realize that the transition to work has an equally large impact on your personal life. Periods of change and transition, even the good ones, are stressful and can have a significant impact on your happiness, health, and satisfaction with life. A change of this magnitude is often a very disorienting experience. Graduates report a sense of having everything familiar in life disappear, of getting lost in a maze of unfamiliar expectations in this strange new way of life. Scared that they can't succeed, they get confused and anxious. (Just living with the uncertainty of a new environment can be quite stressful enough.) The result is that, amid all the excitement and positive aspects of going to work, many students struggle through their first year lonely, confused, and unhappy simply because they weren't taught what to expect during the transition or how to manage it. Ignoring the importance and potential impact of the transition to professional life can quickly make you unhappy at work and significantly reduce your ability to enjoy your personal life. It is necessary for you to learn how to go to work, what becoming a professional means, and how to make the transition.

Unfortunately, most colleges and universities teach the basic skills you need to perform the tasks associated with your new job, but they do not have the time or resources to teach all you need to know about becoming a professional. Even worse, many of the behaviors you learned and were rewarded for in school will hurt you on the job. Company orientation programs often don't give you enough of what you need either. The really good news is that these things can be taught, and that is why this book was written.

THE NEW KID ON THE BLOCK

It sounds like stating the obvious when I tell you you're going to be the new kid on the block. It's hard to understate the importance of understanding how big a role being new plays in everything that happens during your first year. Most new hires I've talked to don't really enjoy the feeling of being new. That's OK because not many people are comfortable with this experience (I sure wasn't in my first job). It feels sort of strange, like you're there but not really there. Everything is unfamiliar and you are not totally sure you belong there. But just because it's uncomfortable doesn't mean you can or should ignore it. Like it or not, you're going to be the newest kid on the block for a while, and that will have a very powerful effect on you and everything you do during the first year. Ignore or deny it, as many new hires try to, and you'll only ensure that mistakes are made and problems created.

Not long ago, I was attending a training meeting for an organization in which I'm a relatively new member. As the training progressed, once again I caught myself realizing how different things were from what I thought they would be and how much more I learned than I expected. How powerful it would be, I thought, if I could go into situations like that, accepting my newness and realizing how much I have to learn. If only I could fully appreciate what being new really means, I'd be so much further ahead.

It's that same sense of acceptance I'd like to convey to you through this book. There's a natural tendency not to want to be new. It's a feeling of being in unfamiliar territory, of not being in control, of feeling inferior—all of which most of us would just as soon not experience. Yet, how many times have you heard people say "I wish I knew then what I know now"? In other words, they didn't realize what they didn't know. Yet the central part of being new is that you don't know. If you can fully assimilate this by opening yourself to new experiences rather than resisting change, you will be 90 percent ahead of your peers. (And you will have taken a major step forward in recognizing the simple truth that it's just as important to know how to be new as it is to be experienced at something.) You don't want to spend your career learning things the hard way or wishing you could take today's lessons and use them a year ago.

Fast-Starter Tip

It's as important to learn how to be new as it is to be experienced.

The most effective new hires are those who understand this. They accept the fact that they are new and have much to learn. Their most important concern initially is not how much they can teach the company about themselves but rather how much they can learn about the company and the people in it. This book can help you become effective, too, because it's about learning the ropes, learning how things are done, and learning about your company and the people in it *before* you try to make changes.

I can almost guarantee that you would not naturally do what this book suggests you do when starting a new job. Invariably, new hires come into a company thinking they know more than they do, forgetting to learn their new environment and making far too many assumptions about it, and later regretting that they didn't do what is suggested here. The natural tendency is to charge ahead. Most likely, nobody has told you much about how to be the new kid on the block. So you just walk in and start doing whatever comes naturally, which means you do whatever you assume is right and hope it all works out. Only it takes a few rough lessons and lots of mistakes before things *do* work out.

What I'm suggesting is that you adopt a new way of thinking and behaving: the art of being and acting like a new employee. That's totally contrary to traditional thinking, which says you need to stop acting like a new employee as quickly as you possibly can. Yes, I agree that you need to move beyond being new promptly so you can become productive and make contributions to the company. Where I disagree is that you must also spend time being the best darn rookie employee you can be before you move forward. Ignore the tasks of the new employee stage, and it's like building a house without a foundation. Being good at being new is easier on you, on your peers, and on the company and is a powerful weapon with which to start your career.

NEW EMPLOYEE QUIZ

To illustrate what I am talking about, complete this inventory before you go any further in this book, indicating whether you Agree (A) or Disagree (D) with the following statements:

_____ 1. To be successful in my first year in a new job, I should concentrate mostly on getting the basic tasks of the job done well.

_____ 2. Since the curriculum in college usually represents the most up-to-date knowledge in one's field, I should be able to share a lot of new knowledge with my coworkers and supervisors on the job.

_____ 3. The best work habit to adopt is to make sure I put in my full 8 hours of productive work each day.

_____ 4. My new coworkers and supervisors will respect my academic background and knowledge because I was a good student and I earned really good grades.

_____ 5. I don't think that mediocrity should be tolerated in the workplace, and employees should be quick to point out mistakes when they see them.

_____ 6. I expect to find a job that will make maximum use of my knowledge and talents and will be a real challenge for me.

_____ 7. One way to impress my bosses is to figure out where some major improvements can be made in the organization and present an idea or plan for making the necessary changes.

_____ 8. The best way to deal with people you can't stand in an organization, especially if you are new on a job, is to ignore and avoid them.

_____ 9. "When in Rome, do what the Romans do." If I model my behavior on everyone around me in the organization, I'll be okay.

_____10. I should be confident that others in the organization will like me and be tolerant of me once they really get to know me.

_____11. A new employee should avoid getting stuck with "grunt work" as much as possible. Your boss will judge you by the relative importance of the tasks with which you become associated.

_____12. It is important that you stop acting like a rookie as quickly as you can.

Now, count the number of "Agrees" and "Disagrees"—how many of each do you have? The correct answer is—all of them should be Disagree! Are you surprised? Most people are, which explains why you need this book.

THE SUCCESS SPIRAL

Edgar Schein, a noted management author, coined the term "success spiral" to describe a very important dynamic that operates during your first year on the job. Imagine a curve traced on the surface of a cone. It starts small at the bottom and coils upward and outward into higher and wider arcs. This represents your career path. As you grow professionally and prove yourself, you will be given broader and broader responsibility (the widening path) while you rise in level inside the organization (the upward direction of the path).

Your challenge in the first year is to get started on this upward-spiraling course. The success spiral happens for people who are well thought of in an organization and prove they have potential. Getting on the success spiral is not a guarantee. In fact, it is entirely possible that you could get stuck in what would best be represented as a single flat circle, not rising and not widening. What you do in your first year can make the difference between getting on the success spiral and not getting on.

Let's examine the success spiral more closely and look at some of the conditions that cause it to work.

1. **You have no professional reputation.** When you start to work, you have no reputation within the company. You have no track record of accomplishments, most likely no substantial experience, and no proven performance upon which to establish a reputation.

2. **You have negative stereotypes to overcome.** Based on the new college graduates who have come before you, businesspeople hold certain stereotypes that you will have to overcome. They expect you to be naive, unrealistic, a know-it-all who is difficult to teach. They fear you will have your head in the clouds, want too much too soon, and not be ready to work. Your challenge is to prove them wrong. As soon as you do, your colleagues will be eager to help you and accept you. It's not that they don't like new college graduates, but they typically expect to have to give them a "healthy dose of reality" to get their heads out of the clouds before they are really ready to go to work. Few new hires disappoint them in these assumptions. You can be several months ahead of your fellow new hires if you overcome these stereotypes in the beginning.

3. **All that counts is what you earn on the job.** "But what about my accomplishments at school, my great GPA, and my student officer positions?" you may ask. Unfortunately, you leave them at the door when you walk in to work. Those things have already served a very useful purpose: they helped you to get in the door and get the job. But they aren't worth much anymore, at least to your professional reputation. Most people in the company won't care what you did in school. On a personal level, they would probably be quite pleased with you and commend you. But the relation-

ship you are establishing with them is not personal but professional. Now, you must earn their respect and establish credibility as a professional.

4. **You have to prove yourself.** You earn respect and credibility by proving yourself on the job, so much of your first year should be spent doing just that. It's not that the people you will work with are cynics or uncharitable, but, since you have no reputation and no track record, they have no basis upon which to assume that you are a good professional. You have to prove it. You have to show them that you are trustworthy, capable, mature, likable, and a team player. You have no past laurels upon which to rest.

5. **Everybody is looking for good people.** Most companies are very busy and they need good people. That's why they hired you, because they think you have the potential to be good. It's also true that there are more average performers than outstanding ones. This means that if you can show people you have the potential to be good, people will notice.

6. **You're given a chance.** Everybody gets a fair chance in the beginning. You'll be given a project, some responsibility, a chance to show your stuff. It could just be a chance to work with someone important, but you can use it as a chance to make a good impression.

7. **The success spiral starts.** There is an old saying that good things happen to good people. It works like this: You come in and make a good impression. Somebody thinks you might be good, trusts you profession-

ally, and gives you a chance to prove yourself. You perform well, so you confirm the first impression and your good reputation begins to build. Everybody likes to find a good performer, and good performers get the good assignments. So along comes another good project. And you do well. And the chain continues. You have visibility and opportunity because you made good impressions and developed a good reputation.

So what you see, then, is a process whereby you're entering the company with lots to prove. Everyone is watching because the company needs good people. You're given a chance very quickly to show your stuff, even in a small way. Impressions start to form, and labels are handed out quickly. Good performance and good labels lead to opportunity, and you're on your way. The problem is that you are in a highly leveraged position. It doesn't take much to get you off on the wrong track, but it also doesn't take a lot to get you moving on the right track either—it's mainly up to you. Do the basics right in the first few months, and you're off and running. Do stupid, college-kid things, and you may be in trouble.

ADAPTING TO WORK

When managers of new employees are asked what makes the difference between an average new employee and an outstanding one, task performance has little to do with it. Outstanding new employees, they say, are the ones that have good attitudes, get along well with people, can learn the organization quickly, fit in, and do other things we will talk about here. Great performance on the basic tasks of the job will only get you an average performance rating.

The conclusion: Most new graduates are focused on the wrong things! Why? Because that is what college focuses on: task-related knowledge and skills. The twelve steps on page xx will help you focus on what your employer is worried about: the nontask elements of the job. If you want to be more than just an average performer, you will need to shift your focus.

Your goals for the first year, then, have to include more than just productivity. Equally important are three other goals: acceptance, respect, and credibility. Organizations are groups of people: Just because you have been hired does not mean that you have been accepted by those people as "one of them." Acceptance is earned, as are respect and credibility. Your colleagues will not automatically respect you, your expertise, or the contributions you make. Your success in college got you hired but means little on the job. You have to prove yourself all over again.

In fact, as a new college graduate, your new colleagues may be biased against respecting you since you are so inexperienced. You will have to do things to convince them that you are professionally mature and that they should respect you. Then, you will be able to establish your expertise, experiences, and contributions as credible and worthy of consideration.

This book will help you survive and prosper as a new employee by teaching you how to excel in four key areas. First, you develop the individual attributes that serve as a foundation for respect. Then, with the right individual attributes, you can more easily become part of the team and fit in with the people. Once part of

the team, you will have a much easier time learning about the organization. Finally, once you really understand the organization, you can understand how to succeed at the work you are asked to do.

In the following figure, this process is expanded into a twelve-step framework that will be the structure for this book. Each of these twelve steps is a fundamental step in insuring your survival—and success—as a new employee.

This framework integrates the best of what is known from experience, practice, and research.

Each of these steps is elaborated on in the first eleven chapters of this book. The last two, work tasks and knowledge, skills, and abilities (KSAs) are combined in one chapter because they are not usually a big issue. Most companies and new hires do a pretty good job of learning work tasks.

The first nine steps of this twelve-step program will help you set the essential foundation for becoming productive. The last three steps are the task-related ones that complete the process and enable you to produce. It is through the first nine steps that you demonstrate your professional maturity, get yourself accepted and respected in the organization, and learn how to get things done. Then, and only then, can you achieve outstanding performance on the tasks of your job.

Surprised that the task-related steps are last? Outstanding task performance is a building process. Make no mistake, you must be proficient at the tasks you are asked to perform. But becoming an outstanding employee—which should be your goal—requires much more than technical skill or know-how. No matter how brilliant you are or how successful you have been in school, it is nearly impossible for you to

TWELVE STEPS TO NEW EMPLOYEE SURVIVAL

Table 1: Individual Goals

1. Attitude

Identify the personal values and attitudinal predispositions toward a professional career, job, and organization; identify success-related attitudes in the organization; match personal attitudes to those desired by the organization.

2. Expectations

Develop appropriate expectations about the job, organization, and themselves in the job; resolve frustrations due to expectation differences.

3. Breaking-In

Become aware of the dynamics and importance of organizational entry; master the special skills and strategies required.

Table 2: People Goals

4. Impression Management

Become aware of the role impressions play in establishing the organization's initial evaluation; understand the impression-management process; learn what impressions will be viewed most favorably in the organization; master the skills and strategies necessary to manage impressions.

5. Relationships

Understand the role relationships play in organizational success and the kinds of relationships that should be built; acquire skills necessary to build and maintain effective professional relationships and networks; learn effective teamwork strategies.

6. Supervisor

Become aware of the importance of supervisor/subordinate relationships and their respective roles; identify supervisory style and requirements; build skills needed to be an effective subordinate and to manage the supervisor relationship for mutual gain; learn effective strategies for building a strong working relationship with a supervisor.

receive an outstanding performance rating at the end of your first year without first mastering the nontask aspects of the job. Why? Because getting results (remember, it's results that count) in whatever task you are assigned will require you to work with other people and within an organizational system. No task (yes, none) is performed in isolation. And you can't really understand the task until you understand the people you must work with and the organization of which you are all a part.

TAKING CHARGE OF YOUR OWN CAREER

It is an underlying theme of this book that you, and you alone, are responsible for your career.

TWELVE STEPS (CONTINUED)

Table 3: Organization Goals

7. Organizational Culture

Understand elements of organizational culture and how they affect performance; become aware of the importance of fitting into the organization's culture; acquire skills needed to learn key elements of culture that are not explicitly taught.

8. Organizational Savvy

Become aware of the informal organization and success factors in the organization; understand appropriate means for getting results through the informal organization; acquire skills to learn the informal organization and effectively use it to achieve desired results.

9. Organizational Roles

Locate oneself in the larger perspective of the organization's goals; understand the role and identity of a newcomer in the organization; learn what appropriate expectations and activities are for that role; accept role limits and realities; reconcile role conflicts and ambiguity.

Table 4: Work Goals

10. Work Savvy

Understand how to apply knowledge and skills to the job; acquire generic professional skills (e.g., communication, time management, etc.) necessary to function in the job.

11. Task Knowledge

Understand the basic tasks required in the job and how to perform them successfully.

12. Knowledge, Skills, and Abilities

Identify knowledge, skills, and abilities needed to perform tasks successfully, both now and in the future; develop formal and informal learning skills necessary to acquire the knowledge, skills, and abilities.

That doesn't mean that you can do everything by yourself, that you don't need others, that working with others isn't important, or anything like that. What it does mean is that nobody else will have the kind of dedicated interest and concern for your career as you. An executive put it this way: "You have to enter into the business with the understanding that you have to take 100 percent of the responsibility for your success. Anything that the business contributes is just a plus. Take 100 percent accountability for your success." It is nobody's responsibility but your own to see that you are doing what you need to do in order to advance or to be effective in your career. Similarly, only you can be sure that you are doing what makes you happy and satisfied: not your boss, not your colleagues, not your boss's boss, nor anybody else.

Does that mean that your colleagues don't have the responsibility to help you or that you don't have a right to expect things from them? Not at all. But if they don't deliver what they should or do what's expected and you don't take responsibility yourself to make up for it, all you'll have left is an excuse. You'll quickly find that nobody's interested in excuses. If your boss didn't help you get the training you needed for the next promotion, the fact that it was his or her fault still won't get you promoted. If your colleague doesn't help you with your project and you miss a critical deadline, an excuse won't matter. If you don't get the feedback you need and end up focusing on the wrong things your first year, is that an acceptable excuse? No.

What I'm talking about here is a sense of ownership about your own career. You can and should delegate aspects of your career management to others (such as your boss), but in the final analysis, it's your responsibility. This requires you to show initiative, assertiveness, and a willingness to make things happen for yourself. You and only you know what's good for you, and you have to do what it takes to get there. The days of the paternalistic, big-daddy type of corporation that would take care of you and look out for you are certainly dying and may soon be gone.

There are many concrete ways in which you can begin to demonstrate ownership of your career during your first year on the job. For example, you can demonstrate a spirit of self-responsibility and self-management by:

- Learning how to approach your first year with a willingness to seek out information rather than waiting to be taught
- Taking the initiative to learn the way things are done in your new company
- Taking an active role in developing a strong relationship with your boss
- Actively seeking the feedback and guidance you need
- Seeking opportunity rather than waiting for it to arise on its own
- Assessing your own attitude and working to overcome any shortcomings instead of waiting for the organization to correct them

Getting a strong start with your new organization is your responsibility. The organization may or may not do what it should, but you are the one who will bear the cost for any mistakes. You are the only one with whom I am concerned, and the only way to ensure your successful transition into the working world is to decide now to take charge of managing your own career.

MAKING TRANSITIONS

Change. Some people run from it, some seek it, and some are addicted to it. Regardless of what your preference is, the only sure bet in adult life is that you will have to make changes along the way. One of the keys to a healthy and happy adult life is learning to make changes successfully. The transition from college to work is the first big test of how you react to change in your life and how you negotiate it.

Any transition is an unsettling experience, regardless of whether it's positive or negative or whether or not it's welcome. That's because a transition, by definition, involves leaving behind old habits and roles and moving to new ones that may be quite unfamiliar. It means replacing one support network of friends with another, replacing familiar routines and surroundings with unfamiliar ones. It is a melting away of one way of seeing and acting in the world so that new ways of seeing the world can start to form. It is a time of letting go of old ways but at the same time holding on to the familiar.

For most people, changes bring with them a variety of emotions and reactions. The transition from student to employee is usually positive for most people, since it's something they've worked for. But that doesn't stop them from being scared, sad at leaving old friends, anxious about the future, etc., amid the excitement, fun, and happiness they feel. Just because it's a positive transition doesn't mean that all feelings about it will be positive.

One of the most important things you can do to prepare yourself for a big change like starting to work is to recognize that life is very unsettled during a transition. You must expect a time of mixed emotions, of "shifting sands," of loss as well as gain, of surprises and unexpected events. If you can go into such a period with a sense of fluidity and expect the unexpected, you'll be a long way toward making your transition successful. Many students struggle with their transitions simply because they don't expect them. They aren't prepared for the unsettled nature of life during such times and are shocked by the changes and their own mixed emotions.

Since transitions are natural events, the most effective way to deal with them is, in one sense, not to deal with them at all—to ride out the change rather than resist it. The best changers are those who go with a transition instead of fighting it. You won't be able to control many of the events that happen. And you won't be able to stop many of the changes that occur. Change will be less unsettling for you if you can go with it and treat it as an adventure.

Fast-Starter Tip

Starting a new career is demanding, stressful, and challenging.

One of the reasons that personal transitions can be so challenging is that they have three basic parts: an ending, a new beginning, and an in-between. Any time you make a transition, you are ending a period of your life. And any ending can bring with it a sense of loss, especially if it has been a good period of your life. Even if it has not been a good period, there can still be a loss of familiar patterns and habits. Leaving college is an excellent example of a transition that brings with it a mixture of feelings. On one hand, it's probably a great feeling to finish school, to finally graduate and go out into the world. At the same time, you've probably enjoyed many good times since beginning college, and you'll be leaving lots of good friends. So one minute you may be happy you're leaving, but the next you're missing the good ol' days. Even when it's a transition you want to make or know you need to make, the passing of any stage of life brings with it some mixed emotions, if for no other reason than that it is indeed passing, never to return.

With an ending comes a launching from the familiar into the unknown and uncertain territory of a new beginning. New beginnings are great. They're exciting. They get your adrenaline running and give you something to look forward to. When they're positive transitions like going to work, the new start is a real milestone in your life. But even positive transitions can be stressful and generate anxiety or even fear of the unknown.

In between those two stages is another, which is neither ending nor beginning. If you take two weeks off before starting work, you're neither a student nor a professional. For some people, it's uncomfortable to be without the familiarity of a role identity. This is sort of the "limbo" stage where you're anticipating the new beginning, saying good-bye to the old, but not being *in* either stage.

What makes it even more interesting is that the effects of these three stages can be and usually are felt all at once. There are no clear starting and ending points for any one stage. Before you ever leave school, you'll already be feeling yourself in limbo as you let go of the old. You'll also start thinking of yourself as a new professional. After you get on the job, it's perfectly natural to still think of your school days and also feel a bit lost because you're clearly not a student but neither have you been truly accepted into the new company either. Sometimes your feelings get quite mixed up.

A very important thing to understand about transitions is that they do generate some kind of emotions in most people—and lots of emotions in many. Most people find transitions a little uncomfortable. The first thing to realize is that this feeling is perfectly normal, a natural part of saying hello and good-bye at the same time. It's sort of like ending a nice vacation; you hate to go but are eager to get home, too.

Only you know exactly how you react to transitions. If you like to take risks and try new things, you'll probably think this section a bit ridiculous; if you're a risk-averse person, making changes can be quite uncomfortable or scary. But if you are like most of the world, you're somewhere in between, which means that transitions are a real mixed bag. If you look back at some other transitions you've experienced in your life thus far, you'll probably find clues as to how you'll deal with this one. There's no right or wrong way to feel about or handle transitions such as the one you are facing now— the important thing is to just deal with your individual situation.

Transitions, then, are something to be managed, not just entered into blindly. The most common problem with new graduates is that they simply don't appreciate the magnitude of the transition nor do they understand it is something to be managed. Consequently, many are surprised once the change begins. Even if it's not an uncomfortable thing for you, there are still lots of things to learn, adjustments to make, and feelings to sort through regarding your passage from college into the working world. To help ease your way, you should pay some attention to learning how to manage a transition.

PART

1

INDIVIDUAL FOUNDATIONS
OF RESPECT

1

Developing a Winning Attitude

I can't remember any instance where we've employed someone who didn't have the raw materials to work with and to develop. I can think of others, though, who were given a road map to success, but they just stuck it in their back pocket, refusing to look at it until they were lost. And while they were getting lost somewhere, everybody else was moving on and succeeding.

This manager's sentiments echo those of every manager and executive I talked to. A startling fact emerges: it is rare that a new employee has difficulty for lack of the basic knowledge, skills, and abilities to be competent at a first job. As imperfect as the hiring process is, most companies know how to hire people who are smart and capable enough to learn the basic tasks of the job. Simply put, you won't be hired unless the company is pretty darn certain you have what it takes, at least as far as basic tools go.

What does cause many problems for many new hires is their attitude. Managers talk extensively about the difficulty they experience with new employees' attitudes about their role in the organization, work ethic, etc.

Fast-Starter Tip

Your expectations are too high!

This is an interesting paradox. Most graduates seem to think that they need to prove their intelligence and knowledge early on so they can quickly impress somebody with them. But intelligence is simply not the key issue for managers during the first six to twelve months on the job. Flaunting what you know and how great you are demonstrates precisely the wrong attitude toward management and your colleagues. And it is attitude they are paying the most attention to!

This chapter is all about attitude: what makes for a winning attitude and how attitude will make the difference in your success the first year.

HUMILITY

It's hard to be humble when you graduate and start work. You've finally "arrived," having finished at least seventeen years of school, during which you earned good grades, won several awards, were perhaps a "big man or woman on campus," maybe president of an organization, or a star athlete, homecoming queen, or student government leader. Then came the recruiters, and, boy, they told you that their company only hires the best and they wanted you! What a great feeling.

It's easy to forget that when you go to work, you will be starting over at the bottom of the totem pole. It's like being a freshman in high school or college again, only worse. You may have been a big person on campus and had whiz kid credentials, but now you'll find that your knowledge is woefully lacking compared with the experience of ten- and twenty-year veterans in the business. On top of that, to an awful lot of people your first day at work just isn't a big deal to many of the people you'll be working with. It's a real shock to discover you're at the bottom again.

Now, I don't want to burst your bubble (deflate it a bit perhaps), because you are entitled to feel good about what you bring to the com-

pany. If the company hadn't wanted you, you wouldn't have been hired. But they don't expect you to walk through the door and be a superstar again, and NEITHER CAN YOU. Face it, it may take a lot longer to fit in and feel comfortable than at any other time in your life. You won't reach the top of the heap in two, three, or even four years. And that's OK, or at least you need to think of it that way. As the following comments indicate, what the company wants to see is a proud but modest new employee who recognizes his or her limits.

> *There is a certain amount of paranoia about new people coming in . . . I think the key is to look and listen and be humble. Don't come in and think you're going to change the world. Just kind of come in like, "Listen, I really need some help." Come in humble, willing to learn and listen.*

> *It's a little bit of humble pie recognizing your place in the organization, and that's at the bottom.*

> *The system has told you that we have now given you everything we can to go out and make a full contribution. The expectation you have, particularly if you've done well in college, is that you should hit the ground running. That's a false sense of what you should do when you enter an organization.*

As you see, being humble is not only OK, but it's also by far the best approach for the first job. It won't, as many new hires presume, lose you respect. Rather, you will gain respect because employers want to see new graduates who say, "Hey, I know I have a long way to go and lots to learn, and I'm going to accept my role until I'm ready for more." That will win you more respect and credibility than anything else.

READINESS TO LEARN

Part of humility is knowing what you do and don't know. When you graduate, it's very easy to believe you've acquired all the knowledge that you need to do the job. (You did finish the curriculum requirements and earn your degree, right?)

Fast-Starter Tip

Admitting what you don't know is more important than showing what you do.

You have to realize that what the college or university has given you are basic skills, a foundation upon which to build and nothing more. You still have a lot to learn. I know you don't really want to hear this, but managers and executives are emphatic about it:

Showing enthusiasm, eagerness to learn, letting everybody know you are a rookie, that's important. New people are so effective when they readily admit they don't know very much rather than boasting about what they have learned, what courses they have taken, and the projects they have studied. Showing a willingness to learn a lot more than they've been exposed to, that's what new hires need to do. Their work will demonstrate how much they actually know.

What I want is somebody to come in and be an enthusiastic learner, someone who doesn't feel *he needs to make a contribution from the first day yet is eager to make contributions once he has a basis of knowledge.*

A guy started with the company the same time I did, who I thought was just as smart as I was. While I moved fairly rapidly within the business, this person was fired because he wasn't willing to admit what he didn't know.

It's perfectly OK not to know much at this point. Nobody, and I mean nobody, expects you to come out of school ready to jump right in and perform like a veteran. The company expects you to have acquired some basic skills and to have learned how to learn. What they want to see is a new employee who says, "I have a lot to learn," and shows he or she is eager to do so.

Unfortunately, many, many new hires don't approach it this way. Those who believe that to build a reputation they need to jump right in and show how much they have learned build a reputation based on cockiness, naivete, and immaturity. Those who truly believe that they know enough from their classroom studies to do the job and that they don't have much more to learn are even worse off. They build reputations for being know-it-alls, and there is nothing that will turn their new colleagues off more than coming across that way. Let's listen to some new hires tell how they learned this lesson.

For me it was the first day when you walk in and someone picks up the phone and goes, "I have a problem" and starts throwing acronyms out and you are just writing them down as fast as you can. And you just say,

"I'm sorry, I'll have to get back to you" because you don't know what the acronyms mean. And that's just day one . . . Since you don't know, you learn to eat humble pie.

I think a lot of people come in like I did with the assumption that they are going to make an impact immediately. Through all four years of my college experience, I was learning things I thought I was going to apply later in my career. But as I look back, I think college is just an experience you go through to get the credentials to get into the business world.

When I first came in, I thought, well, I've got this degree, I came from a good college, I'm well prepared, I've done all my research, I know my stuff. And I walked in and was assigned a project that was brand new to me. I didn't care; I was a 4.0 student. But, big deal! I didn't know a thing about my job. So get in there and learn from the ground up.

Be honest with yourself and others about the limits of what you know, and be ready to learn.

WORK ETHIC

Employers want to see new hires who are ready to work hard and do what it takes to contribute the distinguishing characteristics of a professional. They know that your first year will be one of the toughest, that everything you do will be brand new, that the people you do it with are new to you too, and that even the business environment in which you are working is new.

They know that the most basic tasks may take you a long time to complete and be quite arduous. What they want you to realize is that it takes a great deal of hard work to launch a successful career. Simply put, employers want to see a solid work ethic early in your career.

The right attitude and the right perspective on the new hires' part is extremely significant. They should come in bright-eyed and bushy-tailed, ready to work, and willing to do and try everything.

To me, once they get here, frankly, I don't care what degree they have. I don't care where they went to school. All I want to see is a smiling face that says, "Give me something to do . . . I am going to attack this job, take ownership of it, and throw it back to you so quickly that I am going to challenge you as a manager to keep me busy."

To come into business and think that you're going to get a nine-to-five day and yet are going to be able to rise to executive positions is kind of foolish.

Take responsibility, take accountability for whatever it is that needs to be done.

And this is tough to do. After four years of fairly demanding work in college, you finally have some freedom to do fun things and some money with which to do them. There is actually a temptation to coast a bit, thinking that now you can let up or have a good time. Many new employees spend a lot of time talking and thinking about their social life, beach trips, nightclubs, etc. That's perfectly acceptable because this is a fun time, and you don't want to lose sight of that. But for most, it goes too far.

First, you have to remember that the workplace is not the same as a fraternity, sorority, or classroom. Some fun is acceptable, but people are generally pretty serious about getting their work done. They are inclined to think that you are not serious, just because you are fresh out of college. If you persist in focusing on the fun in your life, you only confirm their assumptions about you. The challenge in your first year is to show that you are serious about working hard. Once you establish that reputation, you can loosen up a bit.

Furthermore, all successful people have a strong work ethic. It doesn't mean that you have to be a workaholic, but for successful people work is important, and the way in which they do their work is important. As one manager summed up, "Your job may not be the most important thing in your life, but it should damn well be one of the most important things."

RESPECT

Part of the right attitude boils down to respect. One of the quickest ways you can earn the respect of others for your abilities is to respect theirs. Everybody in the organization has more experience than you in doing business inside that organization. There is no pride to be lost by deferring to that and respecting the wisdom and experience of people who have been working longer than you. Sure, you may wish you knew as much as they do or had as much experience. But be patient: Your time will come. What they want is the same thing you will want in a few years, the respect for what they have accomplished and what they know. Respect them, and they will respect you.

Respect the traditions and ways of the organization. Maybe they don't make sense to you at first or seem a bit ridiculous. Chances are that they exist for a purpose, and you should respect them even if their purpose is not readily apparent to you. In time you will either come to appreciate the ways of the organization or establish enough authority and/or credibility to suggest changing them. But as long as you are new, any criticism or attempt to change things will likely be seen as an outsider's interference.

Fast-Starter Tip

You can't earn the organization's respect unless you first give it.

Respect the authority of those above you. It's really hard sometimes to realize that amid all the freedom you thought you were gaining by striking out on your own is a whole new set of authority figures and people who have control over your life (at least during working hours). These people were given authority for some reason, and you have to respect that. Perhaps you don't understand why they were given authority or don't understand why they use it the way they do, but it's not your place as a new hire to challenge it. In time, you may be able to but not while you're new.

If you are brought into a supervisory role, then you need to respect those reporting to you. Even if you don't supervise people, there may be people who are lower on the organizational ladder and earn less money than you. They deserve your respect, too. They will help you get your job done just as your peers will and deserve respect for their contributions, too.

The overall attitude of successful new hires is one of deferring to and respecting the institution and organization that they have entered. It is not your place to criticize or tear down the traditions or people in the organization. Not only is it a poor way to make friends, but it is also highly unlikely that you will have the wisdom, experience, and inside knowledge of the organization to make credible observations. Even if you do, as a newcomer you will not have established your professional credibility so that your observations will be respected. In short, you can only lose.

FRIENDLINESS

Everybody knows that new hires should be friendly, right? Well, you would be surprised at the number of complaints I have heard about new hires who just aren't friendly, likable people. I can only speculate why. Maybe it is because the popular press often holds up tough, abrasive managers as role models. It could be because not many graduates realize how important people skills are (more about this later). I sincerely doubt that it is because there are that many unlikable people in this world.

Professionals spend a large part of their lives in the workplace. They like to be around people who are friendly and likable, colleagues who have pleasant personalities and add an air of pleasantness to the workplace. Furthermore, you will learn that you need other people to accomplish your job. Other people won't help those who are unfriendly or abrasive.

Being friendly, as one manager said, "doesn't mean that everyone will like you or that you have to like everyone. It doesn't mean that you would want to socialize with everyone outside of work. It doesn't mean that you have to have things in common with everyone as you would a friend." It does mean that you need to have a basically pleasant demeanor so that people enjoy having you in the office. There are enough problems to deal with at work without adding an unpleasant or abrasive new hire to them. Be courteous, say "good morning," smile. Don't brownnose, don't go overboard, but think and act in a likable way. It sounds simple, but it's a powerful tool to help you get accepted.

PATIENCE

Patience is tough to learn and admittedly not one of my strong points. But an underlying theme of this chapter and of your winning attitude is that you must have patience. Your turn and your time will come. New college graduates are usually overeager and push too fast for too much. They expect too much, want too much, and usually end up demanding it. And that is not well liked. I don't want you to lose your energy and enthusiasm, since these are very valuable assets and a big reason that companies love to hire new college graduates. But things take a little time. Think about slowing down, backing off a bit.

Everything in life has a pace to it, a time in which to take place. You can only rush it so much. There is a saying in basketball about "letting the game come to you." What it means is you have to play within yourself and not push too hard. It's like that with companies, too. Work within yourself, within the skill and experience you have, no matter how little that may be. Give yourself a chance to grow into the job—let it come to you. You will be amazed at how quickly things will start happening and how much respect you will earn from those around you.

STARTING WITH A CLEAN SLATE

You may not realize it, but you have already established in your mind lots of expectations and assumptions about the world of work. You have listened to your professors talk about their experiences with and observations of the working world. You have watched your parents, other relatives, and their friends in their careers. From your own personal work experiences, whether professional or nonprofessional, you have learned a lot. You have read in books and magazines about different companies and have talked with recruiters about their companies.

You have learned many useful things that have probably helped you make the career choices you have. But you have also probably developed a lot of what I call "shoulds" and "ought-tos." These are assumptions about the way your first job and company are "supposed" to be. And they are dangerous.

Fast-Starter Tip

Expect to be surprised—it won't be what you think it will.

You see, it is quite likely that your assumptions have been developed from what is really only a limited amount of information gleaned from perceptions, often secondhand. Until you (not your parents, friends, etc.) have worked day in and day out in your job in today's society, you really won't know what it's like. If you go into the job with assumptions about the way it should be, you are only setting yourself up for disappointment.

Think about this for a minute. You are entering a brand-new situation. If you can go in with a clean slate, starting fresh and learning how things are instead of comparing them with a model in your head of how they should be, you and your management will be much happier.

READINESS TO CHANGE

To really learn the things you need to know and to have a clean slate means you have to develop a readiness to change and an openness to new ideas, environments, ways of doing things, and ways of viewing problems, situations, and the world. Some people fight against this, trying to preserve the status quo. Others are excited and stimulated by it.

Fast-Starter Tip

Be ready to adapt and change.

No one will deny that change can be threatening, and it is easy to resist. But the most successful new hires come in with an amazing flexibility and openness to the changes that confront them.

What's different about the successful ones? Just an attitude. Many of them had a little talk with themselves before they started work to prepare for it. And so can you. Think about it as an opening-up process. If you stay closed—fighting the newness, the changes—you will miss many things you need to learn. The organization will sense in you a resistance, almost a defensiveness. On the other hand, if you open up and are ready to change and grow into the organization, you'll most likely feel the organization respond to you. If the company recognizes your clean slate, your readiness to learn, grow, and change, it will want to work with you and will sense your wanting to work with it, not against it. It will know you are someone who truly wants to become part of the team.

POSITIVE ATTITUDE

It may sound a bit like a cliché, but the simple fact is your colleagues don't want a whining, complaining, or grouchy person to work with. Everybody has enough problems and unpleasant things to deal with already. And everybody spends a lot of time at work. Given that, they don't need a negative person to boot.

You would be amazed at what a positive attitude can do for you. You don't need to be an eternal optimist or bounce off the walls with your enthusiasm. You do, however, need to be a pleasant person. Smile. Say "please" and "thank-you." Be someone people like being around, who can exchange pleasant small talk. Try to add something positive to the workplace.

When moving from school to the working world, there is a change in culture of which you may not be aware. In school, it's popular to complain about the professor, the cafeteria food, your parents, your boyfriend or girlfriend, etc. There is a certain sense of camaraderie that comes from complaining. Remember walking out of class and talking with your friends about how bad the professor was or how poorly he

graded your paper? Remember making jokes about the bad food? Complaining about the administration of the college and how they never understand the students? All of that was openly tolerated and was sort of an "in" thing to do. You may have developed it as a regular habit.

You will find that this is not the standard in the workplace. You don't walk out of a meeting griping about how poorly run it was. You don't walk the halls complaining about senior management. You don't stand at the coffee machine and laugh about how bad another department is. Now you're in a new environment, and things have changed. In the first place, nobody admires, respects, or has time for that much negativism. Sure, people still complain. But it's done a lot less and not nearly as openly. Being negative is not popular; nobody needs it. Furthermore, you will have to be careful about when and to whom you do your complaining. As you will see later in this book, there are a whole lot of other things to consider when you are talking about colleagues, teammates, and bosses as opposed to professors and classmates.

CONFIDENCE

Everybody knows you must show you have confidence in yourself in order to get a job. But the wrong kind of confidence can hurt you badly in your first year of work.

If you were to ask the average college graduate what kind of confidence a new hire needs to show on the job, you would probably get an answer something like this:

- Ability to do the job
- Readiness to contribute
- Ability to function independently
- Self-assurance

How would you demonstrate such self-confidence? Probably by aggressively jumping into your tasks, offering suggestions at meetings, not asking too many questions at meetings, stating your opinions freely and assertively. In these ways, you would be saying to the company, "I'm capable, I'm good, and I believe in myself." Right?

Wrong! Herein lies one of the major mistakes new hires make. Yes, your colleagues want to see that you have self-confidence. Nobody wants to hire an insecure wimp. But that confidence needs to be tempered by a realistic view of what you don't know and have yet to learn. When you demonstrate your self-confidence by trying to show how much you do know and how much you think you can do, you're on the wrong track. All you demonstrate is your immaturity and naivete, because everybody has a long learning curve when they first start work. Nobody can jump right in and know how to do a great job right away.

The type of confidence people want to see is one that is tempered by humility. It's a confidence that says, "I know I have good raw material and the potential to be good, but I also know my limits." This is a mature confidence, not an immature cockiness that is mistaken for confidence. It is mature confidence if you demonstrate the following characteristics:

- Potential to be good (not that you are there now)
- Ability to learn (not that you know it all now)

- Capacity to grow into the job (not that you are already there)
- Basic skills (but you know you have many skills yet to learn)
- Ability to become a competent professional (not that you already are one)

Can you feel the difference between these two types of confidence? The immature one is cocky and can be perceived as an "I-dare-you-to-teach-me-anything" statement. It says, "I don't need you or your experience." It is also seen as a real put-down of those who have less education than you. (You can almost hear people saying, "Here comes that college girl, thinks she knows it all.")

Fast-Starter Tip

Your attitude will make the difference.

A mature confidence is one that people can respect, because it shows that not only do you respect yourself and your abilities, but you also respect your colleagues and the company as well for the knowledge they already possess—which is the very knowledge you have yet to learn.

This type of confidence is an unassuming confidence. How do you show it? By asking for advice and guidance from more experienced people. By admitting your inexperience. By starting your sentences with phrases like "I don't know if I have enough experience yet, but . . ." or "I hope I'm not out of line with this . . ." instead of just blurting out your opinion. By volunteering to help but acknowledging your need for support. By doing lots of listening.

It's easy to see this type of behavior as self-deprecating or apologetic. That's a mistaken perception. There is nothing insecure, self-deprecating, or wimpy about recognizing your limits. Have confidence in yourself and what abilities you do have, but recognize what you need to learn. All professionals do that throughout their careers as they encounter new jobs and unfamiliar tasks. In time you will be expected to grow and show more confidence in your ability to do your job well. At what point this will occur depends on the complexity of your job, the company, your boss, etc. The critical point though is that you recognize your limits at each step, particularly in the first six to twelve months.

ULTIMATE SURVIVAL TIPS

What's in a Winning Attitude

1. Remember, attitude counts as much as ability.

2. Accept your role as a new hire.

3. Know what you don't know.

4. Be eager to learn.

5. Work hard and willingly.

6. Respect the organization and the people in it.

7. Be a positive person and influence on the organization.

8. Forget "shoulds" and "ought-tos."

9. Be confident but not cocky.

2

Managing Expectations: Professional Life Versus Student Life

People with whom you work want to see that you have made a mental break from the college environment. It's not to say that you have to give up that mind-set completely. But you have to realize there's a time to be professional and there's a time to leave that at the office . . . a lot of folks don't see that and carry over too much baggage from college life.

Part of the challenge in making the transition from college to work stems from some very basic differences in the lifestyles and work styles in the two environments.

In college, you are taught a process that is unique to college life, and the process is the same for most situations; it doesn't change. You apply the same process to every class, to every task, and life is very predictable. Now you've moved from student to professional life and the process is utterly dynamic.

My senior year I never went to bed before 3 a.m. I scheduled my classes in the morning. I would come in and go to sleep in the afternoon and be ready for the next night. You can't do that anymore. You have to get up at six o'clock, and you have to work until it's time to go home. You have to go to bed at a reasonable hour. You can't go out every night of the week anymore.

You don't see time passing . . . In college everything followed the semester schedule—

you knew where you were all the time, and life was too slow. Now, you blink and you have missed something.

In school if you ever took a class and you didn't like the professor, didn't like the subject, you could always drop it or something. Here you can't do that. You've got to realize that you may think your manager's a dough-nut or something, crazy, but you have to deal with him, and you can't walk away from the situation like you could when you were back in school.

Taking tests in school, I mean there was a right answer. When you come here, there is no one right answer.

As these new hires quickly realized, living and working as a professional is fundamentally different from living and working as a student. Some of the major differences include performance expectations, maturity level expected, feedback received, control over your own time, measures of success, personal initiative and responsibility required, clarity of tasks and roles, lifestyle, teachers versus bosses, and level of involvement in work.

Fast-Starter Tip

Work and college aren't the same thing at all!

COLLEGE IS A DIFFERENT WORLD

You probably know that college is a unique and special world . . . but you won't know how different until you start to work. At the heart of the problem most new graduates (and their managers) experience during their transition is the failure to recognize how much the educational culture has shaped their attitudes, expectations, behaviors, and overall view of the organization of which they are a part. Think about it. You have spent at least seventeen years in education. How could a person not be shaped by it?

Look at the survey on the next page. First, think back to when you were in college. Now look at each pair of characteristics on the survey and make a mark on the line closest to how you remember college. After doing that for all eighteen pairs, look at the pattern. If you are like most recent graduates, most of your marks will be to the left of center. Now, if I was to take this same survey to graduates who had been on the job for two years and ask them to complete it based on their perceptions of what working was like, where do you think their marks would be? To the right side! The message: college and work are dramatically different.

The skills you learned in order to be successful in your seventeen years of education and the behaviors for which you were rewarded are rarely the ones you'll need to be successful at work. The knowledge you acquired will be critical to your success, but the process of succeeding in school is very different from the process of succeeding at work. Worse yet, the culture of education is so different that if you continue to have the same expectations of your employer that you did of your college and professors, you'll be greatly disappointed with your job and make costly career mistakes. By taking the time to learn the work culture and

WHAT WAS COLLEGE LIKE?

1. Feedback frequent and concrete	Feedback infrequent and not specific
2. Freedom to set one's own schedule	Little freedom or control over schedule
3. Goals and expectations were clear	Goals and expectations were fuzzy
4. Structured, systematic ways to achieve goals	Unstructured ways to achieve goals
5. Lots of opportunity for fun	Less opportunity for fun
6. High degree of certainty	Low degree of certainty
7. High degree of personal support	Low degree of personal support
8. Focus on development of person	Focus on achieving goals of system
9. High degree of flexibility and control	Low degree of flexibility and control
10. Correct answers were usually available	Correct answers were often not available
11. Performance level required varied	High performance level consistantly required
12. Individual performance mostly	Team performance mostly
13. Acquisition of knowledge	Use of knowledge
14. Lesser degree of individual initiative required	High degree of individual initiative required
15. Rhythm varied: intense periods w/extended breaks	Rhythm was like a marathon
16. Short-term perspective	Long-term perspective
17. Few significant changes	Frequent and unexpected changes
18. Independence of thinking and ideas	Conformance to norms

what it means to be a professional, you'll avoid making a fool of yourself by taking classroom behavior into the workplace.

Let's look at a few examples of how this mind-set that worked for you in school can hurt you on the job. In college you usually received a lot of direction about what to do and how to do it. Your curriculum tells you what courses to take, your professors tell you what is expected of you. If your professor didn't give you a clear syllabus or tell you what to study for an exam, you would probably get upset. At work, you'll rarely get that type of direction, but you've become so accustomed to receiving it that you may well complain that your manager won't tell you what to do.

Your college education has taught you very well how to argue your position in order to convince a professor that you are right and he or she is wrong. Try that with your boss in a meeting and see how far you get! You've become so accustomed to being frequently told "how you're doing" that you might bug the daylights out of your manager for feedback, leaving the impression that you are insecure. Other new graduates are so used to growing and developing through education that they get very upset when their boss won't send them to much training during the first year. Still others can't understand why they aren't getting to do work that stretches their minds and challenges them, not realizing that work will never mimic college.

"Not me," you say? Believe me, you will make mistakes like these if you're not careful because these are the strategies and behaviors that you have known most of your life. You can't just do what comes naturally, because what comes naturally is what you've done for seventeen years—be a student. You'll think you

are changing, but nearly every student will automatically react to the workplace as if it were an educational institution. Eighty to ninety percent of new-college-graduate complaints are either caused or greatly exacerbated by their failure to recognize and let go of their deeply ingrained college-type attitudes, expectations, and behaviors. And it is these college-like behaviors, which you won't even realize you are doing, that will get you labeled as "naive" and "immature." It takes lots of work and effort to let go of those old ways and accept the institution of work for what it is—different. But this is the key to a successful first year. Can you let go, or will you insist on holding on to old ways? It's your decision.

MANAGING YOUR EXPECTATIONS

College courses have trained students to think ahead to positions of responsibility far beyond where they will start out. So it's natural for new college graduates to expect too much from their first year on the job. When you are planning your career, your focus is on where you want to be in five, ten, or twenty years. Nobody spends much time thinking about the day-to-day grind of the early years.

The problem is that you have to crawl before you can walk. Everything you wish and dream for in your career can come to you eventually, but the odds are that the work you do in your first year will be somewhat frustrating and disappointing because it:

- Won't be very glamorous
- May consist of a lot of grunt work

- Will not give you as much challenge as you want
- Won't lead to a promotion as fast as you want
- Will be much different from what you expected

Some authors have suggested that this whole transition process is one of managing expectations. Clearly, some combination of the way college courses are taught, the rosy pictures painted by recruiters, and inaccurate perceptions picked up from a myriad of sources leads to overblown expectations. Throughout this book, you'll learn what appropriate expectations are in these and many other areas.

Fast-Starter Tip

Frustration is the difference between expectations and reality.

Your challenge is to bring your expectations down. I'm sorry, but the chances are things just won't be as great as you think once you actually enter the workplace. Here's the interesting part though. If you lower your expectations, things really won't be as bad as you might expect either. In fact, graduates who go into business with realistic expectations report they are quite excited about their new jobs and usually enjoy them. It's new employees who come in with inflated and unrealistic expectations about their own worth, the level of work they will do, and how fast they will move up who end up frustrated and disappointed.

As you can imagine, the company doesn't like to see unrealistic expectations. One thing particularly troublesome to a company is new employees who believe that their degree, grade point average, and extracurricular activities in college entitle them to certain privileges and respect in the company. You will quickly find out that the only things you are entitled to on the job are the things that you earn. One new hire learned this the hard way:

You can't go into your first job demanding respect because of what you were in college. With most of the people you deal with, you earn their respect. And that's kind of hard when you walk around like a peacock, with your head all high, thinking, well, I've gotten this job, I was 4.0 in college, and I was this and I was that. People are not going to respect you for that.

Part of developing a winning attitude is forging realistic expectations. As a manager of new hires advised, "Set low expectations for your first six months. Set low expectations about how good it is going to be, and then you won't be so disappointed. Don't expect a lot from the organization." Expect to get humdrum assignments for a while, and be grateful if they're not. Expect promotions to come slowly, and be pleasantly surprised if they come quickly. Do the grunt work with a smile. Ironically, this approach will get you where you want to be much faster.

A FEW FACTS ABOUT RECRUITING

When you were hired, you were probably recruited fairly heavily. The people who hired you wanted you to work for them, so they spent considerable time courting and wooing you to the firm. You may even have encountered professional college recruiters whose job it is to do nothing but recruit new graduates (and they do it quite well). All in all, it's usually a very heady and ego-stroking experience that feels pretty darn good.

There's nothing wrong with this recruiting process except for one thing: it can leave you with a rather distorted view of the organization. You have to remember that the recruiter's job was to sell you on working for the company. And when you sell something to someone, you don't spend much time telling all the bad things about it. You talk about all the great things. If the recruiter had told you just the bad things, would you have taken the job?

It's not that recruiters are dishonest. Most have learned that it pays to try to present as realistic a picture of the job as possible so your expectations aren't too far out of line. But the fact is, you're going to hear about more good things than bad things. And you'll hear them presented in a very enthusiastic manner. You have to realize that their recruiting literature, annual reports, etc., are all promotional and try to paint a very pretty picture of their company. Frankly, you have to take it all with a grain of salt. There are lots of things they're not telling you. The evidence clearly shows that most new hires come in expecting a much rosier situation than they find. If you believe that you know exactly what to expect based on what recruiters have told you, you're setting yourself up for disappointment.

There's another unrealistic element in the recruiting process. During it, you receive a great deal of attention from the company. They court you, pursue you, and generally make you feel like a very special person. They seem to be very focused on you and spend a lot of time talking

to you and working with you. That's fine, except it's easy for you to forget that after you're hired you're going to be just one of many employees, perhaps thousands or tens of thousands of employees. As one new hire observed, "They wine you, they dine you, they treat you real nice; and as soon as they say you're hired, you expect to get treated that way some more, and you're not." Most new hires come to the company feeling as if they're very special, based on their experience during recruiting. It's a shock when they show up at work and the rest of the organization doesn't treat them that way.

Quite unintentionally, the recruiting process sets up many unrealistic expectations in you. It's important that you realize that:

- Things won't be as great as you've concluded from the recruiting process.
- Recruiters are salespeople.
- It's fun to be courted, but don't expect it to last.
- There are warts beneath the rosy picture that's been painted for you.
- You need to look past what you've learned so far.
- Your expectations should be about half what they are when you're finished with recruiters.
- You're important to the company but not as important as you were to that recruiter.
- It'll probably still be a good job, even if the recruiter did oversell it.

PERFORMANCE EXPECTATIONS

In other chapters, you'll see that finding out what is expected of you is difficult, even if you're an experienced professional. For new hires, it's especially frustrating because of what you were accustomed to in college. In college, you grow quite accustomed to receiving on the first day of class a syllabus that told you precisely what chapters to read and what work to do when, how many tests you would have and when, what topics would be covered on which days, what kind of project or paper you would have to do, and what should be covered in the paper. You might be told before tests or exams exactly what material would be covered on the test and perhaps given study guides as sample questions. This is all a standard part of the educational system, and students expect it. How many times have you had discussions with friends about how "unfair" a teacher was because he or she didn't tell you how long the paper should be, what would be covered on the test, what types of questions would be on the test, how essay questions would be graded, or what a good answer should contain? The culture is one of fairly clearly defined expectations. If you paid attention and did what you were told, the chances were good that you would receive a fairly decent grade in the course.

Let's contrast that with the workplace. In the first place, many assignments you will be given cannot be laid out in neat, well-defined steps. Professionals aren't hired to follow predefined procedures or methodologies; they are hired for their ability to think originally and solve problems. Quite often you will be asked to figure out how to get the job done, but you will not be told how to do it.

On top of that, the goals are not always so clear in the workplace. You might encounter goals like finding a way to keep Smith's department happy, finishing this by Friday, doing a good job, fixing this, or keeping this customer satisfied. Not only will the how-tos not be spelled out as clearly as they were in college, but also neither will what you are supposed to do. This is equivalent to a professor's telling you, "I'm not going to tell you what I expect you to do to get an A nor am I going to tell you how to get one." Can you imagine how upset you and your classmates would be if you heard that in a class? I've seen editorials in student newspapers and letters to the dean for a lot less! One senior manager explained it this way: "School and the academic environment tend to reward doing things right, working hard, and being efficient. If you do that and follow the track, you are successful. Work typically rewards not necessarily doing things right, but doing the right things . . . you don't have a cookbook or a syllabus to support you in the process. You have to be smart enough to pick out the things that are important."

As a professional, you will be expected to deal with a world that is full of ambiguity, uncertainty, and gray areas. New hires usually start out expecting the same kind of clear instructions that they were used to in school. And they get frustrated when they don't get them. It's not that anybody is withholding information from you or trying to make your life difficult (as the professor would be doing if he or she acted in this manner); it's just that the professional working world is full of situations, issues, and problems that have never been dealt with before and/or are not easily defined. That's just life as a professional. That's what you will be paid well to do—to deal effectively with any situation you may encounter; to think on your feet.

You can't expect the same precise instructions you got in college. Fight the urge to get precise, explicit instructions from your boss or colleagues. Get as much information as is available, but you should be prepared to receive much less than you are accustomed to.

EXPECTATION CHECK

You develop your expectations of what the world of work will be like from a variety of sources, most of which are not completely reliable. One obvious source is the recruiters you encounter from the company. Recruiters have a tough job. While they are supposed to tell you the truth about the company (and they usually do), they are also supposed to paint a rosy enough picture of the company to convince you to come work there. Their job is to sell, not to turn you away. They play a major role in defining your expectations of the job before you go to work.

Professors are another source of expectations that affect your perceptions of the world of work. Whether you realize it or not, you have been getting lots of subtle messages in your classes. Every time professors discuss an example or case in class, relate a theory to the real world, or tell you of their personal experiences, they are helping to define your expectations of the world outside of school.

Other students also play a role. The rumors and "facts" about jobs and careers that circulate among students are usually based on a very little bit of information gleaned from peers, friends, secondhand conversations, etc. Frankly, that information is unreliable, but it often plays a major role in defining your expectations.

Parents and other relatives, neighbors, and adult role models have taught you much about the working world. While you were growing up and interacting with them, you learned much about what to expect in a career, how companies treat people, and what you should get for what you give. Whether your parents were blue- or white-collar workers, poor or rich, they have been powerful professional role models.

The media play another powerful role in shaping your perceptions about work. There aren't many occupations that haven't danced across our television screens, nor are there many people who haven't seen them portrayed in mass media. The way a job is depicted on television or radio has taught you much. Career books and programs have a similar effect.

What I want you to realize is that you've probably already defined most, if not all, of your ideas about work before you get there! And that's not good, because you really haven't had reliable enough sources to be certain about the company for which you're going to be employed. Even if your closest friend or your father has worked there for twenty years, it still won't be the same for you. So not only do you need to realize that you've defined much of your contract in advance, but also you need to discard most of it or at least label it a "draft" effort. Until you have the opportunity to test what you think are appropriate expectations against the reality of the work environment, you're just asking for trouble by proceeding with your current expectations.

I can't emphasize enough how frequently new hires are disenchanted because the preconceived ideas that they had developed about work aren't met. What follows is a list of some

---

Fast-Starter Tip

Adjust your expectations.

---

of the most important elements of the employer/employee relationship. You should use this list twice. First go through it carefully before going to work, and evaluate your expectations. If you're honest, you'll probably be surprised at how much you think you already know about working for XYZ company. Once you're aware of how many expectations and assumptions you already have, put them aside. They're not valid yet. Then use the list again after you go to work to compare your expectations against your actual work experience. In that way, you won't be disappointed.

1. **Performance.** How much is expected of you? How will it be rewarded? What are the standards for a high rating?

2. **Rewards.** How much recognition should you receive? How often should you be rewarded? What are the nonmonetary rewards? When should you expect a raise? How will rewards be tied to performance? How much advancement will you earn and when can you expect it?

3. **Job satisfaction.** How satisfied should you be with your job? Whose responsibility is job satisfaction, yours or the company's? How much "dues paying" do you have to do?

4. **Work commitment/sacrifice.** What kind of work commitment is needed? How much are you expected to sacrifice for the company? How will your sacrifices be rewarded?

5. **The job itself.** How challenging is it? How interesting is it? How much power and responsibility will you have in your work? How much will others have? Does the work provide you with status and prestige? Does the work offer job security? Is there a meaning and sense of purpose to the work? Is it fulfilling?

6. **Work environment.** Who has control over your tasks and time? What are the people like? How is the work environment structured? How much conformity is required?

PERSONAL INITIATIVE

If you are going to deal with less clear instructions and expectations, it follows that you will have to take more personal initiative. Part of graduating to the professional ranks is that you now are granted the privilege of directing yourself more. The further you advance professionally, the more you will be granted that privilege. Of course, having the privilege also means that self-direction will be expected of you. In fact, the more you demonstrate the ability to take personal initiative, the more you earn the privilege to do so.

Even in your first job, you will find that a great deal more personal initiative is expected than in college. College is, in some respects, a fairly passive and constraining environment. The curriculum is laid out for you. Your classes have a high level of certainty. Course schedules and the school calendar are very structured. There are lots of rules and regulations about what you can and can't do.

College is a bridge to the adult world. There are many personal freedoms that you gain and learn to exercise wisely (we hope), but the educational system is still fairly structured. The culture is one of learning to follow the system. If you do as you are told, you will graduate. What it encourages is a more passive follow-the-rules, meet-expectations type of approach to success.

That doesn't work in the professional world. Professionals are expected to be self-motivating, self-directing, and self-monitoring individuals. Now you won't be expected to fully master these skills the day you walk in the door, but that's what successful professionals aim for. You can expect that people will want to see you developing these skills.

This is a 180-degree shift from the college environment. If the expectations aren't going to be made clear to you, then how do you think you will come to know them? You have to figure them out yourself. If you feel you are weak in certain skill areas, whose responsibility will it be to strengthen them? Although the company may provide some training in these areas, the primary responsibility for strengthening them will be yours. If you need to know something, it will be your responsibility to ask. If you see a need in the department, you will be expected to take the initiative to meet the need.

The culture shift will manifest itself in many ways, and I should caution you that how and when to show initiative are very important for a new hire and will be discussed in a later chapter. What you need to accept early on is that with your first professional job comes not only the privilege but also the mandate to take personal responsibility for yourself and to take personal initiative. While it might be unfair to totally characterize college as "spoon feeding," the fact is, you can get through college nicely by being passive as the knowledge is fed to you. Professional life is just the opposite. That's why employers love to hire students who have held leadership positions and why colleges stress research projects—they develop personal-initiative skills. Students who have held leadership positions have demonstrated a desire and an ability to take personal initiative.

MEASURING SUCCESS

Measuring success in school is pretty easy. Every time you are asked to do something, the teacher gives you a grade that tells you exactly where you stand. Typically, you are also told how your grade stands in relation to the rest of the grades in the class. At the end of every quarter or semester, you receive a total grade for each course, an average for that three- to four-month period, and a cumulative grade point average. You may well know what your rank is in your class or at least have percentile ranks against which to judge your performance. In addition, there are specific minimum standards that you must meet in order to stay in school.

Feedback and grades are a regular and constant part of the educational process. For about seventeen years you have been used to feedback that comes at regular intervals, comes frequently, is very precise, is objective, tells you exactly where you stand all the time, measures your performance often, and tells you your standing relative to your peers. If you had any doubt about where you stood, you were encouraged to ask.

It won't be like that at work. In fact, it will be just the opposite. Feedback on your performance will not come frequently at all, often only in once-a-year performance reviews. The performance standards will not be precise and are usually quite subjective. There are no published standards to tell you specifically how to perform. It will usually boil down to your boss, to one person's opinion and perception of how well you have done. And each boss will be somewhat different. Furthermore, you will have little idea how well you are performing relative to your peers, at least until the first rounds of promotions are handed out.

That's not to say you won't know how well you are doing. The difference is that in school you were regularly given explicit feedback, whereas at work you will often have to figure out. That's a big change that is often quite frustrating to new graduates. Some feel cheated or angry when they don't receive "grades" from their bosses. Most are frustrated and anxious about their performance because they are used to more constant reinforcement.

The first thing you have to do is accept it. That's just the way the working world is. Then you have to learn new ways of judging your performance. You have to be alert to observe more subtle clues as to how well you are doing. People just don't walk into your office and hand you A's. Look for signs such as thankyous, your boss's giving you more responsibility, colleagues' coming to ask for your help, and "warm fuzzies"—small acknowledgments of a job well done.

A good boss will tell you when he or she is pleased, particularly when you are new. Thoughtful colleagues will give you feedback. But even good bosses and thoughtful colleagues get busy

Fast-Starter Tip

There's much more to success than the knowledge, skills, and abilities you learned in school.

and forget. It has probably been a while since they were new, and they have grown accustomed to less feedback (as will you). It's just a different way of doing things. That's not to say you shouldn't want or need feedback when you are new. But if you ask for "grades" on your job performance as frequently as you received them in school, you'll be seen as insecure. It's also fair to say that you're entitled to more than you'll likely get. Ask for it. It's perfectly OK to walk into your boss's or colleague's office and ask:

- How am I doing?
- What do I need to improve on?
- What do I need to learn?
- What mistakes have I made?

Many organizations will build in three- and six-month reviews to assess your job performance, which will help (if your boss remembers). If that is not enough, it's your responsibility to seek out what you need.

STANDARDS OF SUCCESS

The standards of performance change dramatically at work. In school, you can decide to put only a moderate amount of effort into a class and take a C. You can mess up one test if you have done well that semester and have other things you want to do besides study. You can stay out late one night and sleep through class the next day. In fact, in most schools you can get your degree as long as you have a 2.0 GPA (C average) or better. Maybe you won't be able to get as good a job with a 2.0 GPA, but the college or university will still award you your degree. Nobody will get upset, nobody will reprimand you as long as you perform better than the minimum.

That won't work on the job. Whenever you have an assignment you are expected to do it right. Said another way, you have to do "A" work all the time. Your boss won't be too happy if the numbers you calculated for his or her report are only 75 percent correct. You can't design a building that will work only 75 percent of the time. You can't run a manufacturing line that makes good products only 75 percent of the time. You can't sleep through meetings after a hard night of partying. You can't be a good performer one week and a poor performer another week and expect it to average out. You can't "flunk" your presentations but "pass" your technical work and still get promoted. A 70–75 percent grade on the job will likely earn you a talking-to from your boss and a clear message to improve.

Your employer will expect you to do your job well and to do it well all the time. Sure, there are differences in performance among different employees, but the differences usually are not between the A's and F's as in college but between those who perform at the B+/A- level and those who perform well beyond the A level. You remember those students you may have hated who did far more than expected and got the A++++ grades? They are now the ones who may get promoted first. This doesn't mean that you should panic if you weren't an A student, since the talent needed to get good grades and the ability to perform well on the job are often quite different. But if your grades were lower because you let them slide some, realize that this won't work now. There is no more "half credit" or "getting by," particularly in your first year. You need to become an A student on the job.

PHILOSOPHY OF THE ORGANIZATION

A university or college is a very special type of institution, with a different philosophical base from most other institutions in our society, particularly private industry. A university is designed to be a place that is somewhat insulated from society. It is specifically structured to provide a free environment for experimentation and growth and the development of knowledge. It is a place that students and professors can feel free to stretch their minds and their imaginations. Its roots are in developing people.

For you, it has been a place to grow up, to gain your independence from your parents, and to develop into an adult and a professional. For four years (or more) you were surrounded by people in an environment that was supportive and helped you grow and develop. You were allowed and encouraged to make mistakes, ask dumb questions, try new things, and discover yourself and learn something about your life's work. All the while, the university provided you with a safe haven in which to do this, a safety net of sorts to let you grow.

Work is different. Most organizations in which you might be employed do not exist for the express purpose of helping people grow and develop. While they do help their employees develop professionally, their main reason for existence is something different. Developing their employees is a means to an end, whether that end be making a product, selling a service, or whatever.

Frankly, you can get away with a lot in college because that's what college is all about—trying and learning. You can't get away with nearly so much in the workplace. People expect you to have matured, not to act like a college student still trying to grow up. Each stage of life brings its own developmental challenges, but the workplace does not exist to help you deal with them. That's now up to you, not the organization.

There is another dimension of the philosophical difference to consider too. A university's mission is to develop and teach knowledge. Its products are the thoughts and ideas developed over many years of practice and research. What that has meant for you is that you have been encouraged to challenge the existing ways of thinking, to freely ask questions, and to think of original ways to do things. Faculty and students are supposed to do research and think, to create original ideas.

These are great skills that will serve you well throughout your life, but the workplace is different. It is typically not a place that creates new knowledge but rather exists to apply knowledge. Except for the research and development areas, your mission at work is to find ways to apply knowledge in a fashion that helps accomplish the goals of the organization. And the organization may not be open to new ideas so readily. One new hire put it this way: "You go into large organizations, and some of them are open to new ideas, but a lot of them have to be continually sold on your ideas. At school, you come up with a new idea, and you don't really have to sell it."

You'll find it to be a different type of intellectual challenge. There often won't be the same kind of mind-boggling, complex issues to be analyzed and absorbed. You won't have the challenge of stretching your mind to master new material every day. There won't be the fascination of exploring new subjects and knowledge. While at first that may be a relief, you might be surprised to discover that you miss some of that. Dealing with people, office politics, and new-hire grunt work is a different type of challenge. Even in highly technical positions, you can be disappointed.

Another aspect of the knowledge business is that you are taught to think critically and to challenge your professors or at least the ideas they present. There is a spirit of academic confrontation when you get A's for questioning what a professor or other authority says. In order to create knowledge and learn to think, you have to learn to challenge the existing ways of doing things. Not so on the job. If you challenge existing ideas and ways of doing things on the job the way you did in school, you'll make enemies fast. In time you'll be able to do more of it but certainly not at first. You need to understand that constant criticism and the challenging of ideas are unique to a university and not appropriate for carrying to work. Find out how much your organization will accept before you start doing it on the job.

What, then, are some of the implications of these philosophical differences between school and work? Let's look at some.

- Work is typically not the same type of intellectual challenge as college.
- The workplace does not always freely encourage you to challenge existing ideas and ways of doing things.
- The workplace is not the place to grow up.
- Your employer will not be as interested in your personal development as your college was.
- Your knowledge must be used to do something, not to create new knowledge.
- You are not free in the workplace to make as many mistakes as you please while learning.

This doesn't mean you are expected to know everything and act as if you were 45 when you first come to work. Everyone grows and develops at work, but, because the philosophies of the organizations are so different, the degree to which you are allowed to show your immaturity (personal or professional) is much more limited. Each organization has different standards for this that you will have to come to understand.

RHYTHMS AND ROUTINES

Student life is really a very free existence. You may have felt that you were very busy and had little free time, but that was largely your choice. Typically, your class schedule would only account for about 15 to 18 hours of your week. While homework and class-related activities might occupy that much or more of the rest of your week, you were largely free to structure that time as you wished. You could study all afternoon and party all night one day and then lie in the sun one afternoon and study all night the next. If you got tired while studying, you could take a nap or go for a jog. You could get away with skipping a class occasionally to sleep in or go skiing or get ready for a big midterm. By and large, your week was yours to spend as you saw fit, except for the hours you had to be in class. That freedom is something most graduates come to miss very quickly once they finish school and begin their careers.

The workplace is quite different (in most cases). Especially in your first year, you are expected to be on the job at least five days a week, at least 8 hours a day, and to arrive and leave at the same times each day. It may be years before you earn the privilege to vary your schedule. Even if you are in a job such as sales that allows you lots of freedom to set your own schedule, you are still going to be accountable to somebody for much of your time. A routine quickly develops. Up at 6 a.m., leave the house at 7:15 a.m., at work by 8 a.m., lunch about noon, leave work between 5 and 6 p.m., dinner at 7 p.m. It doesn't have to be a rut, but your structured days will mean a more structured routine. Your time is just not as flexible or free as it was in college.

Furthermore, your workday will not be quite as flexible. As a professional, you will be given much discretion as to how you accomplish your assignments, but you can't just stop to play tennis in the middle of the afternoon, take a long lunch whenever you feel like it, or head out for happy hour at four o'clock in the afternoon. It doesn't matter anymore whether you like to sleep late or not, because there's no avoiding the eight o'clock class—now known as "work." You can't choose to do your work at 2 a.m. because you're a night owl. I don't mean to make it sound like a prison (it's not), but there are certain expectations about where you will be at certain times that make work much more restrictive than college. Most new professionals also feel that they are working more, too. The hours can be long (10–14 hours per day sometimes), and because this grueling schedule may continue day after day, month after month, work seems to be more wearing than school, even in the toughest curriculums.

One reason may be that college tends to be a series of sprints with breaks in between. The routine of college is such that you have very intense peaks followed by quiet lulls. You remember the routine: The beginning of the semester is pretty quiet until you get closer to midterms, when you have to burn the midnight oil. After midterms, you can relax for a few weeks until you have to finish your term project and then bust butt through finals. Best of all, this is followed by vacation—sometimes two or three weeks over Christmas. And even better, after twice through that cycle comes summer break: three long months to break the routine to work, travel, or play.

Working is much more of a long-distance race. There are still peaks and valleys (more so in some jobs like consulting), but the peaks tend to be as high or higher and the valleys nowhere as low. And there aren't many breaks. Two weeks of vacation is the norm for new employees. Think about it. Only two weeks compared with fifteen to twenty weeks a year when you were a student. Working is for the long haul (forty or more years), and it proceeds

at a steadier, more intense pace. A lot of stamina is required to keep this pace through long days and weeks, month after month and year after year. That's why most new hires find it much more demanding than college life.

This takes some adjustment. Your first Christmas or two at a full-time job will feel strange because you ought to be getting out for a break. Summer is even worse. You'll find that you have to pace yourself more and get used to the constancy of the work demands. You can't attack it like your midterms, burning yourself out and then taking two weeks to recover. Even in project-oriented environments, where intense periods of work followed by lulls are more common, you'll still find work more demanding than college, and you will have to adjust.

Your time perspective must change dramatically, too. In school, the "sprint" routine keeps you focused on the short term. It's the rare student who's thinking beyond the next midterm or end of the semester. If anything, students are looking just to the end of the year. Relationships with professors start and end in ten to fifteen weeks. The gratification is rather constant because you are reaching milestones quickly and frequently and then moving on. As one executive observed, "From the age of 6 or 7 when you enter school it's a continuing, natural progression for you . . . but it's always been a relatively short time frame . . . Now that you're entering the professional arena, you can't expect to reach the top of the ladder in just three or four years."

Work has a much longer-term perspective. Your career itself is a long-term thing. Relationships you build are for the long term. Projects and tasks assigned to you may last months or even years. Often the payoffs from things you do now are not fully evident for years. You can no longer count on the "quick fix" of the end of the semester to reach a conclusion.

A similar phenomenon also applies to the pace of promotions. Promotions in college happen often and at regular intervals. Every year, at an exact and expected time, you graduate or are promoted to the next level. Every semester you know you are moving up. For at least seventeen years, you have been conditioned to expect this.

At work it doesn't happen that way. To start with, promotions are no longer certain. You may or may not get promoted to the next level. It's probably fair to say that most new hires can expect to be promoted at least once, since nobody stays in entry-level jobs for an entire career, but even that is not certain. It will all depend on your performance. If they do come, promotions will not appear as often as in school. There is no regular or expected interval when the moves will occur. You will find there are certain norms or averages in each company, but even if the norm for a promotion to manager is after five years' service, you will have no idea when in the fifth year it will occur. This is a difficult adjustment.

In fact, the whole change in rhythms and routines is a difficult one to adapt to. Whether you realized it or not, you became very conditioned to a certain pace and flow of life while a student. And that rhythm has stayed the same for most of your life to this point. Now much of that will change, and it can literally take years to adjust.

TEACHERS VERSUS BOSSES

When you go to work, you will encounter a relationship you may not have had much experience with yet, and that is your relationship with the boss. This relationship is unlike any other in your life; a whole chapter is devoted to it later to help you understand it better and make it work for you. Suffice it to say for now that the old rules don't apply.

In some ways, bosses are like professors. They have a great deal of control over your working life and will set performance expectations and standards for you. They have the power to reward and punish you and thereby to influence your future. Because there are such similarities between the roles of professor and boss, it's easy to see them as one and the same, but that's a mistake. Bosses are not really like professors. A teacher's or professor's agenda is to help you develop, and his or her own performance is judged, at least in part, by how successfully you learn and develop. Professors teach because they gain intrinsic satisfaction out of conveying their knowledge to you and watching you grow intellectually and professionally.

Bosses have a very different agenda. They have been charged with getting certain things done, and you work for them to help them achieve those goals. Their main mission in life is not to teach and develop you, although that is part of their job. If you turn to your boss as a teacher, mentor, or hand-holding type, your boss will be quite frustrated. The relationship with your boss is just an extension of the basic philosophy discussed earlier.

A professor's job is to give to you rather constantly. While professors certainly expect you to do work and turn in assignments, for the most part they spend their days imparting counsel, advice, and knowledge to students. You are encouraged to probe deeper and ask questions to get more from them. Professors are supposed to listen to your ideas and thoughts. With a boss, the flow is in exactly the opposite direction. In this relationship, it is your role to give to the boss, not vice versa. Particularly in your early years as a staff person, you are there to give support, information, and assistance to your boss. Your job is to make his or her life easier by giving all the support you can. Your boss also gets busy, however, and may not have time for you or want your ideas.

Do you see the risk in viewing your boss as a professor? If you treat your boss like a professor, you will find yourself pulling on your boss, expecting him or her to be working for you in a sense, as your professor did. But you're supposed to work for the boss! As you might imagine, he or she gets very frustrated with this approach. You need to realize there is a fundamental shift in roles between a boss and a teacher. A boss isn't your helpmate, your counselor, your adviser nor is he or she there to serve you. Basically, you're there to serve the boss.

LEVEL OF INVOLVEMENT

In some respects, your college degree prepares you to do all the wrong things when you enter the working world. The things it prepares you to do are typically not what you'll do when you start your career. That is usually a shock to new hires. In college, architecture students design new buildings, but it will be years before they get that kind of responsibility on the job. Marketing majors may plan grand marketing strategies for entire product lines in school but start their careers doing market research in a shopping mall. The design work an engineer performs in the first few years may be a long way from the complex designs done in school. But, says one senior executive, "you need to realize that all those skills you learned are not things you are probably going to be able to put into practice in the first few years of your work experience. It's a very rare individual who gets that opportunity."

The difference between school and work is one of level of responsibility. What college is preparing you for is the thought processes that will be needed ten to twenty years down the road. College simplifies the problems and assignments so that they are manageable with limited experience. That's an appropriate role for colleges, but it leaves you with two mistaken beliefs: that you are ready to tackle high-level assignments and that you'll be given the opportunity to do so. Wrong! The truth is that the real world is so complex that it will take years to gain the experience needed to perform at as high a level as you thought you had reached in your senior year in college. You simply don't have enough background to do it right away. Instead of making big decisions you will be doing detail work (often operational in nature), supporting others, etc.

That's usually very frustrating to new hires. Those high-level tasks that look more exciting are what they're really aiming for in their careers. Nobody told them they can't perform at that level now, and part of their frustration comes because they feel they're being held back unnecessarily. The other part comes in realizing that it will take longer to get there than they thought. In fact, it looks as if it will take forever to get to the "good stuff." But they soon learn there are plenty of other challenges to meet first.

When you first start work, you'll probably find that you'll have your hands full just learning and doing the things you need to before you get to the higher-level tasks. The only way to get to what you think is the good stuff is to do the best job you possibly can at the lower-level assignments. That may not be what you expected, but you'll never get beyond the less desirable assignments if you don't excel at them. If you're like most, you'll find you enjoy them quite a bit more than you thought, once you adapt to the reality of the level you'll really work at. For the sake of your mental health, you need to enjoy what you're doing on a daily basis. Reaching goals is fine, but you have to enjoy the getting there, too.

OTHER DIFFERENCES

And there are other differences between student and professional life to be considered, too.

1. **Results versus perfectionism.** While the quality of your performance at work may need to be "A" in terms of meeting expectations, that won't always mean doing work perfectly as it did in school. One finance executive commented, "In the academic environment, it is really important to do the homework or paper very thoroughly. But when you come into our world, we want [you] to be thorough but [you] don't have as long to deliver a product as [you] are used to." The results you achieve may or may not be perfect ones. You have to

figure out what quality is needed in each task and strive for that.

2. **Team effort versus individual effort.** "In school you can be an absolute success just by yourself . . . You really are much more in charge of your own success or failure. When you come to the business world, you can't do anything by yourself . . . If you don't understand how to work as a team leader, be in charge of a group, or work with colleagues to meet the needs you have to accomplish, you are dead," explained one manager. It will be a big change from what you were used to in school. It's now people, not just books and data.

3. **"Real world" versus the theoretical.** Work is the real world, not imaginary cases or exercises that fit nice, neat theories. The things you do affect real people, have real meaning, affect real dollars, unlike a paper or class presentation, where you can decide whether or not to care about it. The real world won't very neatly fit the theories you learned at all. You'll have to use theory as a base, a starting point, and then figure out how to apply it.

4. **Organizational versus individual control.** "Your fate is only in your hands to a very small degree," commented one insightful second-year employee. While professors had control over some of your fate, compared with work, you had much more control over your own destiny than you thought. At work, many things are simply out of your control. Things will happen to you and decisions made about you over which you have little control.

5. **Competition versus onward and upward.** In school, you advance often and fairly certainly. Everyone wants you to move on and move up. There's plenty of room for everyone to advance, since there's no limit on the number of degrees that can be awarded. That's not necessarily true in the working world. There isn't unlimited advancement, so there's a great deal of competition. Your colleagues may not help you because if you succeed, they or someone else whom they respect or like may not get promoted. There may be people who will feel threatened by you and try to stop your success.

6. **No answers versus right answers.** "Nobody knows all the answers," said one new hire. "There is nobody you can go to that knows all of them—there just isn't. In school, you had your little class, and they taught you everything; you went to the teachers, and they told you the answers. But in the real world, there is nobody that does that." And to compound that, you may be facing problems or situations for which nobody knows if there is a right answer; you just have to find the best answer.

7. **Mixture versus similar people.** In school, you were with a large group of people all very similar to you. You tackled the same problems and issues and advanced together. You were surrounded by peers. At work, you'll have many fewer peers and be surrounded by many people who are older, wiser, and more experienced than you. It can be intimidating and uncomfortable because you don't have the support of your peers as you used to.

8. **Tested every day versus occasionally.** Some new hires have described the first year on the job as one big test, somewhat like taking final exams all the time. That's a pretty accurate description. Unlike college, where you are tested or evaluated only occasionally (perhaps only twice a semester), at work it happens every day. There certainly will be some projects that are more important than others, but it's best to think of each as being as important as the most important exams you took in school. And expect them every day.

LETTING GO OF THE OLD YOU

You have a choice to make when moving from school to job: to fight these changes or accept the fact that you need to make adjustments and let go of the old you. Changing and adapting won't be easy, but you can take a giant step toward a smooth transition by deciding one thing here and now: to let go of the old you. That is, to recognize that you are leaving behind your student days and entering the professional world. If you continue to think and act like a student or treat other people and view the world as such, you will not make a very good professional. It's often easy to hang on to old familiar ways of doing things, but you have to let go. If you don't let go of your student image, how can you be open to accepting a new professional way of life?

Picture yourself standing at a crossroad: in one direction lies your student life, which is very comfortable and familiar to you, and in the other direction is the professional world, which you have worked hard to get to. You have to choose your direction; only you can choose to let go of the old you. You have to make a decision to turn away from your student life and commit yourself to becoming a professional. When you do, only then will you truly be on your way as a professional.

ULTIMATE SURVIVAL TIPS

Beware of letting these old student ways of thinking contaminate your new job.

1. They don't tell me what I'm supposed to do.

2. Nobody will tell me how things work around here.

3. I never really know how well I'm doing.

4. I can just blow off this assignment because I performed my other assignments well.

5. My boss doesn't care about me and my development.

6. Work is boring.

7. Nobody wants to accept my ideas even if I know a "better" way.

8. When do I get my vacation?

9. This is just grunt work; it's beneath me.

10. When do I get to do what I was trained for?

While each of these objections could be a sign of a problem for the organization, for a new hire it usually means you're still thinking like a student. Remember: Your new employer didn't hire you to be a student. He or she hired you to be a new professional.

CHAPTER

3

BREAKING-IN STRATEGIES

You know, they kind of threw me in the middle of the river. It was like "which shore do I swim to?" I was always dodging logs to get to the sides.

As this new hire confirms, there are many pitfalls and hazards that you will need to dodge during your first year at work. It should be clear by now that a major reason for this is that the first year on the job is a peculiar one. It is a transition year during which you bridge the gap between student life and a long, successful career. It's a year that has elements of both lifestyles but not all the elements of either one. You are now a professional with a different set of challenges and expectations, yet you aren't fully accepted as a professional. You are a "professional trainee." Your first year is when your colleagues will decide whether or not to accept you as a professional. To continue with our new hire's analogy, during your first year you are caught in the middle of a river, with dangerous logs floating in your way. The logs are the obstacles and pitfalls you will encounter.

Your challenge is to avoid the logs and, if possible, swim to shore unharmed.

But if you want to avoid the logs and swim ashore safely, you'll have to adopt some special breaking-in thoughts and strategies. This all goes back to Chapter 1 about the basic dynamics of the first year. As stated there, the first year is a time to prove yourself, a time in which you must earn the right to be called a professional and also earn your acceptance as a member of the work team. You have to prove that you are a competent professional capable of accepting responsibility and that you are worthy of your colleagues' trust and confidence. Most of what you have heard or read in other books about climbing the career ladder and being successful overlooks this crucial step; indeed, much of it applies only *after* you get through the breaking-in stage.

What I'd like to suggest is that you put on the back burner many of your thoughts, plans, and strategies about how to achieve success within your company. Delay them about six to twelve months. There is a whole other set of tasks, strategies, and challenges facing you that are built on the foundation material we've already discussed. I expect that you are anxious to get going, full of energy and "chomping at the bit" to charge into your career. That's great, but if you can find the patience to start a little more carefully and do the right things, you'll be much better off later on. In this chapter, you'll learn some specific strategies you can use to get a fast start and be effective during your breaking-in period.

EASY DOES IT AT FIRST

I was watching a horse race on television the other day, and I noticed that the jockey on the favored horse would not let the horse run hard at the beginning. Like most good thoroughbreds, this horse kept trying to race, but the jockey pulled back on the reins to keep him in the middle of the pack. Finally, as they came into the turn off the backstretch, the jockey began to let him loose. He had waited until he could pick the right time and spot and then allowed the horse to surge ahead and break free from the pack. By the time they entered the homestretch, the horse was in the right position on the track at full stride, with the other horses tiring and fading. This horse won easily.

That's sort of how I see the breaking-in process. You are like that thoroughbred, anxious to burst out of the starting gate and race hard from the start. I don't blame you. I was

exactly the same way years ago. What nobody bothered to tell me back then was that I needed to take it much easier at first. I always thought that employers wanted to see a hard-charging, "big splash" type of start from a new college graduate. You know what I mean—the type of start that will impress the boss in the first two weeks, drawing attention to you immediately. Well, I made a big splash all right, but all I did was get everybody soaking wet. I may have drawn attention to myself, but it surely wasn't the type of attention I wanted. And that's exactly what is likely to happen to you if you try the "big splash" approach.

Fast-Starter Tip

The quickest way to make a "big splash" is to have the maturity not to try.

Why is that? Let's go back to some basic facts about your situation.

No matter how good a student you were (or are), you don't know much about how to use your knowledge in the real world.

Even if you miraculously did know, people won't pay much attention, because you don't have the track record to command their respect.

Even if you did have a track record, at this point you have no idea what the rules of the game are at your particular company.

Even if you did know the rules, until you are accepted as part of the team you will have difficulty implementing your ideas.

That suggests, then, that you have these fundamental goals for your first year: (1) learn how to apply your knowledge, (2) build a track record of competence, (3) learn the culture and rules of the game, and (4) get accepted as part of the team. The first goal, learning to apply your knowledge, will be forced on you by the tasks you are asked to perform. The other three, although seemingly very simple goals, are really quite complex and will occupy the better part of your first year. It's your choice whether you do them well or make a fool of yourself.

If you buy this at all, you should see that you can't walk into a company and expect to be effective immediately. You have a lot to learn and much work to do in building a foundation of respect and credibility. This is true of any newcomer to an organization, but it is particularly true of new college graduates. What I hear over and over again from executives and managers is how they wish new graduates would slow down a bit when they come to work.

You can say to yourself, "I'm going to show them that I'm the hottest person they've hired in the last twenty years," and most likely you're going to make an absolute fool of yourself. On several occasions you may end up creating an organizational problem by getting somebody from another part of the business ticked off at you. Or you may dig yourself into a hole if you're not careful, because you don't have the basis of understanding how the company operates or what its philosophy is as yet. You may end up creating problems for yourself that are going to be very difficult to overcome later on.

I tell people to jump in, jump in early . . . but only after you have a real understanding of the business.

You have to slow down and pay attention to culture, team building, and other matters we've discussed. You see, there is little or no risk from starting slowly. It is the rare manager who will criticize you for taking the time to learn, to

foster relationships, to study the culture, and to build a track record before you attempt to become a major player and make a big splash in the organization. This may seem ironic and illogical to you, but one of the quickest ways to impress your boss is to have the maturity and patience to take it easy at first and not try to impress him or her. That is worth repeating: the biggest splash you can make is to have the maturity to take it easy at first and not try to do what you can't.

Fast-Starter Tip

Keep your eyes and ears open and your mouth shut during the first six months.

The time will come in your first year when you need to stop lying low. In some companies the time may come very quickly, and in others, not until the second year. You may have a great boss who will give you lots of room to try your wings very early, or you may have one who holds you back a long time. Some new hires will feel ready very early, others not until later. You can bet you're not as ready as you think you are. I can't tell you exactly when you should start becoming more assertive in the organization. For most people, it happens slowly: bit by bit, almost imperceptibly, you become more and more a part of the work group and work flow, until one day you suddenly feel as if you now know what you are doing and have arrived. It could be the way your boss starts to treat you, the respect you get from your colleagues, the way your subordinates begin to come to you with questions, or the new responsibilities you are given. You'll know when it happens. What I can promise you, though, is if you don't start slowly, the time at which this acceptance happens will be delayed. Accept the fact that you aren't ready to take major responsibility on day one, that you have lots to learn about the people and the organization, and you'll be on the right track.

LEARN!

Of course, starting slowly doesn't mean wasting time. One of your biggest goals for the first year is to learn everything you possibly can. Your new employer wants and expects that. As one employer put it, "You ought to be a sponge. You have to soak up or learn as much as you can get your hands on." Your employer wants to see you hungry to learn. You need to be insatiable, constantly looking for everything new you can find to learn. This seems obvious, but few new hires do it.

Look at it from your employer's viewpoint for a moment. He or she knows that the organization is very complex and that your job is equally complex. He or she knows that it takes much of the first year for you to absorb all you need to and will give you the time to do it. But your employer will want to see the time used well. One manager put it this way: "You've got an awful lot to learn . . . The sooner you learn it, the sooner you can start making contributions and the sooner you are going to be recognized as a fast-tracker." Another manager concurred: "It's almost like learn as much as you can and then look up and look for some more . . . You want to keep broadening the areas where you can add value."

Fast-Starter Tip

Be a "need-to-know" instead of a "know-it-all" new hire.

Thus, learning all you can as fast as you can makes good sense, because:

- It's what will earn the respect of your employer.
- It shows maturity.
- It's what you need to be successful anyway.

In your first year, the performance level expected of you has been reduced to give you the opportunity to learn—probably for the only time in your career—why not take advantage of it?

BUILDING A TRACK RECORD

The quickest way to earn respect is to demonstrate your competence on the job. In most organizations, results are the most important thing. People will excuse lots of mistakes, put up with your idiosyncrasies, and give you respect if you can deliver results. Conversely, you can have the best people skills in the world, build great relationships, learn the culture well, etc., but if you can't do your job and do it well, the rest doesn't matter. All of these other elements of the workplace are very important, but they are important only because they help you get results.

This means that learning your job and doing it well are critical. I'm not necessarily talking about flashy, glamorous, or grandiose accomplishments. Most managers observe that new hires seem to look for the glamorous opportunities to show their competence but do a poor job on the day-to-day tasks they face. While "hitting home runs" may one day be a good strategy for getting ahead, you have to start by doing a good job at the fundamentals, "hitting singles," if you will. You might be able to design a great new manufacturing process, but if you can't keep the current one running effectively, you're not doing your job. You might be able to make one huge sale to a big new customer, but you have to keep all your regular customers satisfied, too. You usually won't be given opportunities for the glamorous assignments until you have clearly demonstrated your competence at the fundamentals of the job.

Fast-Starter Tip

Competence breeds opportunities for success.

What you want is to build a track record of successes. They don't have to be big and glamorous during your first year, just successful. You need to work at putting together a string of assignments, big and small, that send forth a clear message to your colleagues and management that you:

- Are a competent professional
- Get things done
- Do your assignments thoroughly
- Do them well
- Succeed when given the chance

Your colleagues and the management need to develop trust and confidence in your ability to do your job. It's not that they think you can't do it; they just don't know. Show them. In your first year, it's a string of consistent, strong successes that will get you ahead.

To do this, you need to find opportunities to succeed. The strategy that is most likely to succeed for you is to look for assignments that give you a chance to do well. Look for projects, tasks, or assignments that fit your skills and talents, are within your ability to do well, have some importance, and require you to stretch yourself a little to finish them. Avoid mundane, simple kinds of tasks (if you can), because you'll gain no credit for doing something beneath you. Start with something that you think you can do with a little bit of extra effort and learning. Then do the best job you possibly can. Follow that with another task or project, perhaps a notch above the last one. And do that well. Keep doing this, and you are on your way to building a track record of success.

One way to increase your chances of getting good results is to focus your energies and efforts. Don't try to tackle too much—too much just dilutes your energy. Focus on the things that really matter and are within reach for you to succeed.

There are other strategies that are more risky but may work in certain businesses. One is to "go for broke"; that is, to go for a big accomplishment very early. This could be a big deal, a big new customer, a new invention, or whatever. The payoff is that if you win, you win bigger. The problem is that the odds of a new college graduate hitting the big payoff and winning are very low. And if your big gamble doesn't pay off, you have nothing to fall back on.

I strongly recommend a more conservative strategy. If you spend six to twelve months building a base of professional credibility and a track record of competence, you will have something to fall back on. Once you've built your base, you can opt for a riskier career strategy to try and get on the fast track. But this way, if the risk doesn't pay off, at least you have your previous record to support you. If you take the risky strategy early on, it's sort of an "all-or-nothing" approach that only the biggest risk-seekers can tolerate. Start slowly, build a track record, and then pick your time to try to break out of the pack.

MAKING THE RIGHT MISTAKES

There is a lot of talk these days about how badly we need more risk-takers in organizations, more entrepreneurial spirit, etc. The evidence is fairly strong that the risk-averse, "let's-keep-from-making-mistakes" culture often leads to organizations that are stodgy, bureaucratic, and generally not very creative. To counter this, many organizations are changing or have changed their culture to encourage employees to take risks. They do this by not punishing mistakes and some reward people for new initiatives even if they fail.

Each organization has its own risk profile, and you have to learn how much risk-taking is tolerated at your company. Some companies may want to see you trying new things and making mistakes. Particularly in smaller, entrepreneurial firms, the expectation may be one of experimentation and risk-taking. Other firms may have a much more cautious approach and not look upon mistakes as a very positive thing. Depending upon the company, then, mistakes can be either damaging to your career or a help to it.

There's a special standard for new hires: making the right mistakes. Regardless of the risk profile of the company, there are mistakes that will be perceived as dumb or naive. These are the wrong mistakes that happen because you just don't think through what you're doing, don't do what you're told, don't manage yourself or your job well, or don't work hard enough. They are the ones that remind people you are young and naive and aren't a strong performer. These are the mistakes that hurt your career.

The right mistakes are the ones that you make because you try something new based on sound logic, but it just doesn't work out. These mistakes come from initiative that fits the risk profile of the company. These are the new ideas, new approaches to customers, new relationships you try to establish that have potential but fail. Frankly, such moves often fail in your first year because you don't have enough experience. But that's OK since they are "smart" mistakes—the ones that show your creativity, intelligence, and initiative.

Generally, it's fair to say that most new hires need to learn that making mistakes is more acceptable and necessary in organizations (particularly business organizations) than in school. In many organizations, if you're doing everything 100 percent right, you're not sticking out your neck enough. It really is OK to make some mistakes. But there are three keys to the first year:

- Learn your company's risk profile to find out how many mistakes, what size of mistakes, and what kinds of mistakes are acceptable.

- Make sure you are making smart mistakes, not dumb ones.

- Be sure the mistakes you make won't hurt your boss or the organization very much. That's too big a gamble in your first year. Look for smaller initiatives.

Equally important as choosing the right mistakes to make is what you do after making them. Your employer knows that mistakes are part of learning. Choose the right ones to make, and then be sure to:

- Accept responsibility for your mistakes (don't pass on the blame).
- Never make the same mistake a second time. As one manager put it, "It's an error until they make the error twice, and then it's a mistake."
- Develop an action plan to learn from your mistake and prevent it from happening again.

It's repeated dumb mistakes or cover-ups that will get you into trouble. Even though managers like to talk about needing more people who are willing to make mistakes, remember that not all mistakes are the same. When you're breaking in, you want to make smart mistakes that show you're taking the initiatives you should be, but with sound judgment.

EMBRACING THE ORGANIZATION

Chances are the organization is pretty happy with "who" it is and how it does things. It has likely been around a while before you started work and will probably be around a good while after you leave. The people in it are probably reasonably content with the way things are, or they would have left by now. Even if they aren't completely content, they don't really want some brash new kid telling them that things ought to be different. People will react defensively to a newcomer's criticisms, even if they agree with them, because the newcomer is an outsider.

What people in the organization want to see early on is that you want to be part of the team. They want to see you accepting them and their culture, values, and ways of doing things before they fully accept you. Think about it. Why should they welcome you and accept you into their organization if you don't reciprocate? You don't have to, and shouldn't, act like the head cheerleader at a football game, but you should make a concerted effort to demonstrate visibly that you are embracing the organization and what it stands for.

Step one is to adopt what I call "we think." The organization is a team, and if you are to be part of it, you have to join in mentally. What are the team's goals and objectives? Whatever they are, they need to become important to you. What are its problems and concerns? You need to be worried about those things, too. What is expected of your work group? You need to have the same expectations. Nobody expects you to adopt all this on your first day, but you must make a strong effort to integrate and sincerely demonstrate that you are thinking like a team member. It can't be an insincere or false sort of thing, but your employer and colleagues want to see you believe in what they believe in.

They also want to see you embrace their culture. You will very quickly learn that certain values and norms are very important. In a small town, community service might be very important for the organization; safety could be a key value at another company; long hours and strong dedication might be the norm at another.

The group will be accustomed to doing things in certain ways, and this will be seen in both official procedures and informal work methods. The organization and its people generally will have accepted their culture, and while many will not be totally happy about it, they will nonetheless have "bought into it" and expect you to do the same.

What they want to see is some enthusiasm for what they are and what they do. Don't overdo it, but show it. Be interested. Ask questions. Get excited sometimes. Keep your criticisms to yourself. Volunteer to help with things. Use your energy and actions, not just your words, to show that you want to be part of what's going on.

Be sure to attend all company events. This means everything from meetings to lunches to happy hours to weekend parties. Even though they may officially be labeled "optional," the team players will be there. Later you will learn which activities can be skipped, but for now you are an outsider who needs to show support for the organization. Once you are accepted as an insider, you can pick and choose a bit.

Fast-Starter Tip

**You are an outsider until
you prove otherwise.**

Does this sound a bit hokey and insincere? Well, maybe it is a little, but it works. People will respect efforts on your part to adapt to and embrace the organization. Sure, it will be a little awkward at times, a little uncomfortable, and, yes, people may even realize that you are trying to be the "good soldier." But that's OK. The important thing is to broadcast the message that you want to learn about and participate in all the aspects of the company you can and that you want to be part of the team. That wins respect.

And what if you don't totally agree with the team values, desires, and norms? Well, that's OK, too, but just save it for later. For now, go along with it (as long as it's legal and ethical). Later, once you are accepted as part of the team, you can be a little more free to criticize. Eventually you will get chances to change the things you don't like. If things get too bad, you can change jobs. But in your first year, you can only lose if you don't go along with the established culture.

GOING THE EXTRA MILE

What you lack in experience, knowledge of the company, and maturity you can partially make up for with extra effort. There are plenty of people who'll work only the standard amount or exert only a reasonable effort. What every employer needs is more people who are willing to stretch themselves to do outstanding work. As one new hire said, "It's just trying to do whatever it takes to go the extra mile." Most managers are willing to give opportunities to new employees who demonstrate that they have the right attitude and are willing to work extra hard. It is effort and dedication to working hard that stand out to managers and earn you their respect early on. Several managers have remarked on the importance of going the extra mile.

*It's real drudgery to deal with people who
you know are basically going to do what you
ask and no more . . . I think a new hire*

should bend over backward when he or she enters the workforce and work as hard as he or she can.

What employers are looking for are new hires who aren't watching the clock . . . who aren't weighing their effort against what they're paid and don't take a "that's-not-my-job" attitude. Employers want new employees who say, "I'll do whatever it takes to do the job well and help this organization succeed." Sure, there's a point in their careers when employees need to weigh their efforts against the rewards received, but it's not in the first year.

There are lots of ways to show you're willing to go the extra mile:

- Working late and coming to work early
- Volunteering for the tough or less desirable assignments
- Making time to help your colleagues
- Working extra hard to make up for your inexperience
- Asking for increased responsibility
- Taking initiative (when appropriate)
- Doing extra training on your own time

Dedication and effort are two things you can show the employer the minute you walk in the door, regardless of your experience or background. You'll make a quick, positive impression, because employers can see that with enough effort, you'll perform well early on and throughout your career.

FINDING A COACH

I expect most readers are familiar with the concept of mentoring. Many authors advocate finding a mentor to help you rise in the organization. Most of those who have succeeded can point to one or more people who took a special interest in them and helped them speed along in their career.

However, the first year on the job is not the time to be look for a mentor. While it may be wonderful if it happens, it's simply much too early in your career to expect to find a true mentor. A mentor is someone who will take you under a wing and help you get promoted. No one will adopt you as a protégé without watching you for awhile to see if you are worth mentoring, a process that takes more than a few weeks or months. Furthermore, you don't just go out and advertise for a mentor, nor do you generally choose your own mentor. Mentors generally pick their protégés or the relationship just develops. As one experienced mentor explained:

Everyone wants a mentor, and everyone wants the right mentor. Unfortunately, if you're a mentor, you're never going to have enough time to entertain all of those people who want you to help them through their careers. Consequently, you're going to pick out those with special attributes or accomplishments who are worth your time and effort, investing effort where you can see what the payback is going to be. I would say that it's very dangerous for a new hire to go into a job with the express intent of picking a mentor within the first week. The new hire doesn't have a portfolio of accomplishments or job mastery to give the mentor in return. It's more important to look for an experienced hand or role model first.

You should be looking for the guidance of more senior members of the organization during the first year. The fastest-starting new employees do seem to establish relationships with people who have been around the organization awhile and are willing to help. These people are more like coaches, since the implied commitment is not to enhancing your promotional opportunities but simply to helping you get off to a good start. Some companies have even formalized this process by establishing a buddy system of sorts between senior management and new hires during their training period.

A coach can play a very key role in your learning the ropes and gaining acceptance quickly. An ideal coach has the following characteristics:

- Has been around the organization a good while (more than ten years)
- Has a sincere interest in helping young people
- Is willing to take the time to do so
- Is respected in the organization
- Appears to be part of the mainstream thinking and activity in the organization
- Is outside your immediate reporting line so you can talk freely and openly
- Is someone you are comfortable with

Are such people hard to find? You bet, but they're worth their weight in gold when you find them.

Good coaches usually have a strong developmental streak and love to help new employees grow and develop. They take great pride and pleasure in assisting in the process of helping new employees ease into the company. Not only are coaches usually not in your direct reporting line, but they also are not often in the personnel department, since personnel plays an official role in your career and has to be more careful to adhere to the party line. Good coaches will tell you how things really are and how they actually get done in your company. They don't just tell you the policy or the public position but will give you the inside scoop, dirt and all. I don't mean gossip but the straight and honest truth. They are usually very careful to acknowledge their own biases (and you should be cautious of these, too), and they have been around long enough to cut through the bull.

Good coaching is an ideal way to learn about an organization's culture. In fact, coaches are often the culture personified. And they are willing to share what they know. Talk to them about:

- All elements of company culture
- How to get ahead in your first year
- The power structure
- Your boss
- Other people you work with
- Problems and difficulties you have
- Their perceptions of your progress
- How things should be done

Respect the time they are willing to devote to talking to you, and don't abuse it.

A coach can also help you get accepted. Just the fact that this person is willing to talk with you indicates that he or she accepts you. If the coach is a respected member of the organization, his or her acceptance will be an indication to others in the organization that they should do the same. Be careful, then, not to do anything to hurt your coach's credibility, since he or she is taking some risk by being in your corner.

Coaches are great when you are having difficulties on the job. For one thing, they can give you good advice on handling problems and getting out of jams. Equally important is that they give you a safe haven within which to vent your frustrations. Many a new hire has been saved much embarrassment by first talking over frustrations with a coach.

ROLE MODELS

While coaches tell you how things are, role models show you. One of the quickest ways to learn what you need to be doing is simply to observe those people who seem to be successful. Organizations generally only allow people to be successful who fit their culture and expectations reasonably well. How do you find a good role model? "Look around your organization, your peer group, the people who are doing the same job you're doing, and find the best people in that group," advised a senior manager. "Once you find them, figure out what they're doing and how they're doing it and what things you can do in a similar way." Added a new hire, "You walk in and kind of spy out the people whom other employees like. Then you have to sit back and kind of wonder why people like that person so much, what it is about that person."

Role models will be all around you. The most obvious ones are people who have been promoted to positions of significant responsibility at a fairly rapid pace. These could be people who are only a step or two ahead of you

or those many steps beyond you. In fact, it should probably be both. Look for people from last year's new-hire group who seem to be doing the best. Look also at people who are in positions to which you aspire and at those in between. Observe them carefully to find out:

- How they approach their work
- What skills they have that you don't
- How they dress
- What strategies they used to get into their positions
- What interpersonal skills they have
- What they say about the company's culture

Use these people as models to develop an action plan for your first year.

You do have to be careful, though, that you pick the right role models. Be careful to avoid people who are dead-ended in their job or appear to be mavericks in the organization, even if they are successful. Organizations sometimes tolerate and even promote people who get results in an unorthodox way. Modeling yourself after them is a high-stakes gamble that likely won't work. For your first year, you need to find role models who represent the more conventional, mainstream way of doing things.

TALK TO PEOPLE

When it comes to finding a mentor, over and over I have heard managers suggest one simple strategy that is not used often enough: Talk to people. A simple fact of human nature is that people love to talk about themselves. Spend time talking to them. Find out what they do. Ask how they got to where they are today. Ask them what they think is important to get ahead in the company. Ask them what they like to see new hires do. Keep asking and you will soon see a pattern develop among the many people you talk to. It's ironic, but by confessing what you don't know and what you need to know, you will gain their respect for your maturity and initiative.

"Everybody at the root of it loves to be a teacher," added one executive. "Take advantage of it. What that means is come in, be eager, be energetic, be bright, but listen. You haven't been taught the last three or four years to listen. Listen and absorb; learn as much as you can. Draw as much information out of people as you can. Don't challenge them. Try to truly understand them, and you'll find that that person will be dedicated to helping you, because it's very rare that people come by and ask what you do and why you do it."

BUILD YOUR RESOURCE NETWORK

To be effective in an organization, you need a network of people who can help you get things done. You'll need information of all sorts, including everything from a specific piece of information for performing a task to inside information on where certain people stand on particular issues. You'll need advice on how to deal with the policies and procedures and, perhaps, the bureaucracy of the organization. Also, you'll want advice on the best way of accomplishing things or on career decisions you have to make. Sometimes you'll need ideas when you're stuck for one, or you'll need someone to play devil's advocate with your ideas. And the list goes on.

Those who are effective in their jobs build relationships with all sorts of people. As they grow in the organization, they use this network of colleagues and contacts to aid them. They also realize early on that good resource people aren't just the high-ranking ones. In fact, it's often the non-VIPs who can tell you how to really get something done in the organization.

Use your first year to build your resource network. Look all around you, not just up the ladder. As one manager advised, "Make allies with the people at your own level or one level up first. They will be the people who teach you about the organization and what is accepted and what's not. And they can teach you about the job because they are closest to it." Secretaries are wonderful resource people who are often overlooked. A secretary who likes you can make your life easy; one who doesn't can make it miserable. Other colleagues are obvious choices, as are managers other than your own. Don't forget other people in support positions such as those in the supply room, purchasing, building maintenance, and so on.

The strategy is to meet and develop a rapport with as many people as you can in the organization. As a rookie, you have the perfect excuse to do it. Find out what they do and how you can help each other in the future. Don't be afraid to approach people: they need to have contacts as much as you do. You may not know immediately how or why you will need a person in the future, but as you progress, you'll find many reasons to connect with your resource network.

WORKING FOR THE FUTURE

The first year on your first job is really just a time to lay foundations for the future. It's almost like another year of college in that you're still learning and preparing for your career, even though you're already getting paid for it. Yet many new hires are narrowly focused, looking only at immediate tasks and the rewards that are coming to them immediately. That's not a good strategy. I hear new professionals who say things like "That's not what I was hired to do," "I didn't go to college to do this," "I'm not getting paid enough for that," and "This is peon's work." What they don't realize is that nobody wants to stay in the same position, at the same salary, with the same status that they have in the first year for the rest of their career. It's just a start.

You need to take a long-term view of everything you do your first year. You ought to work harder and do more than you're being paid for. Your reward will come later as you earn promotions and grow in the organization. A narrow, short-term perspective won't earn you the respect that will open up the opportunities to advancement. Mature professionals understand making short-term sacrifices for long-term career growth. Just imagine that

you're being paid twice what you're really making, and then act and perform at that level as much as you can. New hires who do this are the ones targeted for faster growth.

It should be acknowledged that things have changed in the workplace. Before this, there was a time when employees could expect an organization to take care of them for the long run, perhaps even for life, if they made sacrifices for the company. A long-term perspective made sense, since it was possible to work for rewards that might be twenty or thirty years away. The eighties, however, will be remembered for the shock and disappointment that took place as restructurings, mergers, and changed economic conditions upset many careers. As a result, the new standard is one of less distant horizons and less long-term loyalty in many companies, although not as short as new hires often have. These days, you don't necessarily have to look ten or twenty years down the road when plotting your career course within the organization; two to five years will do fine. Just look beyond the first year, and understand that you are building for the future.

ULTIMATE SURVIVAL TIPS

1. Look for areas in which you can contribute early on.

2. Know your limitations. If you take on too much and spread yourself too thin, you are not going to do a good job at anything.

3. Work very hard early on, because if you do and it gets noticed, you will have a reputation as a good worker for the rest of your career.

4. Leave the brownnosing and politics for later on—just demonstrate who you are and what you're capable of doing.

5. Show a positive attitude. You have to be happy at what you're doing; if you're not, it's obvious to everyone.

6. The danger is that you'll come across like a college kid. Try to avoid that.

7. Figure out exactly what you are supposed to do, exactly how you are supposed to do it, and whose help you need and don't need to get the job done.

8. Get to work early, work overtime if necessary, and do whatever it takes to go the extra mile.

9. Check your ego at the door.

10. If you want to succeed, you have to play by the rules.

11. Perceptions are often as important as reality. Above all else, you must be perceived as a professional.

12. Don't try and run things. Listen. Understand the organization and understand the politics. Act very humble.

13. Don't get discouraged!

PART

2

JOINING PEOPLE
ON THE TEAM

4

Managing the Impressions You Make

A common and difficult issue new professionals face is getting noticed by senior management and colleagues. When you join an organization, you are an unknown entry-level employee, one of perhaps many newly minted college graduates in the same situation. Nobody knows who you are or what you can do. If you are part of a large group of new hires, you may feel like just one of the crowd, and, frankly, to others in the company you probably are.

In both small and large companies, you have to worry about catching the eye of mid-level and senior management. They have a great deal of influence over your long-term career, yet they are at least several levels removed from you. If it is a large company, you may be one of hundreds or thousands of people in their department or division. How to get noticed in circumstances like these is just one of the several important breaking-in issues addressed in this chapter. Additionally, this chapter will look at performance evaluations, ways of showing initiative,

first-year initiation rites, how to handle a bad work assignment, and other key matters of concern to new hires.

IMPRESSION MANAGEMENT

It would be nice if all the people you work with inside and outside of your company had the opportunity to get to know you well. If they did, they'd probably look past your rookie mistakes, realizing that you're really a pretty smart and capable person. The problem is that only about 5 percent or fewer of the people you work with ever do get to know you that well. These are your boss, a few colleagues, and your teammates. The rest will come to know you superficially through brief encounters and will draw conclusions about you based on these limited interactions, which might be a single meeting with another department, a 10-minute conversation with a colleague across town, or a drop-in visit from a senior vice president.

People like to draw conclusions about others quickly. It's not that we're anxious to judge but that most of us like to fill a void. The process starts the minute you pick up the phone, walk into the room, or whatever. It's as if people need to start finishing the "He/she is . . ." sentence immediately. Even if they don't have sufficient information about you, they'll use whatever they do have to draw some conclusion about you as a professional. And that means they'll hang labels on you very early. You'll hear people make such comments as "That new person seems pretty bright" after perhaps only a few minutes of conversation.

The effect is compounded because you are new and under the microscope. You are unknown and unproven, and others are uncertain about you. Everybody will be watching you. That includes your peers, subordinates, and bosses. Particularly with new college graduates, people are anxious to see if you're a "typical" new college grad, in part just to fill that void they have because they lack information about you. This means that you must place a premium on impression management in your first year on the job. It's really a critical element, compounded well beyond what you'll normally encounter later in your career. As one manager

said, "You are really in a fishbowl now. Whenever you start any job, I don't care what it is, there are a lot of people watching you and trying to assess your ability to succeed." Another manager put it even more strongly: "The first impression that you make is the last impression you make." As you progress in your career and build a good professional reputation, your track record will give you a safety net to cushion you against mistakes and interpersonal gaffes. But you don't have that now, and that means your first impressions count big.

Let me illustrate how making a bad first impression can hurt you early in your career. Suppose that part of your training program includes a meeting with one of the senior partners in the firm, someone many levels above you with whom you would not normally interact. Your assignment for this session includes some background reading about the company, but you decide to go out the night before so you only have a chance to skim the materials. As a result, you end up asking the senior partner a dumb question, while someone else, who read the materials, asks a very insightful question.

Fast-Starter Tip

It takes double the effort to overcome a bad first impression.

Now that seems harmless enough, right? So you asked a dumb question. How can that hurt you? Well, here's how. Suppose that several months later a new project comes along that is very important to the company. The partner sits down with other managers to select some junior people (that's you) for the project team. Your name comes up. "No way," says the partner. "He was at a meeting with me and wasn't very impressive. I'd rather have this person (the one who asked the insightful question); she was impressive."

Your manager, who likes you, protests, "I'm sure that was just a bad day. He's really performed well for us and would do a good job for you."

"I appreciate that," says the partner, "but this project is too important. I have to go with people I have confidence in." You lose, all because you made a bad impression. Surprised? Sound far-fetched? It's not. There will be many, many scenarios just like that throughout your first year.

Sure you can overcome bad first impressions. You do get second chances, and reputations are not cast in concrete. People are not cruel, and they do want you to succeed. But they also develop perceptions of you quickly, and overcoming them has its costs. "It's not that you can't overcome them," said a manager, "but it's just hard. It starts you on an upward battle, and with all the other things you need to spend your energy on, you don't need to add this to your list." While you are trying to undo mistakes, somebody else is learning how to play the game and surging ahead. People do expect new graduates to make mistakes, but there are acceptable, expected mistakes and unacceptable mistakes (more about that later). Besides, you are allowed only so many mistakes, and I'd hate to see you waste your "quota."

Your challenge, then, is to be constantly aware of the image you are projecting and the impressions you are making early in your career. In some respects, this entire book is about one basic thing: doing the right things to make the right impressions to earn the right labels early in your career. You may not understand exactly how this works and all the ways that first impressions count and can affect your career, but you must understand that they are critical to your success.

Getting Noticed

How do you emerge from the crowd and get noticed for your potential and abilities? New hires tend to make one of two mistakes, both of which are at an extreme. Many pay too much attention to getting noticed and try too hard to do something to stand out from the crowd. This is the "big splash" strategy referred to earlier. As discussed previously, it is *highly* unlikely that a new college graduate has anything close to the skills and savvy needed to make a grand contribution to the company in the first six to twelve months on the job. At the other extreme are those new hires who simply ignore the need to get noticed and languish in the crowd, growing increasingly frustrated all the time. What they fail to understand is that average or good performance doesn't really draw attention. That's perfectly OK if your objective is a slow and steady career without a lot of concern for promotion. However, if your objective is to attain a higher level of responsibility, you have to find a way to distinguish yourself.

You need to discover an opportunity to make a significant contribution to the company in a way that is visible beyond your immediate work group before the end of your first year. A significant contribution doesn't necessarily mean a big splash, a grandiose achievement or revolutionary invention. Rather, it means an accomplishment that significantly exceeds what is expected of you on an assignment of real value to the company. If your goal is to get on the fast track, your accomplishment also needs to exceed those of your fellow new hires. You want to give the kind of performance that gets you labeled as someone with above-average or high potential. That's really all you can hope for in your first year, and in some companies you may even have to wait until the second year to get that far.

Visibility is another key concept. One of the unfortunate facts about medium- to large-sized organizations is that people do get lost in them, out of sight of higher-level management. That's one reason you want to get on the right side of the success spiral. You may be a very good person, very smart and capable, but if you don't get the chance to show somebody what you can do in an important assignment, not many people will know how good you are. You need to look for projects and assignments that are important not only to your boss but to management above your boss. Those are the projects in which people will really notice and appreciate your performance.

Timing Your Move into the Spotlight

The difficult thing is picking the right time and place to attempt to separate yourself from the others. Try it too early and you'll likely fall on your face; try it too late and people will wonder what took you so long. The most pervasive problem is trying to do too much too soon. You need to wait long enough after you have joined the company to have a good sense of what's going on. Look for signs from others that you are no longer an outsider but have been accepted as part of the team. These might include your manager's pushing you to take on additional responsibility, a sign that he or she has developed trust in your abilities. Or there might be

signs from your colleagues, such as seeking out your ideas or opinions. It could be small, informal things, such as lunch invitations from senior team members or, if you are a supervisor, a card on boss's day. Until you are recognized as an insider and a valuable team member, it will be very difficult to make a significant contribution.

I would be remiss if I didn't acknowledge that in some organizations, the only way to earn acceptance is by making a significant contribution. But even those organizations will give you some sign or clue that says, "We think you're OK, so show us your stuff." What you need is an initial level of acceptance acknowledging that you are no longer a rookie but rather a professional entitled to make a contribution.

Fast-Starter Tip

Most new hires get noticed for all the wrong things they do.

The time when you receive that acceptance can vary from the first to the tenth month, depending on the company, the department, and you. If I had to pick a specific time, I would say it comes sometime after the first six months on the job. However, if the formal training program lasts longer than six months, you will have to wait until it ends to make your significant contribution. If the training program keeps you separated from the regular work group or rotates you among groups so that you never really become part of one, you may have to wait even longer.

Say Yes to High-Visibility Projects

When you spot an important, high-visibility project, be ready to work hard. Volunteer for it if it isn't handed to you. This is your chance, and it can mean far more than you may realize. Dedicate yourself to doing a truly outstanding job on it. Work long hours and weekends if necessary to ensure that you make a significant contribution. Make sure you do the best work you are capable of doing. Challenge yourself to do even better.

Is it really worth that kind of effort? You betcha! Developing a good reputation and separating yourself from the pack are vitally important if you want above-average success. You won't always have to put in that kind of effort, but experience has shown that this is what it takes early on. The success spiral really works, so when you get a break, a chance to hop on, take advantage of it. Good opportunities don't always come that often. Then, after you've done a good job, make sure you get credit for it. That doesn't mean you run up and down the halls bragging about yourself, but make sure your boss or the project leader knows of your accomplishments and makes it known to other members of management.

A note of caution: Never upstage your boss while breaking away from the pack. Make the boss look good while you are making yourself look good. Also, remember that your fellow new hires are not just your friends but your competitors, too. Don't be surprised if some of them are not too happy when you accomplish something good. It is not like college, where there were plenty of A's and B's for everybody. You are competing with other new hires for a limited number of promotional slots, and some of them can be quite jealous of your success. And that can be a bit uncomfortable for you. You will quite likely be friendly with other new hires, and you may expect them to share in your success. If you avoid boasting and using cut-throat tactics, most of your peers will be happy for you, but I can almost promise you it won't be universal.

Performance Evaluations

Your first year on the job will bring with it perhaps your first professional performance evaluation. The general practice is for professionals to be evaluated formally once a year. Most companies modify that for new hires and do either a quarterly, six-month, or one-year review. Performance evaluations will be a permanent part of your professional life and are particularly critical in your first year. You need to learn a little about them and how to make them work for you.

A performance evaluation is a structured, formal process by which you and the company review your standing. It often takes a long time, perhaps several hours, to go through. It will usually include these components:

- A formal rating of your performance, usually by specific categories as well as by overall performance
- Discussion of your strengths and weaknesses in each category
- Setting of objectives for your performance during the upcoming year
- A training and development plan for improving on problem areas and continued professional growth
- Discussion of your career plan for the near and long term so that your interest areas can be recorded for eventual promotion and transfer
- A rating of your potential for promotion

- A discussion of what raise (if any) you'll receive or how your rating will affect your salary

One thing you will notice is that evaluations don't take place very often, at least not formally. Earlier we talked about how much less frequent feedback would be on the job than in college, and the infrequency of formal evaluations is the most tangible evidence of that. This doesn't mean you'll only get feedback once a year, but it is the one time in the year that you'll get graded or rated and know exactly where you stand relative to your peers and to the company's expectations. Good managers will give you frequent feedback, so there should be no real surprises in your performance review. But many managers don't, and the further you go in your career, the more likely it is that you will sit down with your boss only once a year to discuss your performance formally. This will take quite a bit of adjustment on your part, since you've been accustomed to formal tests and frequent evaluations.

Frankly, performance reviews are not something a lot of people look forward to. Understandably, most people get nervous and anxious before them, particularly if their boss is not one to share lots of feedback. None of us likes to have our weaknesses pointed out, nor do we take criticism very well. And the anxiety is no fun, either. Also, it's something that many managers don't particularly look forward to, since it's no more pleasant to give criticism than to receive it, and giving someone a disappointing rating is often hard to do. But if handled well by both parties, it can be a very positive and helpful thing. You can't control what your boss does, but you can control how you approach it.

Accept Constructive Criticism

You need feedback and lots of it during your first year. So you need all the performance evaluations you can get. The toughest part about this is accepting constructive criticism in a nondefensive manner. I think most people are surprised by the amount of criticism they receive during their first performance review—frankly, they're not used to it, nor do they expect it. You're embarking on a professional career for which you've only just begun to prepare. Obviously, there is lots of room for growth and improvement, and you still have much to learn. And your boss is going to tell you about this, probably in excruciating detail. Even if you're doing great and progressing faster than normal, you're still going to hear about many ways in which you could improve. You can be getting A's and still have many things to work on. The standards are very high in professional life, and it's your boss's job to push you to achieve them. The problem is that you're used to being able to reach the standards more easily (schools design it that way), and you're not used to having your shortcomings pointed out so directly. And that's not very comfortable at first. It's all too easy and very human to react negatively to criticism, even when it's given in a constructive, supportive fashion, so you can imagine what it feels like if your boss isn't very good at giving it.

You need to learn to accept constructive criticism in a nondefensive manner if you are going to be able to grow professionally. You need honest, direct feedback to let you know what to work on. Receiving constructive criticism from a manager is not a sign that he or she doesn't like you. Rather, it is a sign that he or she cares enough about you and your career to help you improve. Sure, we'd all like to be able to do things perfectly, but that's unrealistic, especially in the first year. Only a limited number of people will get a top rating (many fewer than got A's in college). What is realistic is for you to do as well as you possibly can, given the knowledge and experience you have at the time. Then use your performance evaluations to chart your direction for growth.

Fast-Starter Tip

The more constructive criticism you accept, the less you'll need.

It can take your entire first year (and sometimes more) to begin to feel really comfortable and confident that you know how to do your job well. But don't get too comfortable, because this cycle of learning and evaluation will continue throughout your career. Once you've mastered a job, you'll want new challenges, and either you or the company will initiate a change. Then the cycle starts over, and you'll need performance reviews to guide you. So your performance evaluation is actually beneficial and developmental in nature, not something to be avoided.

Subjectivity and Getting Enough Feedback

One tough adjustment is coping with the highly subjective nature of performance evaluations. In college, much of your feedback was based on objective criteria (such as getting the right answer); even the more subjective items, such as essay tests or term papers, had many objective elements. It's not like that at work. Like it or not, much of your evaluation is made up of one person's opinion on how well you have performed. And good performance is not a precise, objective standard. Political factors can come into play in addition to how your performance compares to that of others. You have to be prepared for this subjectivity.

The bigger problem may be in getting enough evaluation. You should have at least two performance reviews in your first year, and four is not too many. Often they are promised but don't happen. Why? For one thing, it takes lots of time: your boss has to prepare and set aside time to meet with you, and both parties have to follow up on the recommendations. Since it's not a crisis, it's easy for hotter items to keep pushing it aside. Before you know it, months have gone by. Also, many bosses procrastinate because they don't like to do reviews. Giving feedback, even constructive feedback, is hard, and there is a real art to giving a good performance review.

Don't wait for someone else to initiate a review if it's overdue. If you've been promised reviews at certain points, follow up and make sure they're scheduled. If you haven't been promised a review at a specified checkpoint, ask your boss to schedule one. Even if it's informal, it's worth it. It's up to you to see that you get the feedback you need and are entitled to. Don't be a pest about it, but remember, feedback is a useful guide to you. It's always better to find out where you stand early so that you can correct whatever mistakes you're making.

Getting Positives from Negative Ratings

Which brings me to the last point and that is dealing with a negative performance evaluation that indicates you aren't doing as well as you should, even for a person of your limited experience. Make no mistake—it hurts to receive a low rating. It's not a fun experience, and I'm sure you won't want to repeat it. But it's not uncommon in the first year. Indeed, there are lots of reasons that make this more likely in the first year:

- A bad match between you and your new job
- A personality conflict with your first boss
- A reluctance to let go of your college mentality
- A failure to start your job in a serious, dedicated fashion
- Difficulty making the necessary transitions to working life
- The impact of personal stress caused by the transition
- A poor manager who cannot handle new hires well

Most managers aren't too surprised if they have to give a new hire a mediocre rating at first, although they prefer not to. It's quite common for a new hire to start slowly, make some mistakes, and take awhile to get on track. Employers realize that it is a big transition for you, and both you and the organization are taking a blind shot with the initial match anyway. However, don't let this knowledge make you complacent, because there are also plenty of people who start strong, and that's the group you want to be in. But realize, too, that a less-than-stellar rating early on is not the end of your career. You can recover.

The key is what you choose to do with a negative rating. You'll probably be angry and hurt, and you may blame others. You may think it's unfair. There certainly are cases of unfair

ratings, and your coach can help you identify them, but usually it's just a matter of bruised ego and hurt feelings. Your choice is to wallow in your feelings or do something about the problem. Blaming others and being angry may feel good, but that won't solve anything. After you blow off steam, get to work correcting your shortcomings. At least someone was nice enough to tell you about them early enough to keep you from truly jeopardizing your career. It's up to you to fix things.

- Meet with your manager again (after apologizing for any angry things you might have said), and put together an action plan.
- Listen to the feedback again without reacting emotionally.
- Meet with your coach to review the feedback and your action plan.
- Ask colleagues for honest feedback. You don't have to tell them that you had a bad review. Just say you're checking up.
- Locate resources (books, classes, etc.) to help you build necessary skills.
- Negotiate task-assignment changes, if necessary, so you won't continue messing up while building additional skills.
- Enlist the boss as your ally and supporter in correcting the situation.

Don't spend time cursing your boss or damning the system to your fellow new hires. If you need to do that, do it outside work. If you take a positive approach with quick action, you'll win respect from your boss and the organization and be well on your way to overcoming the poor evaluation.

INITIATION RITES

Anybody who has attended a military school, served in the military, or been in a fraternity or sorority is very familiar with the practice of putting new recruits through a period of initiation. Initiation activities have several purposes: to test the recruits' allegiance and desire to join the organization, to make them feel privileged to join, and to separate them from their old identity and indoctrinate them with the new identity the organization wants. Not too many organizations put new college graduates joining the professional ranks through such initiation rites, although this is a very real issue for hourly employees and occasionally for more experienced newcomers entering at higher levels of the organization.

You should be aware that something of the sort can occur in the early months of a new job. There are a few organizations that put new hires through what could properly be called an initiation rite. It usually won't be labeled as such, but the effect is the same. The most common method is placing the new employee into a very intensive and rigorous training program. These programs can last from several weeks to several months and typically consume most of the new hires' waking hours. Program participants work hard and play hard as a group and are usually separated from their family. While one agenda is clearly to teach needed skills, another is to establish the "work hard" culture early, to develop a sense of organizational and team identity, and to place a hurdle over which people must climb in order to join the organization. Often these programs result in some type of certification or license that "authorizes" the employee to join the regular work group. You won't find too many organizations that employ this strategy, at least not to the extent of creating a boot-camp environment, but they do exist, and you should be prepared for this if you join one.

It is quite common to find some sort of subtle unofficial initiation activities in professional organizations. It was pointed out earlier that organizations don't always welcome newcomers with open arms. There is a tendency for social groups to make newcomers pay some "price" before they are granted full member status. You may be tested to see if you have truly adopted the culture and accepted the ways of the work group as a reminder that the organization doesn't accept "just anybody." Some examples of ways in which you may be tested by members of the organization include:

- Giving you lots of mundane tasks to see if you are a team player
- Making you and other new hires perform skits at company picnics
- Forcing you to work extra-long hours, weekends, or holidays
- Having you make presentations to senior management to frighten you a bit
- Making you run errands for more senior group members

Most of these activities are quite harmless, and if you just go along and play the game, the testing will end quickly. Note that some of these examples are similar to ones used under "paying your dues," and to some extent, going along with such initiation activities is part of paying your dues.

More troublesome is blatant harassment, also known as hazing, usually by particular individuals in the organization. Unfortunately there are people who take it upon themselves to "show that smart-aleck kid" and truly harass you to "show you who's boss." Most organizations don't tolerate much of this, since it is highly unprofessional. If you encounter hazing, speak to your boss about it and most likely it will stop. If the person doing the harassing is the boss and has lots of power, you won't have much choice except to put up with it (or leave). Or you can go over your boss's head. It might be better to go to your coach or another manager on the same level as your boss. Remember, though, that initiation rites do end; don't overreact.

HOW MUCH INITIATIVE?

One of the most confusing issues during your first year has to be how much initiative to show. If you talk to most employers, they will tell you they want to see their professionals showing initiative and taking risks. They don't want their professionals sitting back in their chair, following the rules and just waiting for things to happen. One of the traits they looked for when they hired you was initiative and the ability to step beyond the norms of the job. Yet they also talk about how new hires want to take too much initiative, to do too much too fast. It's almost as if they talk out of both sides of their mouth, and in fact, new college graduates get confused by it. They hear for four years about how important it is to take initiative. Every professional seminar they attend has an employer telling them they want to see initiative. Now I'm telling you to slow down, and the employers will, too. What gives?

The problem is one of timing. Employers do want initiative, but they want smart, well-informed initiative. Their complaint is not that new hires take initiative, but that they take it too soon. They want mature initiative that comes from people who have acquired the necessary background and knowledge to be successfully proactive, a problem for new hires who believe that their college degree gives them the background they need and qualifies them to take initiative early. The employer wants to see initiative after the new hire has learned more about the company and its business.

So the first lesson about showing initiative on the job is that you have to wait, probably longer than you thought, until you can act. You have to learn some things before you can branch out and take your own initiative. Then you have to be sure that the initiative you take is within the reach of your capabilities. It's a good idea not to reach too far beyond your limits at first so that you can build your track record of successes. Look for opportunities to take the initiative in a smart, well-informed manner.

It is a matter of controlled initiative. You need to initiate action, but you don't want to charge blindly ahead just to be able to say you tried. It's more of a step-by-step process. First you come into the organization, follow the rules for awhile, and learn all you can. Then you find something about which you're fairly knowledgeable and take a little initiative, probably in small steps at first. Then you learn some more and, after that, extend yourself a little further, taking another perhaps bigger initiative in another direction. And then you learn some more and take a little more initiative. It is controlled, thoughtful, well-informed initiative that wins respect. Managers trust subordinates who know their limits and don't overextend themselves into areas where they risk making large and costly mistakes. They respect employees who won't take the initiative when they're out of their league.

Fast-Starter Tip

You can't take the initiative until you learn.

That means that the first initiative you can show is to learn all you can as fast as you can and to step beyond the learning that is expected of you and given to you. That may be plenty of initiative to show in the first year. Take the initiative to learn all you can about the culture, people, tasks, and so on, and you will show both the ability to take the initiative and the maturity to know you need to learn first.

The organization will have an implicit time line for when you are expected and allowed to take certain kinds of initiative. You have to find out what those expectations are. Some organizations will give you lots of room early, and others will demand more control. It will depend on many factors, including the visibility of the project, your ability, the organization's culture, your boss, etc. It's important that you work within the organization's expectations for the first year. What makes this difficult is that the expectations are often unspoken and transmitted to you through many small and subtle clues. You have to be attuned to the feel of your situation; you will feel your confidence—and the organization's confidence in you—growing, which will let you take a little more initiative. Your growth will continue gradually. Of course,

you should also feel free to sit down with your boss and discuss things if you're unsure.

CONTROLLED ENTHUSIASM

It's much the same situation with enthusiasm as with initiative. You've heard frequently how employers want enthusiasm in their new employees. You've been coached to be enthusiastic in interviews. Yet managers complain that new hires are too enthusiastic and need to throttle down their excitement.

The problem actually lies in how you express your enthusiasm. Managers do want people who are enthusiastic about their work, because that usually translates into initiative, but they don't want college cheerleaders in their staff meetings. They don't want the uncontrolled, unpredictable kind of enthusiasm; they want the kind that gets translated into action and results, the kind that says, I'm excited, but I'm in control of myself.

As with initiative, employers want smart, well-informed, and mature enthusiasm. The people who have it stop to think for a minute before getting enthusiastic—instead of just reacting. Their enthusiasm does not explode inside them, getting them into trouble; rather it is tempered by mature, rational thinking. So keep your energy and enthusiasm; that's one reason you were hired. But remember that you're in a professional, adult world. Professionals mix mature judgment with their enthusiasm. Adults at work don't express their enthusiasm the way college students at a football game do. Learn to channel and redirect your enthusiasm, leaving the college style behind, and it will work for you.

WHERE DID ALL THE CHALLENGE GO?

Did you expect to be challenged right away? Do you feel like your talents and capabilities aren't being fully utilized? Are you frustrated with the low-level tasks you are performing? Are you wondering when you'll get to use what you learned in school? If so, you're just like many of your fellow new hires, whose common complaint is that the first job just doesn't have the challenge they expected. Some find themselves mixed up in lots of grunt work, such as photocopying, proofreading and punching holes in reports, running errands, entering data—none of which is what they went to college for. These new hires find that there really isn't any challenge, and they are shocked.

Others find that they feel challenged but not in the same way to which they had become accustomed to in college. The intellectual challenges are replaced by the challenges of learning how to behave as a professional, learning the organization, getting along with people, etc. While this is challenging and tiring in its own right, it still doesn't feel like your intellect and imagination are being stretched or like your real abilities are being utilized.

In other cases, you may face real challenges, but they aren't the ones you want to be dealing with. Perhaps you're being asked to write computer programs when you'd really rather be designing them. You're asked to write reports when you'd rather be making the decisions that go into them, or you're given a small part of a project to do when you'd rather be running the project.

Don't be surprised if you feel you're not working with the level or type of professional challenge you'd like in your first year on the job. It's your rookie year. You know you want to move on to bigger and better things, and your employer knows this, too, or the company wouldn't have hired you. What you need to realize is what your employer already knows: you can't get there overnight. The challenges you want will come in time, but you simply aren't ready for them yet.

The organization doesn't want to hold you back any longer than it has to, because the longer it holds you back, the more you cost in training expenses. You will be thrown in as soon as your employer thinks you're ready. You'll undoubtedly think you're ready before the organization does, but you need to have some faith in the organization. After all, the organization has hired lots of new employees, but you've never had a professional career before. The organization has learned a few things along the way and has a little more experience than you, so if it isn't giving you the challenge you want yet, trust that there may be a reason.

I know it's not comfortable for you, but as hard as it may be, you have to be patient. One of the traits that convinces management that new hires are immature is their impatience. The new hires who succeed are those who can accept their role and build toward the challenges they want. If you continue to demand challenges before you're really ready for them, you'll only lose. Be prepared to wait until you're ready. It's okay to push a little but not too much.

The danger is that you will lose your motivation and perform poorly when you're not challenged. This is very easy to do. Most people find it difficult to discipline themselves to perform well when they aren't challenged. Many new hires view their unchallenging work in the first year as unimportant. It's an easy assumption to make but a seriously wrong one. Just about anything you do in your first year is important. You will never get the opportunity to do challenging work if you don't have the discipline to perform well at whatever is asked of you in your first year. It could be something substantive, such as having to learn the basics for awhile before you can move on, or it could be a seemingly unimportant task designed to see if you're a team player and can follow instructions. Whatever the nature of or reason for the task, what you are asked to do in your first year is important, whether or not you believe it. You must do well, even if you have to force yourself to do things you consider unpleasant and unchallenging. Then the challenges will follow.

CHANNELING YOUR AMBITION AND ENERGY

All of this leaves you with a problem: What in the world do you do with all your ambition? Most new graduates come to work tremendously motivated, full of energy and ambition. But now you're being told to sit on that, control your enthusiasm, take more focused initiatives, and wait for bigger challenges. For some new graduates, that's like trying to put a cork in a volcano! There's no denying the frustration this can cause, and I don't have any really good solutions for it. It's just part of the process, and you'll have to slow down and live with the frustration. Insightful bosses and companies understand the dilemma and try to provide you with enough challenge, but not all of them succeed. It's a matter of accepting that your time will come.

Here are a few coping suggestions to help you channel your ambition and energy in productive ways:

- Volunteer for other job duties and responsibilities so that quantity will compensate for quality
- Talk to your boss (in an undemanding way) to let him or her know that you're ready for more challenging duties whenever the time seems right to give them to you
- Volunteer to help other colleagues so that you get involved with more complicated tasks
- Channel some of your energy into outside or volunteer activities

The best strategy, though, is to focus your ambition and energy on your training. Set ambitious goals for what you intend to learn and how fast you intend to learn it. Ask for more extensive training or for training in other areas. Use the energy to learn all you can so that you'll be ready when the challenges do come.

TOO MUCH, TOO SOON

The opposite can happen, too. Some organizations may throw such immense challenges at you in the beginning that you'll think you're drowning in challenge. It may be because of a unique business situation, the company's culture, a big new project, or any number of other reasons. In situations like this, you will find yourself asked to perform at a very high level, often beyond where you should be, almost as soon as you walk in the door. You may be expecting a nice, orderly transition and find yourself thrown into the fray.

Even if you're not thrown in at an overly high level, the volume of work you're asked to do can be immense. You know that you're capable of doing the tasks, just not as many of them as you're being asked to do. The issue is not the level of difficulty of the work but an expected level of productivity more appropriate for someone well beyond his or her rookie stage. You wonder how you'll ever do it all, and you're giving up most of your personal life just to keep up. This often happens in smaller organizations or ones in which the position has been unfilled for some time.

Some organizations plan it this way, using such upending experiences to tear you away quickly from your old college mentality and socialize you into their culture. Fortunately, most of these organizations will warn you that this is part of their culture before you take the job. Then, if you want a hard-charging environment, you can choose to work for them.

The good news about being thrust into significant responsibility quickly is that you'll have a chance to do something important very early. Opportunity doesn't come along every day, so if you're given an early chance to make a contribution that people will notice, it can be great for your career. In some companies you might wait months or years to get that opportunity. And it feels a lot better to be doing something important rather than menial tasks.

At the same time, the pressure can be immense. You're on an important project with-out the training you need, not knowing the organization well, and with important people watching closely. Sort of a tall order for a new college graduate, isn't it? You don't have time to build the foundations we've talked about or to undertake conservative strategies. You have to perform. The stress of the transition is enough without the added pressure of such a situation.

Nonetheless, view this situation as an opportunity. You have little to lose. Your bosses usually know they've put you in over your head and are prepared to bail you out if you get into too much trouble. If you don't succeed, nobody will blame you. If you do succeed, you'll impress everyone.

On the personal level, it takes an enormous amount of energy to deal with a situation of this sort. Don't be surprised if most of your life is consumed by work, either because you're putting in long hours or because you're recovering from them. You'll be insecure, wondering if you can do the job, and you may be a little scared about not doing well. It's a big challenge. Most of the time, however, you'll end up doing much better than you thought and benefiting from the experience. Even if you don't do as well as you would have liked, you'll earn respect for tackling the challenge with a positive and willing attitude. Do your best to hang tough and make the most of the opportunity.

IT'S NOT FAIR!

The perfectly sensible project you propose gets turned down. Your fellow new hire, whom you've outperformed throughout the training program, gets the better assignment because he befriended the new boss who taught part of the class. You know how to design a circuit board much better than your colleague, but nobody will pay any attention to you. The position you were assigned after accepting the job is changed due to a reorganization, and you're not pleased. "It's not fair! It doesn't make any sense! It's not logical!" you say to yourself. You're probably right. But I have to warn you: it happens and you have to be ready for it.

It may be a shock to discover how unfair, illogical, and irrational organizations can be. Decisions aren't always made in the most objective fashion. Unavoidably, things happen that aren't very fair. People, power, egos, and seniority can hold sway over logic and facts. No organization tries to be unfair or unreasonable, but it happens all the time. The simple fact that organizations are composed of imperfect humans doing their jobs guarantees that imperfect things will happen. Do you have to like it when it happens or accept things passively when you're treated unfairly? No. Should you try to avoid having it happen? Of course. But you shouldn't be surprised or caught off guard. Nor should you decide in knee-jerk fashion that you've joined a rotten organization.

The seemingly illogical or unreasonable events are going to happen much more frequently to new hires, and that's going to be frustrating. Most new hires don't have a good grasp of how big a factor politics play in organizations, and even the most logical politics won't look very logical to newcomers. Another major factor in this apparent unfairness is the extent to which human beings, with all their imperfections, affect what happens. As discussed previously, college can leave you much too focused on factual "hard" stuff, ignoring the people factor. Beyond that, the working world is often complicated and uncertain, requiring you and others to make complex judgment calls. There isn't much black and white, but there are plenty of gray areas. That means the logic isn't always clear, or at least what's clear to you may not match what's clear to others and vice versa. Finally, there are simply lots of things you won't understand at first and, hence, may be quick to label as unreasonable.

The big question, though, is how much unfairness is too much? You have a right to expect that these things won't happen all the time. In good organizations, unfair events should happen to you only occasionally. If they become a common occurrence, you might need to look elsewhere for employment. But be prepared to accept some of this as a part of daily professional life. If you do, you'll greatly reduce your frustration. Find ways to work within the political framework of the organization instead of against the way things are.

DEALING WITH THE REBEL WITHIN

In some ways it's a real shame you have to start your career in your early twenties, because you're really more likely to have the maturity you need years later. One thing that some new hires have to struggle with is the rebel that's within most of us in our early twenties. The personal passage that we are going through in our early twenties seems to conflict directly with the passage we go through in starting a professional career.

For people in their early twenties, one of the most important parts of personal growth and development is breaking away from their parents and establishing themselves as independent adults. If you look back over the last four to eight years, you should see a gradual process of breaking away from your parents' authority and control. This starts in the early teenage years and continues through college, usually culminating with graduation and the beginning of your career. Of course, the breaking away is not always smooth (just ask any parent), and it is at the root of much of the rebellious and disruptive behavior of adolescence.

Just when you think you've finally broken free and are fully independent, you start work. Suddenly you find yourself under just as much control and authority as when you were accountable to your parents. During the working day, it may seem as though your employer has even greater control over your life than your parents had. And that may not feel very good to you. For most, it's a shock to discover that the very job they saw as a key to their independence takes away much freedom, too.

Difficulty can arise in dealing with the authority figures at work. Since many college graduates are still struggling to break away from their parents, authority figures at work can subconsciously trigger the same rebelliousness and desire to break free. It's particularly likely because the first job is the time when graduates will be subject to the most restrictive rules, policies, and guidance and have the least freedom in their career. It might feel like becoming 18 again and moving home to live with Mom and Dad!

I can almost certainly assure you that you won't enjoy your new employer's control over your life. To some extent, that is just something all of us who decide to work for other people have to get used to. But of any point in life, the early twenties have to be about the toughest time to make the adjustment psychologically.

Too many new hires let the rebel inside them take over. They don't like taking instructions from the boss, following work rules, or having work interfere with their personal life. Even worse, they complain at work and let it be known that they aren't pleased. They grumble under their breath and scowl when told to do something. Those negative behaviors and attitudes will hurt them quickly.

Ask most working people, and I think you'll find they'd all like to have more freedom in their lives. But they have learned that their job gives them other rewards, including an income to live on, so in exchange they allow their employer some control over them. Part of professional maturity is learning to accept trade-offs. And, of course, the further you go in your career, the more independence you can gain.

You have to make this adjustment and be careful not to let your natural tendencies at this point in your life make the adjustment more difficult than it has to be. Think about where you are in terms of establishing independence in your private life. Are you still struggling with your parents' authority? Is establishing your independence an important issue for you now? If so, be careful to fight those battles outside work and not project your personal problems onto your new relationships at work.

DISAPPOINTMENT

It's not at all uncommon for new hires to be disappointed in their first job and feel let down. You start out very enthusiastic and upbeat, expecting a fantastic new job and a great experience. Then you find out it's not nearly as good as you thought or hoped it would be. Most of the time, this is due to unrealistic expectations, although sometimes the job really isn't very good or is just not right for you.

Being disappointed with the reality of the job and the organization comes as a real surprise to most people because they aren't cynical enough to expect it. It's always hard to feel let down, but it seems to be particularly tough for new hires. The first professional job is such an important time, and most new college graduates have such high hopes and ambitions.

The reality, of course, is that all jobs and all organizations have their warts and their problems. But you don't know that at the start. Usually for a month or two after you start work there's a honeymoon period during which everything looks pretty good. Your job is new, the organization is all new to you, and everyone is on his or her best behavior. But sometime between the first and sixth month, reality sets in and you discover the not-so-good news about your job choice. You realize that your job can be routine and boring at times, that your boss isn't always a nice guy, that you won't become manager in a year, that the office politics can be nasty. You begin to feel disappointed because the reality doesn't fit what you thought or imagined.

Fortunately, after about six months, the disappointment begins to ease, at least for most people. You begin to realize that it's just the real world. You find out that much of the disappointment comes from the shock of reality not meeting your fantasy. Once the surprise is past, you can look at the situation from a more balanced perspective and find that most of the good things that attracted you about the job in the first place are still there.

The danger is that you let the initial disappointment weigh you down so that you don't perform like you should or actually quit. Don't do it! The disappointment you experience in the first six months is not a reliable signal. Just about everyone experiences it. It's rare that the reality is as good as the recruiter made it sound or as you imagined it to be. Give it some time before you act on your feelings of being let down. Talk to other new hires to see if they're experiencing it, too. Talk to your parents, your coach, and other experienced professionals so you can get a perspective on the realities of work—that will help ease the disappointment. To prevent disappointment, keep your expectations realistic and your mind open.

WHAT ABOUT YOUR PERSONAL STYLE?

Much of what you've heard so far has been a message about conforming to other people's style and the organization's way of doing things. That's the way your first year will be, more so in some companies than in others. "But wait a minute," you say, "I have my way of doing things, my own ideas, my own style. What about those? When do I get to use my style?" The answer: not for awhile in most companies. This is another tough adjustment. For one thing, you've just spent four years or more in college, which not only allowed but encouraged you to develop your own style. Working in an organization, though, requires a certain degree of conformity. Some organizations require more, some less, but all require it to some degree. Part of maturing as a person and a professional is learning to deal with and accept conformity.

For new hires, there is a special dynamic going on. The organization knows that its way works; perhaps not perfectly, but it works. It knows you're inexperienced and still have lots to learn. Thus, its view is that you do things its way until you have enough experience to find a better way. To the organization, nonconformity coupled with inexperience equals immaturity; add the absence of a track record of results and it equals immaturity plus. But nonconformity plus a track record plus experience equals individual style and is acceptable to the organization.

Fast-Starter Tip

You have to earn your pinstripes before you can shed them.

There's not much that can be done to eliminate your frustration. All you can do is accept that you have to gain experience, a track record, and acceptance before you can assert your individual style. As one manager put it, "Sometimes you have to pull back on your personal style until you have proven yourself, until you have established credibility." Your time will come, and the further you go, the more you can do things your way. It may seem to you that style shouldn't matter if you get the results. But in the first year, how you get the results is just as important as obtaining them. In time you'll earn the freedom to get them your own way. The quickest way to get there is to set aside your own style for awhile and not force it on things.

HOW HARD DO YOU REALLY HAVE TO WORK?

When you talk to new hires, they tell you to be careful not to work too much, to take time to relax and play more. They talk about how hard it is to find such time. But when you talk to management, they complain that new hires are too frivolous. They want to see new hires who are serious about their work and will work hard. Your problem, then, is finding a balance that convinces management that you're serious about your career yet gives you enough personal time.

You must realize that your first year will be a time when you have to work very hard. In many jobs, the first year will be much more demanding than later years. The reason is simple: you are so new and have so much to learn that everything will take much more time and be much more demanding than it will be after you've worked at the job for awhile. Even such simple things as coordinating a meeting or writing a memo can be quite a challenge when you're fresh out of college, new to the organization and to professional life. Many companies won't give you a half-time workload just because you're new. Rather, you're expected to meet the normal demands of the job and complete your training. Even the kindest of bosses can forget how inexperienced you are after you have been around for a month or two or when the pressure of deadlines must be met.

What this means is that your first year, and particularly your first six months, is a time when you must be prepared to work very hard. It may take long hours, weekend work, or coming in early to learn everything, meet your deadlines, and impress the management. To get a strong start, you need to be prepared to make a priority of your career and devote a great deal of time to it. Anything less and you'll not get the start you deserve. It's fair to say that the right balance for the first year is to be out of balance, with work getting a much bigger share of your time than your personal life.

That doesn't mean that you should let work bury you to the point that you have no personal life. You will discover very quickly that there is never any shortage of things that need to be done and always a shortage of people to do them. Most professionals could work literally all the time if they were to do their job perfectly. In your zeal to do the best job you can, don't be surprised if all of a sudden you turn around after six months or so and discover that you've had no personal life. You won't feel very good about that.

Neither working all the time nor making your personal life too high a priority will work for you. Working all the time will burn you out quickly. While you may think it's impressing people, in reality, it can hurt you if you're the only one doing it. It may give the impression that you just can't do your job effectively and have to work longer to get the same amount of work done as others. On the other hand, too much attention to your personal life will only convince management that you're not serious.

You can't trust your instincts fully. For most new hires, the amount of work will be a shock. Even a normal 8-hour day, five days a week, fifty weeks a year is a big adjustment and can feel like your life is out of balance, and this is accentuated by having to work as hard as new hires do. Your life probably is unbalanced and should stay that way for awhile. Just because you're working very hard doesn't mean you're working too much. There will be plenty of time to play later on, after your career gets on track.

DEALING WITH A BAD ASSIGNMENT

Just as you may not like the boss you've been assigned to, you may not be too pleased with your job assignment. The natural disappointment of not having enough excitement or challenge has already been discussed. What is of concern here is the type of situation where you've been assigned to work in market research but hate research or have been assigned to write computer programs for a year and don't like to do it.

Frankly, you won't have a whole lot of control over your starting assignment. Most companies will make a very sincere effort to give you a starting assignment that matches your interests. After all, it is in their interest that you be happy at what you're doing. But there is a wide array of things that can mess that up: simple miscommunication between you and your new employer, unavailability of the position you wanted, a need for extra people in some area due to business changes, a belief by management that you need to gain experience in a particular area before doing what you want, unrealistic expectations on your part again, or simply the need to pay your dues.

So what do you do? Many new hires would complain and make their displeasure known quickly. Wrong strategy. It's just like dealing with a bad boss: Your best and only way out is to do the best job you can. You will have opportunities to let your manager know what your preferences are later. Try to imagine for a minute the impression you'd make if you started complaining about your job assignment so early. You probably won't even understand the job for months, so how could you really know if you like it? Do you want the reputation of being a complainer?

One experienced manager suggests: Why not say to yourself, this is an assignment I don't think I like. I don't think I understand it. It doesn't seem fair, but I've decided I am going to come to this company and stay a little while. So why don't I make the best of it and look good in this situation . . . unlike John Doe, who hated it and let everybody know he hated it. "The people who are running that area know that it is not a particularly good assignment and that nobody likes it, but if you come through shining, that's great. You signed on for a certain salary, so what's the big deal? There are some things I don't like, but I still realize that it's a whole lot better than other things. I have also learned from past experience that it's going to change. And it doesn't do me or anybody else any good if I am angry about something.

You'll earn tremendous respect if you do a great job at a rotten assignment (or one you don't like). Sure, it's not fun. That's why you don't want to let it go on too long. If it's widely known that yours is a rotten assignment (but somebody has to do it), there's little chance you can influence how quickly you are given a new one. You were put there for a reason and will have to serve your time. However, if it's a mismatch, let your boss know. But wait until you've tackled the job, have learned and understand it, and have proven you can perform in it. Then your request to move to an assignment that better matches your interests will not be seen as an immature complaint.

NEGOTIATING CHANGES

For most of this book, we've been talking about accepting and adjusting to the way things are when you join an organization. What hasn't been discussed much is how you can change the organization, which might lead you to conclude that you can't, at least not during your first year. That's not quite true, however. You are not totally powerless and do not have to be totally accepting of everything just the way it is. We have discussed at length how you have to build a base of credibility, performance, and acceptance before you can attempt to make any changes. Once you have done that (usually after six months or so), you can consider suggesting changes as long as you use the right approach and the changes are of the right scope.

Any suggestion for change has to be presented in an unthreatening, noncritical fashion. In negotiation strategy, we talk a lot about "win-win" negotiating. If you're being critical of the organization, that's a "win-lose" situation: you win, they lose. That won't work. You have to present your ideas for change as supporting the organization, not attacking it. In fact, one way of showing your loyalty and commitment to the organization is to work to improve things, not just complain about them. You have to offer your suggestions for change as being evidence of your belief in the organization and your desire to help you both grow better as a team.

Additionally, any change you suggest during the first year has to be of an appropriate scope. You have little chance of changing the overall objectives of the organization or your work group, of proposing significant strategy changes, or of changing traditions. You simply won't have the credibility or experience to do that. But you may be able to make an impact on how you accomplish goals and objectives, what techniques you use to solve problems on a daily basis, etc. You have to suggest changes that are within the scope of your knowledge and experience and for which you have established sufficient credibility. These will usually be local, day-to-day issues.

On a more personal level, you can have some impact on your own job assignment, your relationship with the boss, and the way you get your work done. Again, you have to establish that credibility base. With it, you can usually start to negotiate some with your boss. You can negotiate over things like work scheduling, how you and your boss will work together, what methods you will use to do your job, when you're ready for new assignments, and so on. It will be a negotiation process, so you'll have to look for "win-win" types of compromise.

By the second half of your first year, you'll probably find you have gained some control and can begin to assert your own style and ideas in small ways. If you'll just spend the initial part of the year doing things their way, they'll accept you and begin to listen to your way. Keep your suggestions "win-win" and small in scope, and you can make some changes.

GETTING PROMOTED

Every new professional wants a promotion as soon as possible. You want more responsibility, more money, and the recognition and ego strokes that come with them. There's nothing in the world wrong with that. The problem is that new hires usually want the promotions to come more quickly than is possible, and they spend too much time worrying about it. The fact is that promotions simply won't come as fast as you'd like. It will take time for you to prove yourself and earn the right to advance. In many companies today, promotions are being slowed because there is less of a hierarchy and, thus, fewer positions to move into. You'll have to be patient.

There is a real danger in trying to move too fast. You really don't want to take on more responsibility than you're ready for. One executive talked at length about this, using an analogy of a car:

> *Moving too fast can best be compared to revving up a car so much that you cut out its engine. If you try to rev up your career too fast, you're going to cut out your engine also. And you'll do it in one of two ways. First, even if you're doing a good job, somehow you're going to grate on somebody. To use the automobile analogy, when the car engine is revved up, it makes a lot of noise and a lot of people see you, but they don't really want to hear that irritating noise. Second, you are going to ruin the engine if you rev up your career too high. It's as though you've made it to Ohio by car but can't make it all the way to California, where you're headed, because the engine— meaning you—just conks out.*

In most organizations there is a time line, and you can push it only so far and so fast. It might be explicit or implicit, but it's there. And you can't even begin to think about a promotion, let alone talk about it, until you have proved yourself.

Many new hires are so anxious for recognition and ego satisfaction that they push for a promotion too soon. It's perfectly understandable to want recognition, but a promotion is not the only way to get it. Look for the little promotions, the extra responsibility your boss gives you, the added trust and confidence you've earned. Take notice when colleagues come to you for advice or ask for your help. Those are all signs that you're doing well and moving up in the organization, even if they're not formal promotions.

You really can't spend a lot of time worrying about a promotion. Maybe later on you'll need to, but for new professionals the key is simply great performance. Said one executive, "Concentrate on doing your job well as opposed to spending a lot of energy trying to figure out how to get the next one." Added another, "People should realize that they need to be satisfied, turned on, and happy with what they do and have a reasonable understanding of what is going on . . . then good things will happen to them. They need to be concerned about how well they're doing the job rather than how it looks or how it's going to help them get promoted."

Redirect the energy spent worrying about getting promoted into worrying about your performance. There is usually plenty of room for promotion out of entry-level positions, so you don't need to spend a lot of time worrying about what's going on around you, who's getting better assignments, who's working for the better boss, etc. Too much competitiveness will be frowned upon in your first year. And, added a senior manager, "A lot of these things are external; they are outside of your control. If it's outside of your control, there's not a whole lot

you can do about it, and if you spend a lot time worrying about it, it's going to take time away from the time you really ought to be taking to deal with things within your control." The bottom line: focus on you, your own job, your relationship with your boss, and doing the best you can at all of these, and promotions will come.

THE SOCIAL PROFESSIONAL

One key difference between being in school and being at work is that when you are a student and it is Saturday, you are off. If you want to go to a softball game and have too many beers and wear whatever you want or not wear enough clothing, no problem. Maybe the faculty won't perceive you as having good morals, but it's no big deal; it won't affect your performance as a student.

As a professional, however, it's sad to say but I am very careful. Definitely I am not going to wear a bikini if our vice president has a pool party. I'm going to be a little more conservative when I am with business friends or colleagues. Also I am very much more political at functions, even if they are fun functions like an office party or bridal shower. Professionals are still evaluated by what they say and who they show up with. They are always on stage everywhere.

College is a great place for your social life. There are lots of things to do, time in which to do them, and, most important, lots of people to do them with. There are plenty of friends—good friends, party friends, sports friends, intimate friends, dates, you name it. They're everywhere—in your dorm, in your classes, at your clubs, in your fraternities and sororities, etc. College is a great time in your life (they don't call it the best four years of your life for nothing) for parties, social life, and activities.

Much of this will change when you go to work. Friends won't be quite as easy to find or keep up with, there won't be as much time, and meeting new people will be more difficult. Becoming a professional will place new restrictions and demands on your social life, affecting to whom you get close and where you can be free to really have fun. The workplace is not like college in the way you mix social and personal life with work. How you blend and mix these elements during your first-year transition, however, is very important to your professional success and your personal well-being.

Socializing at Work

When you are in college, all of your classmates, people living in your dorm or apartment building, and the rest of your peers in the school are potentially good friends. You can feel quite free to initiate and develop close, personal friendships with anybody and everybody. While not all the friendships you start develop into close ones, they all have that potential. The entire culture of a college heavily revolves around social activities and relationships. Parties, get-togethers, recreational activities, etc., are built into the system and encouraged as a way for young people to grow and mature personally. It's easy to presume that the same holds true in professional life and at work. Unfortunately, it

doesn't. Making friends and building personal relationships at work present quite a different challenge.

To start with, building personal friendships with business colleagues is not the norm. Professionals who work together do build friendly relationships, but most do not build true friendships. Thus, you need to adjust your expectations to realize that your colleagues aren't like your classmates. People don't come to work expecting to develop personal relationships. The company will encourage building some level of personal rapport to make it easier for people to work together. But they couldn't care less about whether you build close friendships, and they may, in fact, discourage it.

Because of this big cultural change, new graduates often lose points quickly when they start work. Many of them come to work with social agendas high on their priority list, just as they did in college. They then devote considerable time to social conversations during the day, making friends, and planning after-work activities. Can you guess management's reaction? They see it as just one more sign of immaturity. In their view, you are there to work, not to join a fraternity or sorority. While there is nothing wrong with casual conversation over the coffeepot, a few minutes spent talking about weekend activities, etc., management wants to see you treating these things as incidental to work, consuming only a limited amount of time.

This could sound like the workplace is meant to be a somber, unfriendly place. That's not what's intended. Most companies want to see their employees happy, enjoying each other's company, working together in a friendly manner, feeling good about themselves, and pulling together as a team. That doesn't happen if everyone is stiff and focuses only on work issues. But if you observe others carefully, you'll notice that the successful people understand that socializing is restricted in amount and only occurs when the work is done. Work is the top priority. That's what you're being hired for, and that's what you're paid for. To the extent that some socializing helps people work better together, it's fine.

Save your heavy socializing for your own time. As you enter your new company, be very cautious about how much socializing you do until you can observe others and find out what the company norms are. Do enough so that you're seen as a friendly, likable person but no more. Usually you can follow the lead of others who have been in the organization longer. Then as you learn how much is expected (notice I didn't say tolerated), you can adjust your level of socializing to match that of your colleagues.

Personal and Work Life: How Close Together?

There's another side of this issue that should be equally important to you. When you were in college, your personal relationships had little or no chance of affecting the grades you received or the professor's evaluation of you. If you got rowdy one night at a party with your classmates, it didn't affect what happened in the classroom. Even if the professor knew, he or she probably didn't care. If you were dating a woman or man in one of your classes and then broke up, it probably wouldn't have any effect on the grade you received. Even if your other classmates disliked you or thought poorly of you for doing it, it would not affect your grades.

In short, your performance evaluation in school likely had no relation to your personal life. Thus, you truly felt free to do as you pleased in mixing school and personal life.

Those days are gone. As a professional, what you do in your personal life can and usually will affect your performance on the job. That may sound unfair, but it's true. It's not that the company wants to control your personal and professional life. It's just that the impressions and perceptions people develop of you will not be restricted to just what they know about you from your working hours. People can't separate or ignore what they know about you personally from the professional side. Their impressions and opinions of you will be shaped by *everything* they know about you.

Let me give some examples. I have known new hires who were quite heavy drinkers on the weekends. They did fine during the week and performed well. But news about their weekend exploits became widely known in the company. The professional performance indicated a somewhat mature professional person, but the weekend exploits continued to reinforce the immature "college kid" image. In another case, a woman confided some very intimate details of a painful relationship to a colleague. That was no big problem until the colleague was promoted. This woman deeply regretted that a member of the management team now knew so many things about her. The only mistake that these two people made is that they chose to bring their personal lives to work. There's nothing wrong with being a bit wild on the weekends (if that's your thing), partying hard, or sharing intimate secrets with a good friend. Just don't do it with colleagues at work. As a general rule, keep some good distance between your personal and professional lives. Never do or say anything in the presence of a professional colleague that you would not want widely known at work.

You need to find friends outside of work to provide an outlet for these things. As one new hire said, "I try to keep my personal and business lives separate. I have two different sets of friends, and by doing that, if I go to play basketball or am working out or whatever, I don't have to worry about little side comments I've made or anything else getting back to the office. I really can be myself and relax, and to me it is very important and has helped me leverage both my personal and my professional life."

In time, you may be able to find someone at work whom you can truly trust and be best friends with. The first year is not enough time. When you first start work, you have no idea who can be trusted and who can't. You have no idea how the culture views personal exploits or who or what can hurt your career. I can promise you that certain aspects of a person's personal life can hurt his or her career; you just have to find out what they are at your company.

It all comes back to impression management. You will be busy building your image in the first year, and you don't want your personal life to affect that. It will, unless you keep it separate. Just as with bosses, you don't have to be "friends" to work well with a colleague. In fact, the vast majority of the time you won't be, and that's OK. You need to develop a sense of moderation when it comes to mixing your personal and social life with work.

This advice may sound a bit cynical, but it's not intended to be. Things are different in the professional world, and this does affect your

personal life. You do not have the personal freedom in the workplace that you may have enjoyed previously. What you do and with whom you do it now have larger, more serious potential impacts. There is still room for fun and making good friends (a good thing or we'd all quit our jobs). Most professionals over the years have made good friends whom they enjoy very much. But you must be careful to remember that there is a whole other dimension that has been added. As a professional, you just have to be more careful and think through the impact your personal and social activities can have on your career.

Your Training Class

One common trap for new hires is the training class. In many companies, there is a training program, sometimes quite lengthy, where you and other new hires work together for weeks or months to prepare for your first position. These programs often present many opportunities to party, have a great time, and really let your hair down with fellow recruits. They are often held at neat places away from home, perhaps with a generous expense account. They can be lots of fun. It looks like, feels like, and is much like being back in college. It's all too easy then to act as if you're back in college, and that's a mistake. While these training programs are a little more liberal in tolerating some college-type behavior, you are still being watched and evaluated. The teachers, school directors, etc., are all building their first impressions of you in that class. They may have a major voice in your first job assignment. Just because they look and act like teachers doesn't mean you can treat them like professors.

Furthermore, you have to be concerned about your fellow trainees. You will be tempted to view them as college classmates and treat them the same way. It's hard to believe when you're first starting out that they could affect your future. The training class might be one of the few chances they get to know you. Months later they may be asked what they think of you. They could even be promoted before you. One could be your boss one day or could be leading a project to which you are assigned. And the impressions they develop of you in the training class will stick and may be all they have to go on. Furthermore, it is not that rare for somebody to use something learned about you in training against you to get ahead.

So, have a good time in your training classes and make some friends. That's part of the experience. But remember that you aren't in college. Those classmates are your professional colleagues. Make sure they see you as their colleague and develop the right image of you.

Working Social Events

You're going to find many opportunities to socialize with your colleagues from work. There will be informal get-togethers over lunch and after work, sometimes just for fun and sometimes to celebrate important events. There will be working lunches and dinners, perhaps with clients, bosses, or colleagues. Most companies sponsor annual picnics, Christmas parties, picnics, etc. Some companies even have regular events on a weekly or monthly basis.

These are extremely important events for you—just as important as anything you do at the office—and you should plan to participate

in as many as possible during your first year. It is at these events that contacts are made, relationships built, and networks expanded. That's one of the reasons employers sponsor such events. You'll quickly find that getting out of the office with your colleagues and enjoying their company in a social setting makes working together much easier. If you don't participate, it's a sign that you're not embracing the organization and its culture. Good politics says attend.

But you're about to learn the answer to "When is a party really not a party?" The answer: when it's with people from work. It may look like a party and feel like a party, but it's still work. "All the rules that apply at the office ought to apply to social events," emphasized one manager. "All a business social event is is work in a different sort of situation. And you need to see it that way. People think, 'Now I can say what I want. I am at ease. I am at a social event.' Wrong! How you dress, who you talk to, how you talk to them should follow the same rules as in the office."

You have to remember that how you handle yourself and the impressions you make at the social events will be remembered just as much as those made at work. In addition, since many professionals conduct business in social situations, your behavior at a company social event is one indication of how you'll handle yourself with clients.

What you need is a new kind of party demeanor: your professional party conduct. You're expected to relax, have a little fun, laugh a little, and enjoy yourself. But not too much and certainly not as much as you would with your nonprofessional acquaintances. Your professional party conduct should be more reserved—

fun but not boisterous, lively but not outlandish. Nothing you do at a company party should ever embarrass you when reported in the office the next day. And remember that a company party doesn't have to be one sponsored by the company but just one that includes your colleagues. Your temptation will be to equate the idea of a party with your old college definition of a party. Don't! Treat it as just another part of your job, and don't drop your professional standards. It isn't a real party, even if it looks like one.

The most common mistake new hires make is drinking too much. It might be acceptable and "cool" (though not healthy) to do that in college, but it's not at working parties. You'll probably see some people do it, and a few may even be executives, but don't follow their lead. One or two social drinks is fine, but do not drink so much that you begin to act tipsy or drunk. When you begin to lose control, you begin to look like a college student rather than a professional. Too much alcohol can also make you talk too much, say the wrong things, and act foolish. You can't afford that.

Don't be the life of the party. Basically, you don't want to do anything that people will want to go back to the office and talk about the next day—unless maybe it's hit a home run at a company softball game. And people do talk! It might have been cool in college to have all your friends talking about your party escapades the next day but not at work. That's not the reputation you want to build.

Don't be fooled by who isn't at the party. One common new hire mistake is to think it's OK to cut loose if it's only fellow new hires at the party and that you only need to be careful when the boss is around. Wrong again. Invariably someone talks at work about how wild or drunk you were, his or her boss overhears it and tells your boss, and before you know it, it's just as if all the managers had been there, too. That's not smart. Also, remember that your fellow new hires are colleagues, too; your professional reputation with them will become important much sooner than you think.

You also need a professional party wardrobe. Your "professional casual" clothes need to be conservative and neat just like your in-office wardrobe. It isn't the same as the casual dress you'd wear to personal social events. Sloppy or loud clothes are out, as are overly sexy clothes, whether you are a man or woman. Pool parties are particularly dangerous situations; be sure you have a bathing suit that is modest and does not invite glaring eyes.

In short, work doesn't stop at the office. There's a new kind of socializing you'll discover that is critical to your career but also full of traps for new hires. Remember, a party is not always a party.

ULTIMATE SURVIVAL TIPS

1. Make good first impressions so that you'll get the chance to show your stuff later.

2. Get noticed for your maturity and abilities, not for your dumb mistakes.

3. Look for highly visible chances to showcase your abilities and talents.

4. Without performance evaluations, you have no way to know if you are on the right track.

5. It is unlikely that your early performance evaluations will be all positive; successful professionals think of them as a learning experience and accept constructive criticism nondefensively.

6. Smart, successful initiatives rarely happen quickly.

7. Enthusiasm works best in moderation.

8. The time will come when your abilities are fully challenged, but it may take time.

9. Work offers different challenges from those that college did.

10. If you are in over your head, admit it and let people help you.

11. Organizations aren't always logical, fair, or rational.

12. You don't have to give up your individuality and independence completely; just put them on hold until you've earned your spot in the organization.

13. It's OK to work harder than normal in the first year.

14. Bad assignments don't last forever, but careers do.

15. Promotions won't happen until you've mastered the first job.

16. A good social life will not happen as easily as it did in college.

17. Successful new professionals limit their socializing at work.

18. You must act professionally when around work colleagues, even outside of work.

19. It is a good idea to keep some distance between your work and your personal life.

20. Social events with colleagues are a golden opportunity to network and cement good relationships.

5

Building Work Relationships

· ·

We are not looking for the lone superstar—you know, the one who is going to hit a home run. We are looking for people who can get base hits and who help others on their team get base hits also.

ORGANIZATIONS ARE PEOPLE

Organizations are people—living, breathing people who have joined together in the pursuit of some common goal in exchange for a reward. Organizations aren't just collections of tasks, jobs, or functions, nor are they just numbers on a page or boxes on an organizational chart to be studied and analyzed. They are composed of people who have agendas; who get frustrated and angry; who feel happy and elated, threatened and defensive; who are proud of what they do and accomplish; and who want to be respected for what they contribute.

> **Fast-Starter Tip**
>
> *You cannot succeed by yourself.*

There is very little, if anything, that takes place in an organization that doesn't depend on people doing their jobs and doing them well. More importantly, very little goes on that doesn't depend on the collective effort of at least several people. Organizations consist of teams. Everybody is dependent on others in the organization to get his or her job done. Except in the smallest of organizations, no one person can do everything that needs to be done. Even the CEO, the most powerful and highest-ranking person in the organization, cannot accomplish much without the effort of others. It's people working together in teams that get things done. That means that the only way you can be effective is to learn to work well with other people in your work group, department, and company. Equally important is the fact that others cannot do their jobs without depending on you.

Working with other people means that the relationships you build with others are as important an element to your success as the technical and task-related skills you learned in school. It further means that developing strong communication and interpersonal skills is essential to your successes, since they are needed to build good working relationships.

It's such a startling contrast to college. While there may have been some group projects or collaborative efforts in school, success is still largely an individual effort. For the most part, the emphasis is on you individually. You have to master a body of knowledge or a set of skills. If you discipline yourself and work and study hard, you will do fine. Even when there are group projects, if others aren't doing their part, you could still usually do extra work to get a good grade. Overall, you were usually not dependent on anyone else to succeed.

Not so in the workplace. For one thing, it is rare that any one person can have all the knowledge needed. If you are designing a building, you need electrical, civil, and mechanical engineers and an architect involved. If you are planning a new product, people from R&D, manufacturing, marketing, and distribution have to be involved. The tasks are usually so complex that no one person can have all the technical and organizational knowledge. It

would be humanly impossible to do it alone. Even if it were possible to do it alone, it would not be wise. Since an organization has many parts and many people in different teams, any project is likely to have an impact far beyond your immediate work group. Thus, other people will want to be involved in the project or assignment to represent their interests.

Fast-Starter Tip

You succeed when you share your success with others.

Finally, as a new hire, you will need other people to show you the ropes—to teach you things, provide information, and tell you how things are done before you can accomplish even the smallest of tasks. You can't learn how to be successful without others helping you.

Make sense? The smart hire will quickly see that his or her attention needs to be directed toward something totally different from what it was directed toward in school. If people like you, respect you, and accept you, you will be effective and successful. If they don't, you won't succeed. It's that simple. Learning and managing the tasks are only part of your job; managing your relations with other people as a team is equally important.

MAKING TIES

There are a myriad of different relationships to build, with your peers, bosses, superiors, subordinates, teammates, and colleagues (lower- and higher-level) in other departments and with support staff, maintenance people, etc. It's critical that you develop a relationship of mutual trust and respect that enables you to work together effectively.

Professional relationships are different from most of the relationships you will likely have experienced before. They are not necessarily like friendships or family relations, and, therefore, different rules apply. The problem is that if you have no experience developing them, you'll try to build them more like the social relationships you're used to, and that doesn't work. One key difference is that in your personal life, if you don't like people, you don't have to associate with them. That's not true at work, where you'll find you need to build relationships with people you don't really care for on a personal level in order to do your job. New hires tend to use a social perspective to decide whether to strike up a relationship with others. That's fine for deciding whether to invite them to your house or to go out to lunch together but not for daily professional activity. You don't have to like your associates to work with them.

College tends to be a fairly homogeneous group of people. Students are about the same age, have lots of similar interests, do similar things (go to class, study, party, etc.), and have similar goals (starting a career). Sure, there are differences but not to the degree you'll find at work. People tend to develop more diverse preferences and interests after they leave college. As they establish their own lifestyles and goals, the differentiation between them becomes more pronounced. Also, there is a wide distribution of ages in the company. And each age group has a different experience level, different goals, and a different perspective on life. As one manager put it, "A big part is learning to become mature and communicating with people, knowing how to balance the different levels and attitudes."

So, two key things complicate relationship building in the workplace for a new hire: the new rules for building professional relationships and the diversity of personalities. And it's more important than ever to build good relationships. Keep in mind that your objective is not necessarily to make friends. "You want other people to respect you. You don't want them to like you; you don't care if they like you. If they do, it's nice; it's icing on the cake," observed a marketing manager. Worry about professional respect and teamwork first, and the rest will fall into place.

Here are some pointers to help you do a better job at building relationships:

1. **Understand differences in people—not only understand but also respect them.** The foundation for all good professional relationships is a deep appreciation for the many differences in individual styles, personalities, and beliefs and an acknowledgment that there are no rights or wrongs but just differences. If you can grow to appreciate and respect differences, you can work well with anyone. All of us need room to be ourselves and have our rights respected. "People have to realize that there has to be mutual respect for everybody because we each have some value to add," said one new hire.

2. **Respect experience and expertise.** If someone has more experience than you or knows more than you, respect that. There is no disgrace in yielding to it. Everyone wants respect for what he or she can contribute.

Don't let your ego get in the way of acknowledging someone as more senior or skilled than you, particularly if you could not be expected to have the expertise.

3. **Give, so you can receive.** Give respect, and you'll likely receive it. Acknowledge others, and they'll acknowledge you. Ignore your colleagues, and they'll ignore you. "You're not any better than anybody. You're on an equal level with others," observed a second-year employee. It may sound simplistic, but it works.

4. **Give credit where credit is due.** In a team-oriented environment, no one person accomplishes anything. Be sure to credit others for their ideas, contributions, and successes. If you use someone else's idea or methods, ask before you do so, and give credit afterward. There is absolutely no reason not to credit others. It's expected that you can't do it alone, and others deserve recognition, too. Forget to do it, and they'll forget to contribute next time.

5. **Make the relationship mutually beneficial.** In a good professional relationship, there is something for both parties. Somehow, both have to profit from it, or the relationship won't last. Whether it's sharing ideas, trading favors, helping out in a jam, or whatever, the relationship has to be a two-way street. That's one of the problems for a new hire: at first you're mostly taking from others. They know that and will accept it for awhile, but be prepared to give something back later.

6. **Don't make snap judgments about people.** It's all too easy to use your first impressions about people to make judgments about

them. Resist this temptation. Get out of the habit of drawing quick conclusions about people's worth to the organization, their professional skill, and their ability to help you. Give the relationship some time to develop before you make those judgments.

7. **Be open to new ideas and styles.** You're not the only one in the organization who has good ideas. Be open to what others suggest. Don't bury yourself so deep in your own ideas and rationale that you can't see a different view or different approach. Similarly, there may be many good ways to do something. Be open to a different style or technique. Yours may work well, but that doesn't mean others won't, too.

8. **Don't use people.** You may get away with using people for a short while, but it won't last. If you get a reputation for manipulating people for your personal gain and their loss, you'll find yourself without any colleagues willing to support you.

9. **Ignore level in the organization.** New hires are particularly prone to look down on people beneath them in the organization. Remember, people are still people, not job titles, and respect everyone. Treat all with dignity; just because their rank is lower than yours doesn't mean you can step on them or use them. In particular, watch how you treat clerical and support people. They are much more important to your success than you may realize. Remember, too, that things change fast in organizations, and your relative status today could be quite different tomorrow.

10. **Make your own judgments.** Don't listen to what others say about people. Draw your

own conclusions, and build your own relationships. Your experience could be quite different from another's, especially if you follow these rules.

11. **Don't get too close to the wrong people.** Be careful whom you become friends with and with whom you ally yourself. It's pretty easy to figure out who the losers and outcasts are in the organization. It's okay to interact with them on a professional level, but don't go beyond that. Also don't get caught arguing their position or defending it. That's risky because if they're being branded a loser, so will you. That doesn't mean you can only be friends with superstars, but do try to stay with people who appear to be widely accepted and respected. The crowd you run with does make a difference.

12. **Smile and laugh.** Yes, this may seem banal, but a warm smile, a happy demeanor, and a few laughs can go a long way toward making work fun. And people do like to have a little fun at work. You spend too much time at work to be somber or cold all day. Loosen up but only enough to be personable and likable.

There really aren't too many people that you can't develop at least an acceptable professional relationship with. You may not like a person, you may not speak more often than you have to, but you can work together. Remember, you don't have to be friends to have a good professional relationship.

TRICKY RELATIONSHIPS

Interestingly enough, one of the trickiest types of relationships to deal with in your first year is that with your peers. When you first go to work, you'll need their support and friendship. That's perfectly acceptable and is encouraged. Since they are going through the same experience, you ought to talk to and support each other. But it won't take long before you realize that they aren't just friends; they are also your competitors. As one new hire advised, "The people you work with are your competitors for job promotions, for better raises, for the opportunities . . . Even though you personally would never stab anyone in the back, that doesn't mean that everybody you work with wouldn't." Fortunately, at the entry level there's usually plenty of room for promotion, so you needn't be paranoid. But it's wise to approach peers cautiously. It's not good to bare your soul to them. It's best to consider them professional relationships and consider yourself lucky if you find one or two peers who can be true friends.

The ironic part is that these are very important professional relationships for you to build. The bonds you build with your fellow new hires will be the basis for a professional network that will help you throughout your career with that company. As you and your peers rise through the ranks together, you'll return to those relationships again and again to solve problems, learn new information, and get support. So while you need to be careful to view the relationships as professional, not personal ones, you also need to nurture them with great care.

Another type of tricky relationship is that with colleagues much older than you, particularly if you have a higher level of education than they do or just a more current education. It's easy to think that you know more than they do, and sometimes you really do. That's why companies hire bright young minds. It's also true that you may have a sharper and faster mind simply because you're twenty or thirty years younger than an older colleague. Out of insecurity and your zest to prove yourself, you'll be tempted to "show your stuff" and demonstrate how smart and quick you are. The problem is that in your quest to blow your own horn, you often will put down that older, more experienced colleague, and, whether you intended to or not, he or she will resent it terribly. From the colleague's point of view, here's this new college kid coming in here and knowing so much. "I have been with this company twenty-five years or more. This is my job. I know what I am doing," they may say to themselves or others. "Is this kid going to come here now and start telling me what to do?"

Even if you are right, and some of your older colleagues' ideas are outdated, you have to respect their experience. Quite often, they really know more than you think they do. You'll never get the chance to implement your new ideas as long as those ideas are a threat to the "old-timers." Give them respect and become an ally, and your new ideas will cease to threaten and become a help to them.

POLITICS ISN'T A DIRTY WORD

It seems that when the word "politics" is used today it's often in a negative tone. Listen to the evening news report and hear the president and Congress accuse each other of "playing politics" instead of focusing on real issues. Or notice that when a neighbor loses out on a big promotion, he may blame it on "company politics." You might read in the *Wall Street Journal* about an executive who lost her job because of "political infighting." These are just a few examples of the way we usually view politics as a rather negative, undesirable, cynical, and manipulative part of our society.

I won't be so naive as to say that politics is not dirty and practiced with a vengeance and unpleasant results in many cases. In many jobs, bruising political wars are a common occurrence. But we have to separate the tactics used in political battles and the politics involved at higher levels within the company from what goes on at the entry level, which is what is of concern to us here.

I suggest that there is a level of organizational politics that is not vicious, negative, or vindictive. At this level, organizational politics can and should be viewed as a natural outgrowth of people doing their jobs and is not a negative force in the organization at all. It is this level of organizational politics in which you will participate during your first year on the job. Furthermore, it is a level of politics that you must not only come to understand but also become skillful at working within. What I am interested in doing is not telling you how to fight political battles but convincing you that this basic level of nondestructive politics is a reality of working with people in an organization and must be mastered for you to be effective in the workplace.

Managers and executives repeatedly mention politics when talking about new hires. One human resources executive summed it up:

What I find lacking most of all [in new hires] is political savvy. Candidates come in with excellent academic knowledge, which applies to only some of the assignments they get. But they are so dependent on it that they are naive when it comes to the politics of how an office is run.

It's really not that employers expect you to learn all the ins and outs of organizational politics in college—they're perfectly willing to teach that. What they hate is that most new hires don't even realize that politics exists. What they would be tickled to see is a new hire who realizes that politics is an integral part of getting things done and that political and people skills are just as important as task-related skills. If you're even just highly sensitive to the political realities of an organization, you'll be miles ahead of other new hires. The details will fall into place later.

Fast-Starter Tip

Politics is not something you win or lose at; it's the way things get done.

John P. Kotter of the Harvard Business School has written an excellent book entitled *Power and Influence: Beyond Formal Authority*, which explains very well why politics exists. In it, he starts with the basic premise that organizations are complex social institutions that depend on people to accomplish their goals. Organizational politics arises because of two basic facts: People are diverse and are dependent on each other to do their jobs (i.e., they are a team).

Everyone has different educational, social, and family backgrounds that they bring to the workplace. From these varied backgrounds, each person develops his or her own unique set of values and assumptions about the world and what is right or wrong, good or bad, and desirable or undesirable. Everybody perceives the world, the company, issues, and their job a little differently. Most likely, everybody will bring different assumptions to solving any problem and will develop different goals and agendas. "No two people are alike." Stop and think about that old cliché for a minute. Consider its implications when you combine thousands and maybe tens of thousands of people in an organization trying to reach common goals. It is an extremely complex situation.

It gets even more complex when you add the fact that people in organizations generally do not work independently. A very, very large majority of people are heavily dependent on others. I don't mean only to meet organizational goals; I mean that to perform the immediate specific task the boss wants done by 5 p.m., you will likely need the help of someone else. You need others, and they need you, which means that you have some power over them and they have some power over you.

Matters are further complicated by the fact that resources are limited in most organizations. Time, money, people, etc., are all necessary for people to do their jobs. If they were unlimited, then everyone could accomplish their own goals and diversity would not be an issue. But if resources are limited, not all the various agendas and goals can be met in full, and that will often lead to disagreement and conflict.

When these realities come together, the result is politics. As Kotter says:

When the many parties who are linked together interdependently are very diverse from one another, they will naturally have difficulty agreeing on what should be done, who should do it, and when. Differences in goals, values, states, and outlooks will lead people to different conclusions. The greater the diversity, the more differences of opinion there will be. Because of interdependence, people will not be able to resolve their differences either by edict or by walking away.

(John P. Kotter, *Power and Influence: Beyond Formal Authority*, Free Press, 1985, p. 18.)

In order to settle the differences and find some common ground, people resort to negotiation, persuasion, compromise, manipulation, power plays, infighting, and all the other elements of corporate politics you are used to reading about.

Most of the political problems new hires have result from a lack of understanding of these basic political realities: diversity and interdependence. In school, you spent most of your time focusing on technical aspects of your work. And you have been doing it mostly on an individual basis. The result is a disturbing tendency of new college graduates not to understand why people don't see things their way. When others don't cooperate or share their view of issues, they want to blame it on "politics" and walk away from it.

What I hope you can see from this discussion is that organizational politics is a fact of life, at least at a basic level. You absolutely must come to appreciate and respect the diversity of the people with whom you will work and recognize how inextricably you will be tied to them to perform your job. Just the simple acceptance

and integration of these facts into your daily work will greatly increase your political savvy. To most readers, these facts are easy to accept on an intellectual basis. Before you pass them off as something you don't need to work on, let me caution you that many people find them much harder to integrate into their daily activity. It is one thing to understand intellectually and another to integrate into practice. Judging by the number of new hires who seem not to perform in a manner that shows sensitivity to these two facts, I suggest you recheck yourself and pay extra attention.

WHO HAS THE POWER?

Power and authority are also everyday facts of life in the working world. Everyone, even the CEO, has to deal with people who have, would like to have, or are afraid of losing power and authority. Power is often defined as the ability to get done what you want even in the face of resistance. It is also the ability you have to influence your future and your job. Power is usually presented as arising from five different sources:

1. Reward power is the ability to reward others.
2. Coercive power is the ability to inflict punishment or unpleasant conditions on others.
3. Legitimate power is the right to influence or control others who have accepted the power as legitimate because of the position one holds.
4. Referent power is the desire of others to identify with the person wielding power (movie stars, sports figures, cult heroes).

5. Expert power stems from the knowledge and expertise of the person who wields it.

You will see all five types of power in your organization. Your boss will have reward power, since he or she has the ability to reward you, and also coercive power, since he or she could fire you. Your boss will also have some legitimate power because of his or her position. Another person may have only reward power because of having the ability to appoint you to a choice committee assignment. You may encounter people placed in figurehead positions, who have legitimate power because of their position but little power to reward or punish anybody. High-ranking officers in the company may also have referent power because others see them as role models and aspire to emulate them. Companies sometimes give referent power by creating legends who personify company values. Expert power is a common power source, particularly in high-tech businesses. A person can acquire a great deal of power in the organization because of his or her expertise without having any other significant sources of power.

One insightful new hire commented, "You need to know how the power structure runs the organization; how it identifies good and bad projects, good and bad people; and how its reward system is set up, because those are the key things that are going to make or break your own personal career." This person was right on target. You must quickly identify the power structure in the organization. Those that have power and those that want it will have an enormous impact on you, since they are the ones who control the rewards you want. And they will reward those who help them meet their objectives. Power politics for a new hire

can be quite simple: find out who has the power to get you what you want in your career, find out what his or her agenda is, and then help that person accomplish it!

You have to realize that new hires typically don't have much power. As the low person in the organization, you may well have no power to reward or punish anybody, little legitimate power because of your position, no referent power because nobody is aspiring to be at the bottom of the ladder, and little expert power because you lack experience. This you just have to accept. In time, you will acquire power of some type, but in the beginning you will have little or none.

You can acquire some power sooner than you think by quickly developing some expertise of great value to the organization. You don't have to look any further than your own job to find the right subject area either. You can actually become quite persuasive and influential in the organization if you work hard to become a true master of your job. Learn everything you can about every aspect of your job and how it relates to other activities of the company, and you will be amazed at how others will be coming to you for advice and assistance.

Reward, coercive, legitimate, and certainly referent power come much more slowly. Legitimate power begins to develop as soon as you firmly establish yourself as a competent professional. As you earn respect for your abilities and expertise, others will begin to respect your position in the organization. Referent power will likely be a long time in coming, so you can just forget about that for now. Reward and coercive power may be a long time coming or could happen very quickly. In some organizations new graduates are often placed in positions supervising hourly or blue-collar workers very quickly, perhaps from day one. In these cases, you will have reward, coercive, and legitimate power. That is quite a heady feeling for a new graduate, but it's important not to let it go to your head so that you abuse it. In other organizations, it may be quite some time before you are given managerial responsibility.

You must learn to respect the power others in the organization have. They earned it, they worked for it, they suffered through their "powerless" days just like you, and they will demand respect. And they deserve it. There is one simple fact of power politics that you must learn quickly: if you have no power, you had better respect the power of others, or you are guaranteed to lose out.

This won't always be easy for you to do. You have already spent the better part of your life with people who had a great deal of power over you: parents, teachers, professors, etc. Most new college graduates are quite anxious to gain their freedom, to get away from these people and institutions that have had so much power over their lives. It's a real shock for them to discover that at a time in their life when they are most anxious to establish their independence and freedom, they once again will be subject to the power and demands of others. And feeling powerless is no fun.

As difficult as it is, it's a fact of working life. You are gaining a great deal of power and freedom over your personal life when you leave college and home, but in your professional life it will be a while before you find the degree of authority and freedom you want. You have to recognize and accept the power and authority others in the organization will have over you in the early years. You also have to realize that

someone in the organization will always have some sort of power over you as long as you are in the organization. That's part of the "contract." They pay you, and in return, you give them the right to tell you what to do for 40–60 hours per week. You can't rebel against this authority as you did against your parents' or complain and fuss as you did about your professors. You can only accept it and work as hard as you can so you can progress to where you, too, share in the power.

Just as in organizational politics, you are best advised to stay out of any power games or battles in your first year. Without any power, your best bet is to just sit on the sidelines and watch. But you do need to realize that power is an everyday fact for an organization and will play a role in its decisions and activities. The degree will vary greatly from company to company: some corporate cultures encourage an almost constant power play, while others strongly discourage it.

People also tend not to be threatened by you during your first year since they will perceive you as having little power. If you can resist the temptation to jump into power games, you can remain a fairly impartial observer. That makes the first year a great time to watch and learn what the power structure in the organization is. Pay particular attention to:

- Who really has the power in the organization
- Who has what type of power
- Who has proved to use his or her power extensively
- Who can get things done the quickest and most effectively (usually has lots of power)
- Whom people turn to when the going gets tough

- Who has the most respect in the organization
- Who is the most feared
- How powerful people got their power
- How they maintain it
- To what extent the power structure follows the organizational hierarchy
- What the most powerful second- and third-year employees did in their first year

LEARNING TO PLAY THE GAME

Like it or not, you need a certain amount of gamesmanship to succeed in an organization. I don't necessarily mean the manipulative, deceptive, or destructive type of games; it's critically important that you not get yourself involved in such politics. As a new hire, you have neither the chips, clout, nor political awareness to play those games and win. If you try, you'll only get clobbered.

New hires describe the games you'll have to play better than I can:

You have to figure out who the important people are and play their game.

Figure out exactly what you are supposed to do, exactly how you are supposed to do it, and whom you need and whom you don't need.

The "game," then, is simply learning who the people that can affect your future career are, learning what they expect of you, and then delivering it. (And delivering it in the way the organization usually does things.) What it doesn't mean is you come into the organization and do what you think is important in the way

you think it's best to do it. In time, you'll have greater and greater opportunity to do that. But as a newcomer, you have to first learn the rules of the game as currently played. Then, and only then, can you effectively make changes. That requires adaptability and flexibility, and, sometimes, swallowing some pride.

Picture a Broadway play that's been running for many months. Being a newcomer is like being dropped on stage right in the middle of the second act of a performance. The play is well under way, all the actors know their parts and lines, and, suddenly, you're sitting in the middle of the stage. Your challenge is to figure out what your role is supposed to be. It's hard at first, because it may not seem as if there is a role for you since you're joining a group of "actors" with well-defined sets of roles. Most important, you have to learn to play your role, just like an actor must. You learn your lines, find out how the director wants you to act the part, and then do it.

The problem is that many new hires don't like to play the game. They want to be independent and do things their own way, as the following comments indicate:

It's frustrating when you say I'm not going to play politics. I'm not going to get sucked into this. So you sit there and do your job well and things seem to be going smoothly, but then you see that the people who play politics keep on getting promoted. And you feel like saying to the person who gave them the promotions, "I am doing just as well as the people you promoted, if not better, and I am the one actually doing the work."

In college, a lot of people hate to play the game. When I say "the game," I mean getting to know the right people, saying the right things, being at the right places. In college, you got away with it; you didn't have to play the game. But here, if you're not going to play it, somebody else is.

A senior executive explained it this way:

To be effective ultimately depends on your ability not only to think through a problem but also to implement your great solution. You're only going to be able to implement it to the degree you are effective within the organization because you fit in and play the game.

So you can be a rebel, be independent, and do things your own way if you want to. But if you do, you won't fit in or play the game, and you won't become part of the culture and be accepted within the organization. And as a result, you won't earn a reputation and be effective in the workplace.

Playing the game doesn't always feel good. We'd all rather do things our own way, and playing the game requires us to do things someone else's way. Two things seem to bother new hires most: First, playing the game doesn't leave much room to demonstrate their capability and make an independent contribution to the organization. Second, there's a great sense of falseness, of not being genuine or true to oneself, that goes with it. But you have to be flexible. Only by playing the game in the beginning and pleasing other people will you gain a taste of freedom from it as you begin to rise through the organization.

EFFECTIVE POLITICAL STRATEGIES FOR YOUR FIRST YEAR

If you want to be successful, acquiring political skill is a must. That means learning to work with, through, and around people. One simple way to view organizational politics is to think of chips in a game. In politics you earn chips by your strong performance, by helping other people accomplish their goals, by doing favors, by not causing people problems, and by allying yourself with them on issues. You spend your chips when you make mistakes and someone has to cover for you, when you embarrass someone, when you don't do your job right or take a position against a powerful person. Politics then becomes a continual process of acquiring and spending chips.

As a new hire, you don't have any chips, save for a few generated out of simple goodwill because you're new. Fortunately, you don't have much of a deficit either. New hires do have a tendency to build big deficits, though, because they aren't sensitive to political realities. If you're not careful, you'll soon find you're too far in the hole to ever get out. Your strategy in your first year should be to acquire as many chips as you can and keep from spending too many. Later, as you become a bit more savvy about the organization, you can pick when to spend your political capital.

Your first year is a time to build a solid political base, not to practice your political tactics. To do that, focus on the following things in your first year:

1. **Prove your competence.** Nothing builds a strong political base quicker than a proven track record of competence. If you are to be

respected for your opinion, views, and objectives, you must first establish yourself as a competent professional. Without this respect, you might as well quit reading because little else can make up for it.

2. **Learn the rules of the political game.** Watch and learn how politics is played in your company. Is the company highly political or not very? How do people resolve their conflicting agendas, openly or behind closed doors? What do the effective people do politically? What types of influence work?

3. **Stay out of trouble.** Try to end your first year without any political strikes against you. Be careful not to strike out by stepping on the toes of your teammates (colleagues) and managers or swinging for political home runs you're incapable of hitting as a rookie. The idea is simple: don't try and rattle the ball club (your organization) politically until you've built a political base. That way, when you're ready to be more active politically, you won't be in such deep trouble that the only position the ball club will let you play is "left out."

4. **Become aware of and sensitive to people.** Watch, listen, and learn about the great diversity of people in your organization. Don't judge, but learn the differences in their outlooks and agendas. Learn to appreciate their differences and to understand why they exist. Make knowing people as high a priority as your other tasks.

5. **Learn to read people.** Learn how to see others more objectively, rather than filtered through your own values. Learn how to pick up on cues they give as to what's important to them. Be aware of the interpersonal dynamics.

6. **Build strong working relationships.** Being effective means building good working relationships with others. The more relationships you can build based on trust and integrity, the more respect you will gain for your position and the more credibility you will have in political situations. Learn how to build good relationships. Develop your network of people you know and who know you.

7. **Collect information.** Besides learning the rules of the political game, learn who the various players are in the company. Learn who usually takes what position in disagreements, what people's "hot buttons" are, what agendas different departments have. Learn to seek out information such as this and to be receptive to the information around you.

8. **Learn how to persuade and influence others.** Selling your ideas and yourself is a critical skill. Learn how to present a cogent, persuasive argument for your ideas and positions so you can influence others to accept them. While the first year may not be the time to do this publicly, you should look for opportunities to practice and develop this skill.

The degree to which you will need to be politically skilled varies tremendously, depending on your company, career path, and career objectives. Some companies are highly political, particularly larger ones, while others work hard to keep politics to a minimum. If you are on a highly technical career path, you may have less call to be a strong political tactician than someone who is on a management career path. If your aim is to become president of the company, then politics will be much more important for you than for a person who is content to stay in mid-management.

But all of that will sort itself out in years beyond the first year. Regardless of those factors, you need to be paying attention to the basic level of politics described here. You might say that it is really just the basic skills of working well with people. And that's something everybody needs, even in the most apolitical of companies. If you are then moving on in your career to positions requiring a higher level of political skill, you will have established a solid political base on which to build. If you choose less political career paths, you will still have the skills you need to be effective.

ULTIMATE SURVIVAL TIPS

1. Work gets done by, with, and through people.

2. Regardless of your profession, you need strong people skills to succeed.

3. Professional relationships are unique but critical to your success. Cultivate a strong network.

4. Learn to work and get along with all types of people.

5. Playing politics is simply the way to get work done in organizations.

6. Politics does not have to be a negative force in the organization.

7. Understand who has the power and sets the agenda for the organization.

8. Protect your ego, because you won't have much power at first.

9. Learn to "play the game," you can change the rules later.

10. Politics does matter in your first year, so learn effective political strategies.

6

WORKING WITH YOUR BOSS

The biggest power center for the first six months is going
to be your supervisor. He or she is the one you're going
to be playing to. [manager]

You're never quite sure what your bosses want,
but you have to give it to them. [new hire]

During your first year, your boss is probably the single most important person to you in the entire company. He or she will be largely responsible for getting you opportunities to showcase your talents, seeing that you get the training you need, setting the tone of your first year, shaping the organization's opinion and evaluation of you, determining your advancement beyond the entry position, and socializing you in the organization's culture. Because you are a stranger to the organization and have no other track record, what your boss thinks of you and how he or she introduces you to the organization are critical to your success.

While bosses vary, all managers have one thing in common: They want good subordinates. The problem is this: In college, you've spent most of your time studying how to be a good leader—that is, preparing to be a manager or senior member of an organization. But before you can be a good leader, you must first manage the art of being a good follower. The only way you'll ever be promoted to a managerial position is to first prove you are an outstanding subordinate.

The problem is that you really haven't been taught how to be an effective subordinate in college. Just as there is a well-defined set of managerial skills, there is a well-defined set of subordinate skills. If you start your career as a subordinate acting and thinking like a manager, you'll be making a big mistake and will probably alienate your boss. As you reach the senior staff level, assuming a managerial approach will be an effective strategy to prove you're ready for a managerial promotion. But in your first year, it's subordinate savvy that counts.

Because the relationship with your boss is so critical, you should give top priority to it in your first year (really for your entire career). It is a unique relationship unlike most that you've experienced. The success of your relationship with your boss is just as much your responsibility as it is the boss's. It's a two-way relationship. What flows from subordinate to boss is productivity, results, and effectiveness. From boss to subordinate flow instructions, supervision, and management. In this chapter, we'll look at things you can do to improve both aspects—that is, to make yourself more effective and easier to manage—as well as other "subordinate" issues. Understanding and applying the information presented here can save you a lot of headaches in your first year as you adjust to your new boss.

WHAT IS A BOSS?

A boss is simply another professional like yourself who has been given the responsibility to supervise and direct the efforts of other people toward achieving organizational goals. It's sometimes a rather awesome responsibility because it puts a person in charge of other people's professional lives. To work effectively with a boss, it's good to fully understand the ramifications of who that boss is and what he or she is charged to do.

Your boss has not been endowed with any superhuman capabilities that make him or her very different from you. Bosses are fallible. They have lots of weaknesses and faults to go

with their strengths and capabilities. They don't know everything, nor do they have unlimited time to do their work. They get stressed, overworked, and pressured to meet deadlines. They have doubts and insecurities just like you, worry about things just like you, and get angry, nervous, scared, elated, etc., just like you. They have good days and bad days, and they make mistakes. They have a boss who puts pressure on them, who has bad days just as your boss does, and who asks your boss to do things he or she doesn't want to do. Your boss worries about his or her career and has personal problems, hopes, and dreams just like you.

New hires tend to place bosses on a pedestal, to see them as an all-powerful, near-perfect person and to expect them to behave accordingly. If you do this, you will be disappointed. Your boss is going to snap at you once in a while; he or she sometimes is going to make mistakes and be upset about that. In short, your boss will not be the perfect boss, just as you aren't going to be the perfect employee. And just as your boss won't always fully understand why you behave the way you do, you won't always know everything that is affecting your boss's behavior. In other words, bosses are just people trying to do the best job they can. Is that an excuse for poor performance? No, but it is an explanation for less-than-perfect behavior. Just as you expect your boss to consider you as an individual, to take into account your strengths and weaknesses and to allow for other things in your life that may affect your work, you, too, will have to allow for these things in your boss.

Your boss has been given some special authority, though, and that is to supervise and direct your efforts. That means that for at least 8 and often more hours per day, you are accountable to your boss for what you do, when you do it, and how you do it. You'll find that as a professional, you are usually given considerable flexibility in structuring your work, especially after you gain more experience. But you have to remember that it is your boss's prerogative to change that structure and to ask you to do what he or she wants you to do as long as it is within company policy and is legal, moral, and ethical. Bosses do in fact have control over your time while you are at work and, in most professional jobs, the right to impinge on a reasonable amount of your personal time if needed (you're not punching a clock).

This really isn't comfortable. Like many new college graduates, you may not be too fond of authority figures; in fact, you may even resent them. I remember when I first went to work, I thought I was independent and free. It was quite a shock to discover that my boss had just as much control over me as my parents or professors. It may be difficult for you to adjust to yet another authority figure, but you will have to. Your boss has been given the authority, and when you agreed to come to work, you also agreed to let the organization have control over some of your time in exchange for your salary and other rewards. It's all too easy to let a subconscious resentment of authority get in the way of an effective relationship with your boss. Think about it a little: how do you feel about authority? If accepting it is a problem for you, work on it and keep your negativity out of the workplace. Don't project resentment against authority figures, like your parents, onto your boss. Bosses aren't the same, and besides, until you decide to start your own business and become your own boss, you're stuck with them.

Your boss's mission is to direct you and himself or herself toward meeting the organization's goals. Although the odds are that your first boss will not be at a level where he or she has much to say about the goals, he or she will be charged with implementing them. The agenda will not be his or her own but rather the organization's. This means that what your boss asks you to do may not always be exactly what you prefer but what he or she has deemed necessary to meet organizational goals. That's what both of you are paid to do.

Fast-Starter Tip

Your boss's evaluation of your performance is the single most important factor in how well your career gets started.

Part of your boss's job is to judge and evaluate your performance, to set standards and goals for you to achieve and then assess how well you meet them. You are accountable to him or her for your performance, so it doesn't matter if you like your boss or agree with him or her; you had better work hard to meet the standards he or she sets. And while the organization may place limits on what kinds of standards and goals he or she sets, the limits are usually quite broad. Your boss will usually have wide discretion to set standards as he or she sees fit.

Your boss's job is also to look out for the well-being of the organization. What everyone hopes for is that your professional and personal well-being and success are consistent with the organization's. But—and this is critical—if forced to choose between what's good for the organization and what's good for you, your boss may well have to choose what's good for the organization. He or she may not like it and might personally prefer to do something else, but as a professional he or she is paid to be a caretaker of the organization's interests.

Being a boss is a tough job. It has its rewards for sure, but it's also a tough balancing act. Any good boss likes his or her people, looks out for them, promotes their efforts, helps them meet their goals, etc. On the other hand, your boss's primary mandate, which he or she will be rewarded for, is to meet the goals the organization has set forth. It's very hard to keep both parties happy all the time, though good bosses and good organizations do a pretty good job of it because they know the happier you are, the more productive you are. You have to understand these conflicting demands put on your boss and not take it personally if he or she has to choose what's best for the organization rather than you.

THE BOSS-SUBORDINATE RELATIONSHIP

Your relationship with your boss is first and foremost a professional one. The sole reason for the relationship is so both parties can meet their professional goals. That doesn't mean that it has to be unfriendly or unpleasant, but you must begin with the basic premise that the relationship does not have to be more than a strong professional one. Usually, however, a good professional relationship is also a friendly one. That is, there will usually be a pleasant tone to conversations, and you will enjoy working together, sharing a few laughs, etc. You want to establish a good rapport that lets you communicate easily and clearly and achieve a certain level of mutual trust and confidence if possible. You'll probably see a lot of these kinds of relationships.

There is a key difference here though: friendly does not mean the same thing as being personal friends. If you are not used to building professional relationships (which most new graduates aren't), this is one of the first adjustments you have to make. Prior to this point, most of your relationships have contained a strong personal element. Friends, family, classmates, etc., were all personal friends. It's only a short jump then, and a quite natural one, to approach your relationship with your boss the same way. But this won't do. It's fine to share some elements of your personal life, such as what you did over the weekend or where you bought a house, but your boss is not your confidant, not the one with whom to discuss personal problems and difficulties that aren't affecting your job. It's perfectly okay to have a drink after work with your boss or possibly to invite him or her to dinner once or twice, but that's not a necessary part of a good professional relationship. In fact, many very good boss-subordinate relationships have nearly no personal elements whatsoever and include no activity outside the office. And that's perfectly okay. All that is required is that you work smoothly and effectively as professionals.

Should You Be Friends

Does that mean you shouldn't become friends with your boss? Opinions are very mixed about this. There are those who suggest that a boss should never get too close to his or her subordinates and vice versa. I tend to think the absolute "never" is a little strong. How close you get will depend heavily on your personal style, your boss's, and the culture of the organization. Some people can handle it, and others can't. I think it is fair to say that it is unwise to let a friendship with your boss get too close. You have to remember that there are some elements of your personal life that you just don't want to bring into the workplace. People's impressions of you, including your boss's, will be shaped by all the information they have, personal and professional. That means it's very difficult for your boss to be your best friend, the one to whom you reveal all your wants and your deep, dark secrets.

Bosses tend to like to put a little distance between themselves and their subordinates because they always have to remember that their primary responsibility is to the organization. It's hard enough to make a decision that might disappoint a subordinate when you're not friends but even tougher when you are. If you do become friends with your boss, be prepared for this type of dilemma. What you'll see most often, however, is a low-to-moderate level of friendship developing. The key point is that you not go into your relationship with your boss expecting to be friends. Approach it on a sound, strong professional basis. If you then discover that both of you are comfortable with more of a friendship, fine—let it develop, but not too close. Don't make the common mistake of approaching your boss as your friend.

Neither is your boss your enemy. It's probably equally easy to view your boss as your adversary, particularly when he or she exercises authority to direct you in ways you find unpleasant or rejects your ideas. At times, therefore, you may be tempted to try and undermine your boss's efforts. Remember, however, that the only way you are going to be effective and advance in your career is to work well with your boss, not against him or her.

No Two Bosses Are Alike

The one certainty is that every boss you have will be different, and, therefore, so will each relationship. Each boss will have his or her own style, ideas, priorities, ways of doing things, strengths, and weaknesses. You have to learn when to go along, when to challenge, when to be patient, etc. There is no one "right" combination that is perfect for each situation. One of the privileges the organization gives a manager is the right to assert his or her own style and methods in the job. The higher you go in the managerial ranks, the more freedom you have to do that.

Too often, new hires approach their boss comparing him or her to some ideal model they have in mind, which is often heavily influenced by a textbook model. Not surprisingly, they can quickly find faults because they fail to allow for individual styles and differences. While they're busy finding faults or wishing for something different, they're not building a good relationship and aren't earning very high performance ratings.

There is no such thing as an ideal or perfect boss. There might be an ideal for you individually in a given situation, but there is no absolute perfect model. There are many, many different ways to be effective as a manager. You need to accept that and focus on adapting to the individual differences instead of fighting against your boss. As one executive emphasized:

I think the mistake that a lot of first-year people make that results in conflicts with bosses is the desire to make some contribution rather than start by giving the boss what he or she wants, by fulfilling the expectations of the boss. They don't do what they've been asked to do first. Instead, they fight what they think is a wrong decision and come back with an alternative.

As a first-year subordinate, you'll lose if you fight your boss's decisions. Also, as a subordinate you must adapt to your boss's style, not vice versa. When you get promoted to manager or supervisor, then you can have the privilege of asserting yours. That's a boss's prerogative.

Fast-Starter Tip

**Don't be part of the problem;
be part of the solution!**

If your boss is a fallible human being just like you, then the relationship is one of two fallible humans with their own diverse backgrounds and interests trying to mesh individual and common goals in order to achieve whatever organizational goals the two have been given. You and your boss may or may not agree, be friends, or share the same personal goals, but you have to find a way to get along, solve problems, and get the job done, at least until you can move to another position. Frankly, the odds of moving are slim if you don't perform at least reasonably well with your current boss. Your job is to find a way of doing that.

You need to do several things. First, you have to understand one another's expectations. One differentiating characteristic of professional relationships is that people are usually much more up-front with each other. It is expected and quite acceptable to have conversations of the pattern "Here's where I am" and "Here's what I expect." Politics and diplomacy have to be considered, but the degree of tact that often characterizes social relationships is not required. You and your boss have to understand one another. It's that simple.

A good relationship will result from a process of matching your strengths and weaknesses with your boss's. By matching, I mean in a complementary fashion, where your strengths help compensate for your boss's weaknesses. (Be careful though, because it's really not your boss's job to cover for your weaknesses.) The best boss-subordinate relationships are those where you work as a team, where your strengths add to your boss's effectiveness. You need to work with your boss to identify the areas where you can support and strengthen his or her efforts.

You have to resolve conflict. Conflict is to be expected. Whenever you have smart, ambitious, capable people working closely together, they will sometimes disagree; so will you and your boss. Conflict has to be resolved, not left to fester and disrupt the relationship. Again, a frank but controlled and low-emotion discussion with your boss is in order.

Part of all this, and perhaps the basis for an effective relationship, is good communication. Bosses and subordinates who work well together keep an open channel of communication. They learn to talk with each other and work hard to understand each other. More of the burden is on the subordinate, though, than on the boss.

WHAT TO EXPECT FROM YOUR BOSS

The relationship between boss and subordinate is not all a one-way street. You do have a right to expect certain things from your boss and no right to expect other things. Getting a clear picture of the difference is another important element of building a good relationship. Let's look first at what you do have a right to expect from your boss:

1. **Performance expectations.** You have a right to know what your boss expects you to do and what it takes to meet your boss's standards of success. I talked earlier about how different and less precise the expectations might be, and you have to take this into account, but nonetheless you have a right to be told on what basis your performance will be judged. Finding this out can sometimes be difficult and will be discussed later in this chapter.

2. **Feedback.** Similarly, you have a right to know how you are doing. Particularly when you are new, you need to know if you are doing your job correctly, meeting your boss's standards, etc. It won't be as clear as grades in school, but you have a right to know.

3. **Policies and guidelines.** Every boss has his or her own way of conducting business. You have the right to expect your boss to set some parameters that you can understand and within which you should do your job. It's your boss's job to set policies and communicate them to you.

4. **Resources to do your job.** You can't do your job without a certain level of resources. All professionals will tell you that they could sure use more resources to do their job, so don't expect to have everything you want. It is reasonable to expect to be given at least a minimal amount of money, time, personnel, equipment, or whatever is needed to get the job done. You'll surely be pushed to do more with less, but there is at least a minimal level that your boss must provide.

5. **Means for you to help yourself.** You will quickly discover that professionals are expected to teach themselves how to do new tasks, locate resource persons, find sources of training, etc. Your boss does not have to do all this personally and may not do any of it. But it is his or her responsibility to provide you with the means to help yourself. That could mean giving you access to training programs or self-instruction resources, identifying other people you should talk to, or just telling you how to get started on a project.

6. **Protection.** Part of your boss's job is to protect his or her staff when necessary. Your boss has been given a certain amount of status and power in the organization. With power comes the obligation to use it when needed to protect his or her people from others in the organization who might abuse their power and authority.

7. **Help with professional development.** The initiative for professional development has to come from you, but your boss should be receptive to it and help you. It is to everyone's best interest that you continue to grow professionally, and it is part of a manager's job to assist in that process.

8. **Use authority wisely.** Authority in an organization carries with it the responsibility of

using it wisely. Decisions made don't have to be popular, but they should not be abusive in results or driven by a simple need to exercise power. Your boss's power and authority should be used to further organizational goals, not personal ones.

What you cannot expect your boss to do is the following:

1. **Tell you exactly how to do your job.** Professionals don't get step-by-step instructions or road maps for their jobs. You are hired for your ability to think, to learn, and to contribute, not to follow marching orders. Don't look to your boss for detailed instructions on how to complete your tasks. According to one manager, "Most bosses have their own job to do and simply cannot spend all day teaching new hires how to do their work from A to Z. Employees are hired to help the boss get his or her work done and not to detract from it. Simply put, bosses want new hires who can learn to do things on their own without an awful lot of direction and without becoming a real drag on the boss's own time, work, and productivity."

2. **Hold your hand.** Bosses aren't baby-sitters. They expect you to pull your own weight in the organization (after the first six months or so), take initiative, help yourself, etc. Don't be in your boss's office with every little complaint.

3. **Cover your mistakes.** While your boss might choose to help bail you out of tough situations and correct your mistakes, you can't approach your work with a casual attitude because you expect your boss to

bail you out. You are responsible for your own work and the consequences. Expect to avoid mistakes and correct them yourself. Then when you do get in a really tough jam, your boss will be glad to help you.

THE IDEAL FIRST BOSS

You're going to need a lot from your first boss. A good first boss can make a huge difference in how successful you are in your first year. Unfortunately, you will probably have absolutely nothing to say about who the person is and will be totally at the mercy of your new employer to choose a good person. Many companies do realize the importance of the first boss and take great pains to carefully select one. But business needs, politics, ignorance, and other factors often keep companies from choosing the ideal person.

It's important for you to understand what you really need from your boss during the first year. Knowing this will help you gain some perspective on what kind of relationship you need to have and also what to ask your boss for if you aren't getting what you need. If you have any input into who your first boss is, knowing what an ideal boss is will help you make a sensible choice. And if you're unfortunate enough to end up with a bad first boss, awareness of the qualities a good boss should possess will help you select your next one. The following attributes are highly desirable in an ideal first boss. (Keep in mind that this is perfection, and no one person is likely to have all these strengths. Find a majority of these, and you should count your blessings.) An ideal first boss would be one who gives you:

- Challenging assignments early on so you can prove your competence, including assignments that make you visible to the right people and parts of the organization
- Honest, direct, and frank feedback on your strengths and weaknesses, even when he or she knows it may be unpleasant
- The opportunity to get all the training you need
- Credit and reward for your contributions
- Opportunities to grow and progress and the push to do so, even when you're reluctant

Furthermore, the ideal boss would:

- Keep you from sticking out your neck too far in high-risk situations, even if you feel he or she is holding you back
- Encourage you and help you to build confidence
- Introduce you to the right people so you can build a good network
- Help you identify and define criteria for success and advancement
- Defend you when you make unexpected rookie mistakes that are critical, i.e., take the heat but give you the credit
- Have a supportive and developmentally oriented personality
- Promote you to others so that your career will progress
- In general, represent a good role model

That's a tough bill for one person to fill, and there aren't many bosses who do. Yet, you still need all these things. What do you do if your boss doesn't provide them? One strategy that is really useful throughout your career is to not be too dependent on just one person. While it is much better and simpler if your boss provides all this, you can find other role models elsewhere in the organization. Not getting the right kind or amount of feedback you need? Ask others. Not getting enough visibility? Volunteer to help out in other areas, with your boss's permission, of course. Getting too much negative feedback and feel your confidence waning? Find some other more positive people in the organization to help balance that. Not getting the training you need? Find out from others what you ought to have and then ask your boss for it.

While I would say that I think it's your boss's responsibility to do some of these things, you've already learned that making excuses doesn't work. It's your responsibility to make your career work the way you want it to. As long as you don't go over your boss's head unnecessarily or commit other organizational sins that are part of your organization's culture, it's perfectly OK to look to others to provide what your boss doesn't. It's your responsibility to do this, and you owe it to yourself.

GETTING TO KNOW YOUR BOSS

Since your boss is so important, you need to get to know him or her quickly. You need to understand your boss's expectations, motivations, and style so that you can perform in the way he or she wants. These new hires learned this lesson well:

One of the things I am learning is that you need to find out immediately what your boss is like—under all types of situations.

So I talk to other people who have worked for this person and I say, "What is this person like on a daily basis? Are they an eight-to-five person? What about going out for lunch for an hour and a half?"

Sometimes it's a game of "managing your own manager." But it's more than that. You need to learn your boss's style but also let your boss know you do good work.

Too many new hires approach their new boss much as they would a new professor, as someone who is passing through their life with only minimal impact. However, because your boss is so important in your career, you should plan to devote considerable effort to getting to know him or her. That's your responsibility. Although many bosses will make an effort to get to know you, your work style, etc., others will not, and you should be ready for that. You have to protect your record and reputation.

You will want to establish a rapport with your boss early on to open up a channel for good communication. The quickest way to build rapport is to find some common ground or interest. That could be work, family, sports, or other related areas. Often the easiest place to break the ice is in a social setting. Look for a chance to have lunch with your boss, attend a party, play golf, or whatever. You'll be surprised how some social conversation can carry over into the work environment. Once you have developed a good rapport, there are some key things you need to learn about your boss:

1. **Relationship with subordinates.** How close or distant does your boss like to be? Does he or she like to talk to subordinates frequently or infrequently? Does your boss socialize with subordinates? Does your boss use subordinates to further his or her own career or have a sincere interest in helping you develop?

2. **The boss's agenda.** What are the highest priorities for your boss? What are his or her key objectives? What are his or her biggest problems or issues? How can you help solve them? On what will your boss's performance be judged? What is his or her hidden agenda?

3. **Your performance.** What is his or her definition of excellent performance? What does your boss expect of you? How can you help solve his or her most pressing problems or issues? How can you help him or her meet objectives? What kind of feedback does your boss give about your performance? How often should you expect that feedback?

4. **Office politics.** Is your boss a politically sensitive individual? Who are his or her friends? Enemies? (Don't make friends with his or her enemies.) Where is your boss in the overall power structure? How much power does he or she have? Where is your boss in the overall structure of the company? Is your boss on the fast track or a slow mover?

5. **Communication.** Does your boss prefer a formal or informal style of communication? How well does he or she respond to suggestions and input? How about compliments and praise? How about criticism? How much information does your boss want from you? Does he or she prefer to get information verbally in meetings or by

e-mail, memo, report, phone, etc.? How does your boss handle conflict?

6. **Personal work habits.** What is your boss's peak time of day? Downtime? What are his or her particular quirks and idiosyncrasies? (You'll have to adapt.) What are your boss's mood cycles? What are his or her work habits? When does he or she arrive for work and leave? (You'd better do the same.)

7. **General considerations.** What are your boss's strengths and weaknesses? (You should help cover his or her weaknesses.) What pressures does your boss have to deal with, and how can you relieve them?

8. **Your boss's boss.** What kind of relationship does your boss have with his or her boss? How much freedom does your boss have to run his or her own area? (If not much, then you'll need to pay more attention to your boss's boss.)

THE SUBORDINATE ROLE

New professionals typically are hired to work for someone else. They report to a manager who is charged with responsibility for part of the organization and given a staff to help achieve some of its goals. The system works like this: Your goals flow from the boss's goals, which, in turn, flow from the boss's boss. The way you get ahead is by helping your immediate boss achieve his or her goals. He or she then rewards you for your assistance with raises and promotions. Eventually you reach the point where you may have a staff reporting to you also, and you can pass along your goals to them.

Notice that in this system, you're not setting goals. Of course, if you join a highly participative organization, you may be very involved in setting the goals. Or if your boss is very people oriented, he or she may seek your input or give you much latitude to question the goals. But in this system, you must never forget that you work for your boss and in the final analysis, your job is to help and support your boss in achieving his or her objectives.

If this seems a little uncomfortable, that's normal. Your boss has lots of control over your fate and your career. Complete and total control? No, but a heck of a lot. It's a very unsettling feeling, to be sure, to know that someone has so much influence over your advancement.

Most organizations have control procedures to help increase the objectivity of performance evaluations and keep personality conflicts from derailing your career, but the reality is that your boss has a major influence on your career. Simply put, you cannot earn the rewards directly; you can only earn them by pleasing your boss.

You may also feel uncomfortable in this support role if you believe you're more knowledgeable than your boss. Of course, it's rare that you really are. (More often than not, your boss is a lot brighter and more experienced than you think.) But you may have more up-to-date knowledge than your boss, particularly in a technical field. In a good team, though, that's exactly what's wanted. Each member contributes some special ability to the team; thus, the manager doesn't have to be an expert on everything.

So how do you handle your boss if you know more about a subject? For starters, you have to remember that people may not believe this until you have a little experience. Then be sure to present your knowledge and expertise in support of your boss and not as a threat. If you try to one-up your boss, he or she will become defensive and resentful like this manager:

If the company wants to bring new hires in at the top of their class, who are sharp as a tack and going to ride me all the time, I don't want them to work with me . . . I don't want them to try to make me feel inferior because they're so doggone smart. And they can't be. They haven't been here that long. I mean, who do they think they are?

Your role, then, is to support, not compete with, your boss.

I've stated this rather harshly to drive home a critical point. The good news is that most professionals move ahead rather quickly in their career and gain much control over their daily work life. So you won't be a puppet on a string always doing what somebody else wants forever. But you must never forget this reality: your boss controls the rewards through your performance evaluation, and, ultimately, he or she calls the shots.

KEYS TO BEING AN EFFECTIVE SUBORDINATE

The keys to being a good subordinate stem from the basics you learned about the roles of boss and subordinate earlier in this chapter. Essentially, you should sincerely support your boss's efforts in all that you do and never under any circumstance undermine your boss's position.

Fast-Starter Tip

You have to learn to be a good follower before you can become a leader.

More specifically, to be a good subordinate, you should:

Never Surprise or Embarrass Your Boss

You will quickly discover that nobody, particularly a boss, likes to be blindsided by unexpected events. Your job is to prevent that, if at all possible. You have to anticipate what may happen that could affect your boss and keep him or her informed. Most important, don't ever surprise your boss in public, because doing so would be quite embarrassing. Also, help your boss anticipate other events that might surprise him or her. Of course, some unexpected things are unavoidable and will surprise both of you. Your job as a professional, however, is to learn to anticipate as many problems as possible, minimize them, and keep your boss aware of those you can't prevent.

Keep Your Boss Informed

Make sure your boss knows what he or she needs to. The only way to prevent unpleasant surprises is to keep a steady flow of information going forward to your boss. Your boss needs to know what is happening in your area of responsibility: your successes, problems, failures, and needs. Your boss wants to learn these things from you, not through the grapevine or from colleagues in another department. He or she also wants to receive this information on a timely basis and in an orderly fashion. There is enough chaos in a normal day without your adding to it.

The problem is that every boss will have different requirements for information flow, depending on his or her personal management style, his or her boss's style, and the particular job and organization in which you're situated. Every time you get a new boss or your boss gets a new boss, the rules will change. If the outside environment changes, there is an emergency situation, or the company gets a new owner, the rules change again. You'll find that the culture regarding information flow is quite different at different companies. Highly decentralized companies tend to want only "exception" reports ("Don't tell me anything unless things aren't as they should be"), whereas highly centralized companies want more constant "status" reports ("Periodically tell me how things are going").

It's your job to keep good channels of communication open and the appropriate amount of information flowing. Too much information can be just as frustrating to your boss as too little. It's also your job to adjust the information flow as needed to adapt to changing situations and different people.

Add Value

Your boss and your boss's organization should be better because you're there. Your performance has to add value, or you won't be rated highly. After all, why should your boss want to have you around if you can't add something to the organization? The quickest way to prove yourself is to prove that you can produce results.

Offer Solutions

Your boss has more problems than can be handled. What he or she needs is people who can find solutions to problems, not add to them. "Go to them with answers, not questions," said one new hire. "Even if you're wrong, it shows you're thinking." Whenever you dis-

cuss a problem with your boss, always be prepared to offer a solution at the same time. (It may not be the best one, but it is a start.) Or always be prepared to offer an alternative or idea when called on.

Do What Is Asked and Do It Well

This may sound ridiculously simple, but it's still worth noting: your boss needs to count on you to get things done and done right. He or she doesn't want to have to ask you more than once or to keep checking with you. Your boss wants to have complete confidence that you will complete whatever assignment you are given in a fashion that will make you both proud.

Be Consistent

If the boss is to count on you, then your work needs to be consistent so your boss knows what to expect. Nothing is worse than erratic performance (except perhaps consistently bad performance). Even if you can't do everything perfectly yet, aim to produce consistently good results on each and every assignment. It is consistently good results over the long haul that win promotions, not just flashes of brilliance.

Know Your Boss's Agenda

What issues is your boss dealing with? What are the most important things on his or her priority list? You want to be focusing your efforts on the projects that help your boss achieve the things highest on his or her agenda. It does you little good to do outstanding work on something that's not very important. Help your boss meet his or her most important objectives or solve the biggest problems, and you will be a valuable subordinate.

Make Your Boss Look Good

"The cardinal rule is: make your boss look good, and your boss will love you," said one manager. Your rewards will come from your boss if you help him or her shine before higher-level management and his or her peers. Help your boss succeed, and you will succeed. One caveat: never try to outshine your boss, because if you do, he or she may block your career.

Work With, Not Against, Your Boss

You are supposed to be your boss's ally. You are part of his or her team, and you had better work for that team's objectives. Bosses don't want someone working for them who pulls against them, argues with them frequently over objectives, or sabotages their efforts, particularly in the first year on the job. They want someone they can count on to back them up, protect them, and be supportive and helpful. Make your boss's life easier, and your life will get easier, too.

Never Cause Trouble

Be sure you know where the snake pits and traps are on the job so you can stay out of severe trouble and keep your unit of the organization out of trouble. That doesn't mean you can't make mistakes. That is okay as long as they aren't so large as to cause serious trouble. Your boss has enough problems to solve as it is: don't add to them.

Work Hard

No boss will tolerate a subordinate who isn't willing to work hard on whatever tasks are assigned. Hard work and dedicated effort will overcome lots of shortcomings in a subordi-nate. Your boss expects nothing less than 110 percent dedicated effort.

Help Your Boss Manage Time

Your boss is like most busy professionals: lots to do and not enough time in which to do it. Good time management forces him or her (and you) to spend time on only those things that are important. Don't waste his or her time. Make sure your thoughts are organized before you meet with your boss, handle everything you can yourself, don't ask questions you could get answers to elsewhere, don't do sloppy work, and don't use his or her time for frivolous items. Help your boss by taking over some of his or her tasks, assisting with others, or whatever it takes to relieve the time pressure.

Never Waste Resources

Resources are tough to get in many organizations, so don't waste them. This means people, money, equipment, etc. Your boss probably has to fight hard to get and keep the resources he or she has available and will rightly be annoyed if you turn around and waste them.

Never Be a Burden

Many times, subordinates need so much assistance that they are actually more of a burden than a help. Your boss wants to feel that he or she is more productive and efficient with you around. Find ways to help your boss and to demonstrate that you won't be a burden to manage.

Be Available

Be on time, easy to reach, and accessible. Be available to work overtime when needed. Come in early or stay late to help out. Be willing and able to do what your boss needs. Build a reputation with your boss that when the chips are down or there's a crisis, you're available to help.

Make Yourself Indispensable

"You want to make yourself indispensable to your boss so he or she relies on you and subconsciously comes to give you a special project because he or she is very confident in you," advised an advertising manager. Simply stated, you want your boss to depend on you so much that he or she can't do without you.

MAKING YOURSELF MANAGEABLE

The other side of the equation is that you want to exhibit the right attitude and behavior so that you're easy to manage. Being a productive employee is great, but if your boss has to push you extra hard to make that happen, you're really not contributing as much as you think. You want to be valued as a subordinate not only because you produce and are effective but also because you are easy to manage. Let's look at some ways to make yourself easy to manage and receptive to supervision.

Respect Your Boss's Authority

Your boss was given authority to control and direct a certain part of the organization. How to accomplish that is usually his or her decision. Whether you agree or disagree with the decision, you have to respect your boss's authority to make it. There is often a point in the decision-making process where you may provide input, but once a decision is made, it's your job to fall in line and implement it. As one executive advised, "That person has the stripes. After you've told him twice what you think you ought to do and he has disagreed twice, the third time you've got only one thing to do—execute and follow through on his decision." Undermining your boss's decision once it's been made can be fatal in your career.

Accept Criticism and Feedback Well

If your boss has any hope of teaching you how to be a good employee and to do your job well, you have to be willing to accept constructive criticism. Too many people react defensively anytime they receive less than 100 percent positive and supportive feedback. If your boss has to provide adverse feedback to help you fix certain problems, accept it nondefensively, and remember that critical comments don't necessarily mean you are a bad employee. Often it's just part of the learning process. Accept the criticism, and then act to fix the problems your boss has identified.

Cultivate Flexibility

Expect the unexpected. Be ready and willing to change your work schedule to accommodate your boss's needs. Do it your boss's way if that's what he or she wants. Don't growl when your boss makes last-minute demands or changes plans. The working world just doesn't always flow in an orderly and predictable fashion. Your boss needs you to be flexible enough to respond when needed. Don't work as if your feet were planted in cement. Do whatever is needed, not just what you want to do.

Take Ownership of the Job

What your boss likes to see is someone who cares about the job just as much as he or she does. Pretend that it's your own company, and treat your job as if you're doing it only for yourself. When you care that much, your boss will like to manage you.

Eliminate the Need for Supervision

Aim to eliminate the need for your boss to supervise you. You'll never quite get to that point; but the closer you get, the more your boss will appreciate it. What a boss really likes is someone whom he or she can trust as much as himself or herself. Managing people takes time, a rare commodity. The less time your boss has to spend managing you, the happier he or she will be.

Take as Much Responsibility as You Can

The more you can and will do, the happier your boss will be. Take on as much responsibility as you can. The more you can take on, the more your boss and the organization can accomplish. Make yourself indispensable.

Accept Instruction

Another simple but overlooked fact: Some people just don't like to take instruction. Your boss needs someone who will. That doesn't mean you can't disagree occasionally, but your boss doesn't need someone to whom he or she has to defend, explain, and justify every request. Having a boss means taking orders sometimes, and you must be willing to do that cheerfully. You may not always understand why, but the reasons will become obvious later.

Play It Straight

Your boss needs to be able to trust you. Don't try to smoothtalk or flatter your boss. Be hon-est, forthright, and candid. It's old-fashioned, but be sure your boss knows he or she can get the truth and nothing but the truth from you. That means you must own up to your own mistakes and not blame others. It means you tell your boss exactly where you stand on a project. It means you give him or her the good news as well as the bad.

Keep Disagreements Behind Closed Doors

Nobody says you'll always agree with your boss or always have to. But keep your conflicts and disagreements (if they must occur) behind closed doors. "A common error among new hires is a lack of loyalty to their boss," said one manager. "It's not like the educational system, where you walk out and say good and bad things about your teacher . . . Never say bad things about your boss in the organization. You are a new-comer; nobody has loyalty to you; it will get back to your boss. And there is nothing worse you can do as a newcomer." Don't air your disagreements at the water cooler, in the hall, or in a meeting. In public, be supportive.

Ask for Help

Ask for help if you need it, but not too often! It's important for you to know your limits and know when to ask for help. Your boss needs to trust that you'll know when to do that. But you also don't want to ask too often. You should have the intelligence to figure out a lot of what you need and not rely too heavily on your boss.

Motivate Yourself

While part of a manager's job is to motivate his or her employees, the more you motivate yourself, the less burden you place on your boss. Don't make your boss responsible for pushing you along and picking you up all the time. Provide most of your own motivation, and let your boss build on that.

Do More Than You're Asked to Do

Listen to this manager: "Once you get in and you know what your assignment is, be creative. Start thinking, 'What can I do that I have not been asked to do? What responsibilities could I take on that no one else seems to care about?' and make your boss happy by assuming the initiative in taking them on. But be sure to get your boss's prior approval before undertaking such an initiative, and don't walk on other people's feet to do it."

SUBORDINATE SKILLS

There are some skills you can use to help the relationship with your boss work smoothly. While these skills are not particularly unusual, they are especially important in the boss-subordinate relationship. They are based on the same underlying theme I've stressed so far: that it's your responsibility to do everything you can to support your boss and take the initiative to make the relationship work.

One of the first things you'll need to do is to take assignments well. During the workday, people get hurried and rushed so that assignments are not always clear. If you do the following, you can reduce miscommunication with your boss and do your job more effectively:

- Clarify what the objectives of your assignment are.
- Find out exactly when it should be completed.

- Understand what priority it has for your boss.
- Find out what limits or parameters you need to work within.
- Find out if there are checkpoints when your progress will be reviewed by your boss.
- Find out who the key players to consider are in carrying out a project.
- Know what the sensitivities of the organization and key people are toward this project.
- Know exactly what you should deliver when the assignment is completed.

Don't expect your boss to give you all this information automatically. You can protect yourself and help your boss by taking the initiative to ask for it.

One useful tool is reflecting and clarifying. When taking instructions, don't just sit there and listen. Repeat what your boss has said so that both of you can hear it again. You'll be surprised how often hearing it said again will raise questions about what you thought you understood or will prompt your boss to clarify the instructions. It can also help your boss structure his or her thoughts and prevent miscommunication. It's as simple as saying, "So you want me to . . ." after your boss asks you to do something.

Good organization skills are essential. Sometimes simple things can make the difference between the average and the good subordinate. Examples include keeping accurate, complete, and orderly office files; keeping accurate documentation of a project; planning and organizing meetings with your boss to reduce wasted time; knowing where to find information when asked; keeping a good "paper trail" of your activities on a given project; and submitting reports and paperwork on a timely basis. Usually a manager will look to his or her subordinates to manage and organize information in the organization. The better you are at it, the more help you can be to your boss.

Also, you have to do your homework. Thorough preparation is a hallmark of a good professional. Doing your homework can mean doing good research before a meeting, not asking questions without first looking for answers yourself, making sure you understand why an answer is what it is, etc. The point is that being prepared is important.

CHALLENGES OF BEING A SUBORDINATE

It's not easy to be a good subordinate. Sometimes it can seem easy because you don't have the responsibility for other people, as your boss does, and you can just look out for yourself and your own job. Yet being a subordinate creates some of its own stresses and strains.

Taking Orders/Control

The most obvious challenge is that someone else is calling the shots, someone to whom you are accountable. But the further you advance in the organization, the more freedom you get to make decisions, to control at least some aspect of the organization, to manage your own time and work methods, and perhaps to manage others. As a new hire, you really don't have much control over your own work and time at all. That's tough. Also it's a bit ironic that in order to advance to where you do have more control, you first have to be effective at letting someone else boss you around!

It's hard to have to respond to someone else's direction most of the time. Your boss may want things done a certain way that might not fit your style exactly. You may be asked to drop whatever you're doing to do what your boss wants done. He or she may reject your ideas or approach in favor of his or her own. Your boss may set deadlines that are difficult for you to meet. You may have to cancel or alter personal plans, such as vacations, parties, visits with friends, and so on to accommodate what he or she needs. Good bosses try to be as sensitive as they can to your lifestyle and work style, but you will inevitably find yourself succumbing to your boss's wishes frequently. That's just life as a subordinate.

Control is probably the guts of the issue. As a subordinate, particularly as a first-year subordinate, you can expect to have a lot less control over your work time and professional life than you would like. In time you'll get more, but until you prove yourself and your professional competence, your boss may watch closely and give you lots of direction. You may not like it, but the worst thing you can do is to fight it.

What Does Your Boss Want?

Your boss's expectations and agenda aren't always going to be clear to you. Frequently you'll find yourself interpreting and second-guessing. Asking for clarification helps but doesn't always solve the problem. Sometimes you'll guess right; sometimes you'll guess wrong and won't do things right. You'll probably get frustrated because your boss isn't clear and precise. To some extent, that's just the way it is. Remember, too, that the problems and issues you and your boss face won't always have precise answers. Part of your job is to help your boss clarify and define things, not just to respond to him or her. Your boss will appreciate it if you share some of that burden.

How Much Initiative?

Every boss wants to see some initiative and independence in his or her subordinates, and every boss wants some dependence. The problem is that every boss wants different amounts of initiative on different types of tasks. One wants to be involved closely in a certain issue, but another in the same job only wants to know if there is a problem. One boss wants to hear your ideas; another just wants you to follow orders. All bosses vary in how much free rein they give their subordinates, and the only way you can figure it out is by good communication and some trial and error.

Feeling Inferior

Particularly in your first year, you're likely to find yourself working for someone who is vastly superior to you in experience and knowledge of your work area. This person has been around, made the mistakes, and learned everything you still have to learn. It's easy to feel inferior and inadequate in the face of that kind of expertise. Remember, though, that your boss was in your shoes at one time and also had to start at the beginning. When you have as much experience and tenure in the job as your boss does, you, too, will feel on top of things. Don't let someone else's expertise make you feel inferior; nobody else is expecting you to be as advanced as your boss, and you shouldn't either.

Not Getting Credit for Your Work

It's not unusual to find your boss getting the credit for results achieved because of your work. Good bosses are quick to pass along the credit and rewards to their subordinates, but it is inevitable that you won't get as much recognition as you think you deserve. It's simply in the nature of the roles that your job as a new hire is to support your boss's efforts. The way the system works is that when your boss shines, so do you. Then, you have to trust your boss to reward you for helping him or her shine. It can be frustrating though, and when the frustration becomes extreme, you should look for ways to make your contribution known. But in normal circumstances, just be sure you are getting rewarded and then be content that your accomplishments are reflected through your boss's.

Dependence

You are very dependent on your boss, and that's not always a comfortable feeling. Because your boss has lots of control over you and makes a lot of the decisions, you depend on him or her to structure your work. You depend on your boss for advancement, for training, for guidance, and so on. Anytime you depend on another person, you feel vulnerable because your destiny is not 100 percent in your own hands. To a new hire, this is particularly relevant. Do you have a choice? You can build other support networks to some extent, but you can't avoid a high level of dependence.

Getting Respect

One of the major topics of this book is earning respect, and the first person whose respect you must earn is your boss. Sometimes it is tough getting your boss to listen, to pay attention to your ideas, to let you make a contribution. Bosses are accountable for the results of their part of the organization. Even if they delegate the work to a subordinate, they are still responsible for the outcome. It's unacceptable for a boss to say, "My subordinate did it, not me," if the outcome is unsatisfactory. Thus, bosses are very cautious about whom they let do the work. Before you get full respect, you'll have to prove that you won't let your boss down and that you'll make him or her look good.

GETTING WHAT YOU NEED FROM YOUR BOSS

It would be wonderful if every boss gave you all the training, support, and guidance that you need to do your job well. But you'll quickly discover that this rarely happens and that you'll get frustrated because you sometimes lack the things you need. What can you do about it?

First, you should keep things in perspective. Many new hires tend to want too much from their boss. You are unlikely to ever get the same amount of hand-holding, explicit instruction, precise objectives, and similar guidance that you were accustomed to receiving from your college professors. Second, you'll have to realize that some of your frustration is misdirected, since in the workplace you have to work more independently, solve more of your own problems, and take the initiative in getting what you need.

You also should have some understanding of why bosses are unable to give you all the things you need. Some simply do not have the

formal training to know they should be providing these things. Mostly, however, it's a matter of their forgetting or not having the time to do everything they should. The day-to-day pressures, hassles, and crises of work have a way of pushing aside some of the things you need. It may not seem right, but to your boss, providing for your needs may seem like one of those things that "can wait a day or two."

Moreover, your boss isn't a mind reader, so sometimes he or she may not even realize that you need something. Then, too, there are some bosses who simply aren't good managers.

Still and all, there are some things you need from your boss that you can't get elsewhere and can't do without. For example, you need to know the objectives and goals you are to meet and the policies you must follow.

You have a choice of responses if you're not getting what you need. You can continue to wait for your boss to take the initiative, remain frustrated if he or she doesn't, and blame him or her for failing to provide what you need. The problem is that this will make you less effective in your job. And at performance review time, excuses won't matter, especially if your excuse consists of telling the boss who's doing the evaluation that it's his or her fault that you did not perform well on the job! A better response is to take the initiative and go after the things you need yourself. Doing this will become easier if you remember that doing the job and doing it well are far too critical to your career success to be left entirely in your boss's hands. Simply sit down with your boss, and say what you need, without criticizing or blaming him or her for not providing it. Nine out of ten times, your boss will salute you for taking the initiative to ask, apologize for you having to ask, and give you what you need.

What about the tenth time when you encounter a boss who won't give you what he or she truly ought to? Again, you can remain mad as all get-out if you want to, but you still need to get the job done and done well in order to protect your career. So you have to find some other way to get what you need. Ask your colleagues, your mentor, or your coach if you can. Be careful not to embarrass your boss or to go over his or her head. Just get enough of the information you need without appearing to blame your boss for not having given you what you need.

COPING WITH A DIFFICULT BOSS

I wish I could say that your relationship with your boss will always be smooth and enjoyable, but that simply is not likely to be true. Sometimes your personality or work style just won't mesh very well with your boss's. And sometimes your boss may not be a very good manager. Dealing with bad bosses or bad boss-subordinate relationships is a reality of working life that most professionals encounter at some time in their career. Here are some other realities of working life:

- You don't have to like your boss to work for him or her.
- You don't have to be personal friends with your boss to work well together.
- Your boss does not have to adapt to you (in the final analysis).

- You will have to learn to deal with less-than-perfect relationships.

There are many reasons that a boss-subordinate relationship may not work well. They include personality differences, unreasonable work demands, age differences, a difference in educational levels, and a job mismatch, as well as the boss stealing credit from a subordinate or lacking experience as a manager. Sometimes blame can be assigned, but many other times it's just a bad match. Either way, you have to find a way to deal with it. If you don't, you're only damaging your career.

Most of the time both boss and subordinate are anxious to find ways to work with each other. You should certainly be anxious to please your boss, and your boss wants you to be reasonably happy at work so that you will be productive. After all, without you, your boss probably could not accomplish his or her objectives.

But what if it doesn't work out like that? It's certainly no picnic to work for a boss you don't like or don't get along with well. One option is to quit, and some new hires do, but that is really a little extreme. One of the realities of life in larger organizations is that people move around a lot. People quit, get promoted, are reassigned due to business developments, or make a move for their own professional development. And this applies both to you and to your boss. Particularly in your early years with the company, bosses most likely will expect to move you around a bit to give you a variety of experiences and to assess your performance in a variety of situations. You may not be promoted but will be moved to different work groups, which means that the odds of you and your current boss being together for more than a year or so are very small. This senior manager's insight and experience are instructive and valuable as a means of preparing you to work for other managers as your career continues to develop.

Bosses are typically temporary in the life cycle of any organization. Certainly in your individual career cycle, you are going to see a lot of bosses and a lot of different approaches to business, so you might as well begin to understand how to adapt and deal with them as early as possible. If you get a good boss, fine. If you get a bad boss, don't think of it as limiting or ending your career but simply as a matter that has to be dealt with by everyone sometime in a career—you're just getting an opportunity to deal with it earlier. And focus on the job. The one thing that your boss can never dispute is performance that delivers good results.

Your real concern with a bad boss should be that you'll get a bad performance rating because of a personality conflict or because he or she doesn't know how to evaluate you properly. Good performance is the best defense against a bad boss. It's hard to argue with results. As the same senior manager said, "Try to focus on outputs and deliverables, because they are very tangible evidence of the job you're doing as opposed to process. The bottom line is that if your performance ever becomes an issue, you at least have the reply 'well, here are the results, here are the outputs, and here's basically what I understood I was supposed to do.' That's a hard case to argue with."

People notice good results. Chances are that if you deliver good results, people other than your boss will notice, and it will be very difficult for your boss to give you a poor rating.

It just wouldn't make sense. It's rare that anybody who's doing good work ever gets fired, at least at the entry level. And the odds are good that you're not the first person your boss has had difficulty with. Others will know if this is the case, and if you can hang in there and do good work anyway, you'll be highly respected. If you don't do good work, you'll never get promoted or moved away from your boss.

Fast-Starter Tip

A bad boss is not a legitimate excuse for poor performance.

Really the only way out of a bad situation in terms of your relationship with your boss is to adapt as well as you can and to do your work so well that the company wants to move you. They will expect you to give any relationship a chance to work. Sometimes the company allows for a few rough months until you and your boss adjust to each other and the relationship has at least some chance to smooth out. What they don't want to hear is a new employee who starts whining and complaining after only a few weeks with a boss. Complaints about your boss in the early months will be met with a great deal of skepticism, since there is an assumption that you just don't know how to be a good subordinate yet (which may be quite true).

Suppose, then, that you've been with a company several months, long enough to learn a few things about getting along with a boss, but it's still not working well. Your next step is to meet with your boss to discuss the situation. As a professional, you are expected to attempt to work out difficulties by yourself before asking the company to take action. When you meet with your boss, discuss your concerns about the relationship in an open but nonthreatening manner. This isn't the place to hurl "you do this" and "you do that" accusations at your boss. That would only result in a defensive reaction and get you nowhere. Take an "I'm OK, you're OK, but we're not working well together" approach. Frequently you can work out ways to accommodate each other so that the situation becomes at least tolerable. Often misunderstandings can be cleared up with the result that the relationship becomes a good one. Remember, though, that the burden is primarily on you to adapt to your boss, not the other way around.

If it's still not working at this point, you have a problem. I'll remind you that the quickest way out of such a situation is to do a great job and earn a new assignment, though you need to preserve your sanity at the same time. If you have found a coach in the organization, now's the time to talk to that person. A good coach can tell you if you're out of line or if your boss is. Either way, your coach can suggest some ways to deal with the problem and may even be willing to intercede on your behalf by talking to either your boss or others in the organization. Personnel people can also make good sounding boards.

The final step (other than resigning your position) is one that should be taken with great caution: Talking to your boss's boss. You are entitled to do this if the problem is really unbearable, but you should understand that going over your boss's head can have grave implications in many organizations. For one thing, it is likely to get your boss in some hot water with his or her boss, which can be quite embarrassing. Then if you don't get any action to move you to another manager, you'll have to continue working for a boss who may be angry at you. However, personnel managers at most companies would say that if you have done everything possible to work things out without success, then by all means talk to your boss's boss, particularly before you leave the company. If your boss is a bad manager, chances are your complaints won't be the first.

Your obligation is to do everything possible to arrive at a reasonable working relationship. That means having realistic expectations about the relationship, doing all you can to be a good subordinate, trying to adapt to your boss, and doing the best job you can. If, after you've done all that, it still isn't working out, do something about it. It certainly won't be the first time two people couldn't work well together. But by taking all the other steps I've outlined here, you'll minimize the risk of being labeled a troublemaker or difficult to get along with. Do not do this too many times in your career, or you will get a bad reputation. Finally, throughout your time of trials and tribulations with a bad boss, keep this executive's advice in mind.

Don't worry about it. Even if the relationship doesn't work out, you learn something from every boss you work for, even if it's nothing more than what you won't do if you become a boss. Try to learn something from the relationship, and you'll find that you've made a bad situation work to your advantage.

ULTIMATE SURVIVAL TIPS

1. Your boss is the single most important person to you in the entire company during your first year.

2. Respect your boss's authority and experience, even if you don't understand why certain things are done the way they are.

3. Take the time to understand the unique experience of working for a boss and how it differs from other relationships.

4. Build a relationship that makes your boss's job easier and more productive, not more difficult.

5. Learn what your boss wants, needs, and expects, and then be sure to do it.

6. Don't put your boss on a pedestal; realize that he or she is an imperfect human, just like you.

7. Observe your boss carefully so you understand the realities of his or her world as well as your own.

8. You will always have a boss in an organization, so to be a successful professional, you must learn how to be an effective subordinate.

9. Your success is inexorably tied to your boss's success, so you have to find a way to work well together.

10. As a new professional, your most important role is to assist and support your boss.

11. It is your responsibility to do everything possible to make yourself easy to manage.

12. Being a subordinate is not always fun or easy, particularly early in your career.

13. Most bosses have shortcomings in their management skills. It is just as much your responsibility to overcome and work around those shortcomings as it is your boss's.

14. Difficult bosses are a fact of organizational life, but they are not a legitimate excuse for your poor performance.

15. Always ask yourself what you can do to contribute to a more effective working relationship with your boss.

PART

3

GETTING TO KNOW YOUR ORGANIZATION

7

LEARNING YOUR ORGANIZATION'S CULTURE AND PERSONALITY

• •

Most readers probably have heard the term "organizational culture." It's a popular topic, one of great interest to most organizations and academics today. It's also of critical importance to every new professional. This chapter takes a look at what organizational culture is, what it means to you as a new hire, and how you can learn it.

WHAT IS ORGANIZATIONAL CULTURE?

Culture is your company's personality. If you observe carefully, you'll notice that each company has a distinct and unique personality, just like different people. No two companies look, feel, or work quite the same way. Part of this is the "hard stuff," like different products, markets, policies, and procedures. What you may not be aware of (because the hard stuff tends to be so tangible) is the equally large "soft" part of the company's identity—its culture and personality. It is culture that tells you what the company believes in, strives for, and actually practices. It tells you basic things like how people treat each other, what the work environment will be like, and how to get ahead. Simply put, organizational culture is "who" the company is, what it stands for, and how things are done. Some companies have strong cultures, some not so strong. Some cultures are still growing and developing; some have been entrenched for years.

Organizations have unique and special personalities—get acquainted.

So why does this matter? Well, whether you knew it or not, when you signed on to work for the company you chose, you not only bought into a set of tasks and responsibilities, but you also bought into a way of life. How well you come to understand, appreciate, and live with this way of life or corporate culture can have just as much to do with your first-year (and career) success as your task-related performance.

FITTING IN

To a large extent, what we are talking about in this book is a process of fitting in. As one executive pointed out:

If new hires are not comfortable in the organization's culture, they are not going to rise to their full potential. It's just a reality of life . . . It all goes back to the issue of fit. It's important to find somebody who we know will not be a bull in a china shop; [somebody who] will not only be challenged here but [will] also be happy, like the other people, and like the way the other people operate.

Organizations like to have the people within them fit the norms, values, and missions of the organization, just as you like to make friends with people who have lots in common with you. Your challenge, then, in your first year is to learn the culture at your company and

show you want to fit in. You don't want to come into the organization in a manner that sets you up as an outsider or a misfit.

Does that mean that all a company wants is conformists? No. Conformists do not make for bold, aggressive leaders. To rise within the organization, you will eventually have to demonstrate your ability to separate yourself from the pack and establish your own individual style and direction. But that comes later, usually not in your first year and especially not in your first six months on the job.

You have to conform to the team before you can earn the right to assert your individuality.

This is a tough issue for many new college graduates. The early twenties is a time in most people's lives when they are anxious to establish their own identity, make their own way in life, and assert their individuality. I'm sorry to be the one to break the bad news to you, but you are going to have to wait a little longer to do that professionally. You are still in your professional infancy, and you must learn to fit in before you can grow and establish your own identity. Let's look at some facts about the balance of fitting in versus asserting individuality:

1. **Requirement to fit in first.** Only when you have proved you can fit in and be part of the team do you earn the right to pull away from the team and separate from the norms of your organization's culture. Don't be

misled by the individuality you might see around you. Your colleagues have earned that right.

2. **Acceptable limits of "rebellion."** Each organization has its own limits on how much individuality it will allow. Some companies not only tolerate but also encourage a high degree of rebellion to generate an entrepreneurial spirit. Others prize conformity to organizational norms. What is acceptable can also vary tremendously between divisions, departments, and even work groups and individual bosses. You have to find out what the limits at your company are and live within them.

3. **Acceptable timetable for "rebellion."** There is also a timetable for asserting more and more individuality on the job that will vary between companies and within your company. You will quickly learn that when you reach a certain tenure or organizational level, the limits of acceptable rebellion widen. The longer you stay and the higher you go, the more you can assert your individuality.

4. **Competence and performance.** Nothing will earn you the right to add individual style to your job more quickly than outstanding performance. Conversely, until you have a track record and a reputation for strong performance, deviations from the norms will appear destructive, not constructive. It's amazing what strong contributors can get away with inside the organization.

I tell you these things not to teach you how to climb the ladder but because you need to understand the later dynamics to appreciate the importance of fitting in and conforming

early on. Your best bet is to "lie low," observing and learning the organization's culture. While you are doing that, you will convince people that you are a team player and can fit in. Then, and only then, will you know what the acceptable deviations are from the norms and when you have earned the right to assert your individuality.

THE ELEMENTS OF ORGANIZATIONAL CULTURE

That leaves two big questions: What do you need to know and how do you find it out? The "what" is much easier than the "how." What you need to find out is all the contextual factors, i.e., those things outside the basic content of the job that affect your life in that company. I believe that the following are the major items you need to know:

1. **Purpose of the organization.** What is the organization trying to achieve? Why does it exist? Does the company have a stated mission?

2. **Philosophy.** What is the guiding light of the company? How does the company conduct business? What parameters are placed on the strategies used to achieve its goals?

3. **Corporate values.** What beliefs or credos exist? Is the company conservative or liberal?

4. **Behavioral expectations and limits.** Does the company tell you how to behave in certain situations? (Most will.) Does it extend these expectations into your per-

sonal life? Does the company encourage conformance or tolerate mavericks?

5. **Attitudes of employees.** What do the employees talk about? Are they happy and motivated or down and lethargic? Are they conservative or liberal? Power hungry or mutually supportive?

6. **Work ethic.** How hard do people work? What role does work play in their lives?

7. **Dress code.** Is the norm a suit and tie or casual? Do the women wear dresses and suits or something less formal?

8. **Character of the organization.** Is the organization stodgy and sluggish or vibrant and hustling? Centralized or decentralized? Entrepreneurial or bureaucratic?

9. **Success factors.** What is it that makes people succeed in the organization? What are the characteristics of the high-level successful people? How do you climb the ladder?

10. **Social norms.** Does the organization require certain types of social obligations and/or behavior from you? Do you have to belong to certain clubs or socialize in the right places? Are you expected to attend informal gatherings frequently? Do employees socialize together often?

11. **Management norms.** How are the employees managed? Are managers autocratic or democratic? How much control is exercised over people? How would you have to behave to best get along with your boss?

12. **Atmosphere.** As you walk through the office, are people relaxed and happy or formal and on edge? Is there an atmosphere of trust or fear?

13. **Career progression.** How do people progress through their careers? Is progression largely seniority-based, or is it results-based? Is movement across functional areas encouraged?

14. **Strategic orientation.** Does management have a clearly outlined strategy? Is its thinking short- or long-term?

15. **Ethical standards.** Is there a strong ethical orientation in the company? Are people concerned about honesty and fairness in business? Is there a sense of broader social responsibility?

16. **Political environment.** To what extent is organizational politics a factor in accomplishing tasks? (It's always present to some extent.) Do different parts of the organization work together well, or is there a strong sense of "protecting one's turf"? Which is more important: who you know or what you do?

17. **Communication.** Do people talk openly and freely or are discussions guarded? Are communication lines formal, progressing through layers of the organization? Or do you see top management talking regularly with lower levels of the organization? To what extent does management keep employees informed about the company's progress?

This is just a list of the major items to consider. There may be other items worth considering. The key is to investigate and understand anything about the organization that will affect you on or off the job.

NORMS AND VALUES

Two of these elements jump out as having the biggest impact on new employees in the first year on the job: norms and values. "Norms" simply means how things get done. As you are learning, each organization has certain ways it expects things to get done and employees to behave. We don't always like to acknowledge this, but when you join an organization you implicitly agree to let it have some say over your behavior—both on and sometimes off the job—in exchange for rewards and compensation.

You need to learn quickly what the norms are for your behavior and the performance of your work. And I do mean in a hurry. If your assumptions about appropriate behavior are substantially different from the company's, you could be in for a rough start. Even if your assumptions don't differ dramatically but differ in many areas, you still could be seen as a "problem" early on. That's why I suggest an eyes-and-ears-open, mouth-closed approach. If you show a readiness to learn and lie low until you have learned the ropes, then you can start strong and not make irreversible mistakes.

Values tell you what is important to the company and its employees (with luck, their preferences will be similar), which tasks should have the highest priority, which aspects of your performance will be most important, which mistakes will have the worst consequences, and to what you should pay the most attention. An understanding of the value system within your own work group can help you please the boss. The value system often pinpoints what is most important to him or her. An understanding of an organization's value system can also help you figure out why conflicts occur, how to get a strong start with your colleagues, and how to get noticed.

Values are not the same as task priorities. In theory (and often in practice), values are the guiding lights that result in priorities. They are the principles underlying much of what goes on within your company. If you don't understand them, you may act in conflict with them either because your own values are different or just out of ignorance. For example, if a decision is being made in a meeting on spending lots of money to fix some mistakes with a customer, and you are a finance person (prone to want to save money) but don't realize that customer satisfaction is near and dear to the company's heart, you're likely to stick not only your foot but also your whole leg in your mouth. Or if your boss truly believes in doing everything right the first time, you don't want to be sending preliminary work for review with lots of errors in it, even if you would prefer to do things differently.

Again, the strategy is to lie low until you have a pretty good fix on what the value system is. Behave and perform in a manner that is counter to the organization's or a key individual's values (particularly the critical ones), and you could get detoured early.

DISCOVERING YOUR ORGANIZATION'S CULTURE

The tough part about getting to know your organization's culture is that nobody is going to hand you a policy book telling you everything you need to know about it. Some elements of culture may be documented, such as the organizational mission, but most of them are not. More often, it is handed down through generations of new employees by word of mouth and simple osmosis as a new employee absorbs it from the surroundings and day-to-day interactions with the company.

If you walked up to the average employee and asked, "What is the organization's culture?", most would be hard-pressed to give you much of an answer. Yet, it is all around them and is a part of them. That means that you are going to have to discover it in more indirect ways and know what you are looking for. It also means that nobody will spoon-feed it to you. You have to take the initiative to seek it out. Eventually the organization will let you know if you are violating the organization's norms and values, but by then you'll have already made mistakes you will regret.

"Pay attention to the environment," advised one manager. "I think sometimes people get lost in their own little world, and they are not paying any attention to what is going on around them." From the new-employee perspective, learning the culture is imperative to success on the job. "It's a different world; it's a structure; everything is done in a certain way," cautioned a new hire. "And if you do it that way, you succeed. If you buck it, then you don't." You have to observe the organization closely, as though it were a case study in school. That is, you need to step back and look at your new company as an objective outsider, not as an employee immersed in it. It's hard to notice a lot of the information available to you when you're caught up in day-to-day goings-on. Don't make judgments about what you see and learn. Culture is not right or wrong; it just is. Later, if you find out you can't fit into the culture very well, you can make personal decisions about staying with the company but not now. Here are some specific strategies to use in learning your company's culture:

Observe Your Colleagues

Sounds simple enough to forget to do, doesn't it? Your richest source of information is your colleagues, particularly those who have been with the company awhile. Watch them closely. How do they talk, dress, act, and conduct their business? How do they deal with customers, bosses, and subordinates? What do they talk and think about? What is their attitude, tone, and general demeanor?

Look for common patterns among people so that you aren't misguided by individual personality differences and quirks. Not everybody will act exactly alike, but you will see definite patterns emerging. What do these patterns tell you about the company, its values, its norms for behavior, its work ethic, etc.? What elements of culture have these people integrated into their daily work lives? Use them as role models to help you learn the culture.

Notice What People Spend Their Time On

If you want to find out what is truly important in the organization, watch how people—particularly successful people, in organizational terms—spend their time. That will tell you what their priorities are, and since the organization is rewarding them, that will tell you what the organization's priorities are. For comparison, look at how people who aren't as successful spend their time. See any differences? I expect you will, and then you'll have some idea of what things are more and less important to the organization.

Talk to Your Colleagues

While most can't answer a broad question about organizational culture, they can talk about specific elements of it. Schedule a time and interview them. Yes, a formal interview. You'll be surprised at how receptive people are, how much you learn, and the respect you'll earn. You'd also be surprised at how many new hires forget to just ask.

Listen for "Legends" and "Heroes"

In companies with strong cultures, you will often hear employees recount with great pride stories of how certain individuals made a great difference in the company's history. These legends about corporate heroes tell you much about the values and characteristics that are important to the company. These are people like Ross Perot of Electronic Data Systems (EDS), Steve Jobs of Apple Computer, Thomas Watson of IBM, or Harley Procter of Procter & Gamble. Each of these individuals created a lasting personality in his company.

Legends may not have a major figure at their core; rather, they may talk about seemingly minor figures who played pivotal roles at some point in the company's history. They might be stories of service people fighting through snowstorms to serve the customer, huge sums of money spent to ensure quality, people promoted quickly because of great innovations. They may also be accounts of people demoted or fired because of things they did (or didn't do). Corporate legends are used to teach employees what the company considers important in its culture and to keep the culture alive. Pay attention to them.

Rites and Rituals

Most companies also have certain rites or rituals that are part of the culture. Rites and rituals are a way of institutionalizing culture. Monthly beer busts say, "We care about our employees," at Hewlett-Packard; monthly safety meetings at DuPont say the same thing. Stopping the assembly line to present a quality award says, "Quality is important." Often the rituals are less grandiose. They could be the way bosses are addressed, a certain way meetings are conducted, the way customer complaints are responded to, etc. All stem directly from the company culture.

The Physical Setting

Look at the offices, the manufacturing plants, the executive offices, the reception areas, etc. Are they formal and conservative in tone or modernistic and upbeat? What do you then conclude about the company's attitude? A great-looking reception area might tell you something about the company's attitude toward guests and customers. Spartan offices, particularly executive offices, might clue you that frugality is admired in the company. Well-kept and cheerful manufacturing plants or ergonomically designed engineering workstations might clue you to the company's emphasis on its employees. Take the time to stop and notice.

Organizational Structure

You don't have to be a management student to learn something from the organizational structure. First of all, is there a lot of structure? If so, that is usually indicative of a bureaucratic, traditional organization. Observe what parts of the organization have the fewest layers between them and the CEO. These may be the parts of the organization most important to the company. Look at which department or division heads have the biggest titles. These, too, are probably the most important in the organization. Look at the background of the top executives. If they are finance people, that tells you one thing about the company; if they are engineers and scientists, that tells you something different.

Read the Company Literature and History

Read all you can about what the company says about itself. You have to be a bit careful here, because you never know if you are reading the way things are, the way the company wishes things were, or the way they intend for things to become. But combined with the other information you collect, this literature will give you an important reference point. For example, it might clue you to a company in transition or one in serious trouble.

Don't forget to look at the history of the company. Particularly in older organizations, the culture is usually rooted in a long history of challenges, growth, successes, and failures. In young and old organizations, the founder of the company, often a driving entrepreneurial spirit, will have had a major and often lasting impact on the culture of the company. Many companies are very sensitive to these traditions.

ULTIMATE SURVIVAL TIPS

1. Learning culture means learning the ropes and how you are expected to behave.

2. Organizations aren't things. They are people with attitudes, values, beliefs, and habits.

3. It is rare that you can ever change an organization's culture before you become a part of it.

4. Culture is everything and everybody around you—look, listen, and observe to understand it.

5. The "organization man" (or woman) may be dead, but conformity is still the rule for the first six months.

6. Remember that every organization's culture is different (often radically), so don't let experience blind you.

7. Understand the culture, and you'll be able to understand many of the mistakes your peers make and avoid them yourself.

8

Organizational Savvy: The Facts of Life in Organizations

· ·

> Joining a company is a lot like pledging a fraternity or sorority. When you are a pledge, you are supposed to do what everybody tells you. And if you are a good pledge, you don't question it—you just do it. The more you rebel as a pledge, the less the group members above you like you or want to respond to or interact with you. The more willing you are to go along with whatever they want you to do, the better. Later on, years later perhaps, you'll find out why they asked you to behave this way—it brings brothers or sisters closer together.

When I sit down and talk to new hires, one consistent theme emerges: working. And working in an organization is much different from what they had imagined. Through no fault of their own, most college graduates begin work entertaining a variety of myths (and in some cases, fantasies) about the way organizations work and the manner in which to behave to be effective in them. Moreover, some basic realities of organizational life often just aren't discussed frequently in the classroom. See if any of these sound at all familiar:

- Work is fun and exciting
- Organizations are always logical and rational
- Individual effort is what counts

- Results and competence are sufficient to get you promoted
- Organizations are usually advanced and on the cutting edge
- Newcomers are welcomed with open arms
- Change is expected and welcome
- Everybody wants to help you succeed
- Your assignments will be made clear to you

These are just some of the myths new hires have shared about the way organizations work and should work. All are false, at least in part. All are also understandable, given your experiences in college.

This chapter presents some of the key elements of organizations that you need to understand to be effective in adapting to your work culture. In essence, what the chapter is concerned with is the first test of the new attitude discussed earlier, particularly your readiness to change and accept that things are different in the workplace—not necessarily better or worse, just different. The single decision to accept this and the new information presented in this chapter will go a long way toward giving you a successful start on the job.

THERE'S MORE TO IT THAN JUST TASKS

In college, most of the emphasis is placed on tasks and the skills and knowledge needed to accomplish them. Aside from the general knowledge acquired from courses such as history, political science, and literature and simply from learning how to learn, your focus during your college years is on specific skills needed to go to work. That's not to equate your college experi-

ence with a vocational program but, rather, that you have devoted those years to the fairly narrow perspective of "technical" skills. Even in broad-based curricula such as public administration or business, the emphasis is still on acquiring job performance skills.

As a result, it's very easy for you to think that the most important consideration on the job is your technical or task-related competence. Yet while such competence is absolutely necessary, it is hardly sufficient to allow you to excel on the job. Much more is needed. Other dimensions are every bit as important as task-related competence, including people, politics, networks, relationships, organizational culture, image, communication, and attitude. All of these are discussed in more detail throughout the book. The central point to remember, however, is that the task-related skills are only half of your education.

The typical new college graduate approaches the new job as if all he or she has to do is to complete the assigned task on time and deliver a good product in order to be on the way to a successful career. Most managers would be darned glad to see that as a start, but the end result is not all that counts. The "how" of getting the task accomplished is just as important as "when." The interactions with colleagues can mean just as much as the bottom line. Understanding how the organization works and what its norms are is just as important as delivering a good product. The attitude you demonstrate along the way can make just as much difference as how technically strong your performance is.

Any manager can tell you stories of people who had all the brains and ability to do the job but never developed the organizational savvy to be a strong performer. Of course, a manager can also tell you about employees who spent all their time worrying about other things besides doing their job well; they failed, too. It takes both task competence and organizational savvy to be a strong performer. Employers don't expect to see you perform well in both of these areas immediately—that's too tall an order for the first year. But they do expect you to be growing and developing in both dimensions. And that's where new hires often make a mistake, because they are so busy worrying about the tasks that they forget to pay attention to the rest of the game. The sooner you start paying attention to both parts of the game, the better off you'll be.

Work Is Not All Fun and Excitement

By the time your professors and the company recruiters finish with you, you're likely to think that your career is going to be great and glamorous. It will be but not quite the way you think. There will probably be lots of very neat things about it and some glamorous parts. The accomplishments you achieve will feel great. The challenges you encounter on the job will be fun and stimulating. The responsibility you are given will feel good. Business trips and expense account dinners can take you to some very nice places. The prestige of working for a well-known company helps your self-esteem.

What everyone forgets to tell you is that there is a lot of just plain old work in between the fun and exciting stuff. And some of that is not much fun. There are a lot of mundane, routine tasks associated with even the best jobs. And that's okay, as this manager pointed out:

Fun is not the right word. Work should be satisfying. And for something to be satisfying doesn't mean that it has to be fun every waking second. It also has horrors to it and ups and downs. But if you go through the day and feel good about yourself and what you are doing and have a certain amount of pride in your professionalism, you'll earn the respect of the people around you.

Letters have to be written, paperwork done, files kept up to date. You have to follow up on sales calls and document your lab experiment or computer program. A lot of your time will be spent on tasks that are either not much fun or neutral at best. Furthermore, the not-so-fun parts are usually just as important as the fun parts and are often necessary evils to get to the end results that are so rewarding. The difference between an average and a great employee is often the ability to do all aspects of the job well, including the grunt work.

A new hire spoke about this particular challenge in the following way:

Initially you are put on a job and in a lot of instances, you do things that are below you. You do photocopying, stapling, hole-punching, whatever is required. And for me, maybe it was just a rash impulse, but I rebelled against it. If you don't fit right into a neat hole immediately, if you don't accept the "administrative trivia" as we call it, people will look at you and say, "Why aren't you keeping your mouth shut and just getting the job done?" And while all this is happening, you'll be thinking, "I spent four years in college to do this?"

But managers are equally pointed in their response:

In an entry-level position, you are the person who is going to get all the work no one else wants to do. The neat part about moving up in an organization is you don't have to do what you don't want to do anymore. So, guess what? The person coming in doesn't have a choice; he has to do it. People who have had jobs before understand grunt work. They have done a lot of it, and they realize that this job at first is not a whole lot different from working at McDonald's.

Chances are you have been trained for and aspire to a level of work higher than where you will start. That is likely to mean that what you do in your early years and your first year, in particular, may not be even close to the fun and excitement you would like. But the only way to get beyond that will be to buckle down and do the best darn job you can.

Fast-Starter Tip

Expect to start with the routine—the good stuff will come later.

Even though the mix of fun and not-so-fun tasks will improve as you advance in the organization, you will always find yourself having to do some less pleasant tasks. All of us have tasks we prefer to do over others, but jobs aren't designed that way. I'll bet that even the most successful people will tell you of parts of their job that they just put up with so they can get the results they want.

Your first year on the job will challenge you to learn to view the less pleasant aspects of your job as just means to an end. If the result for which you are striving is worth it to you, then the other stuff is just a necessary evil. The only way to free yourself from the unpleasant tasks that come with your job is to develop the discipline to excel at them so that you can get promoted and delegate them to another new hire!

PAYING THOSE PROVERBIAL DUES

I see them not willing to pay the dues that are necessary in many organizations to advance. The typical attitude in many companies when a new graduate is hired is "You show me what you can do and we will go from there." And the attitude sometimes of the graduate is "Here I am, so show me what you've got for me." Sometimes new hires are not willing to pay the dues, to really do groundwork and show what they can do. Nor are they willing to tolerate situations that they don't think are proper for them at that time.

The higher you go in the organization, the more "fun" stuff you get to do and the less mundane, routine grunt work you have to put up with. Conversely, the lower you are in the organization, the more grunt work you'll have to do, since someone has to do it.

Every organization has its pecking order, with privileges accorded to ranks within it. Part of climbing through the organization is simply paying your dues. That is, if new hires are expected to do photocopying and run errands as part of their job and as part of earning the right to rise to the next level, they do it. If they are expected to travel constantly or work third shift or long hours, they do it.

Fast-Starter Tip

Nobody starts at the top!

Let's face it: entry-level jobs are not always the greatest in the world. If they were, more people would want to stay in them. New hires get handed some of the most tedious, time-consuming tasks in the organization. That's not to say that new hires are abused or not offered challenges, but whatever all those people above you don't want to do and have earned the right to delegate will trickle all the way down the ladder to you. And you will have to do it and do it cheerfully. "It's a boot camp philosophy" explained one new hire. "You will go out and do whatever they want you to do, and you will be happy doing it, and you will do the best job you can. And the people who are most successful at this are the people who just open their minds and accept it and move right up the ladder. Because if you do a good job and you are conscientious about what you do, you get a good reputation."

It doesn't sound like the glamour job you thought, does it? I don't want to sound too pessimistic, but you have to realize that it could be many years before you reach the level of tasks that you studied in school—make a strategic decision on a product line, develop an entire computer system yourself, design a new building, or head a research team. It will take some time to get to that level. And while you are getting there, you will be doing some tasks you

find really enjoyable and others you hope you never have to do again (and you won't once you rise from entry level because you'll then pass them down the line).

Surviving this process is called "paying your dues." Everybody hired before you has done it, and everybody hired after you will have to do it. You'll have to work your way up the organization one step at a time and do whatever it takes at each step. The quickest way to get to a level where you are doing the fun things is to pay your dues as cheerfully and efficiently as you possibly can.

Keep in mind, too, that you may not always understand why you are asked to do certain tasks. While a large part of paying your dues comes about from the trickle-down effect, an equally large part occurs because you need the experience or knowledge even if the process of gaining it is not the most fun. I doubt that there are many plant managers who would like to go back to working the graveyard shift, but they are glad they had that experience and the knowledge that came with it. I doubt that there are many engineers who would relish the thought of going back to their days hunched over a drafting board, but they learned a lot there. I'm sure that there are many scientists who wouldn't care to go back to the tasks they did their first year, but they are glad they had the experience.

Paying your dues, then, also means getting the experience and knowledge you need. A second-year professional agreed: "When you come in, you're going to have a job that you think is probably not as important as you'd like. Once you get experience, you're going to realize how important your job really is . . . If you think about it, you've got to start at ground zero, because you've got to get some technical experience."

What it boils down to is that success, however you define it, doesn't happen overnight or always so easily. Sure, we'd all like to start at the top, where we are paid well, do fun things, have the perks we want—or whatever the "top" means. But it doesn't happen that way. We have to pay our dues to get there. As a new professional, it's important that you be ready for this and accept it. The most you can do is pay your dues quickly because very few people get by without doing so. The happiest people are those who can see paying their dues as fun, recognize it as a means to an end, and enjoy the "getting there" process and not just the moment they arrive.

ORGANIZATIONS AND CHANGE

There is a principle in physics called inertia, which says that a body in motion resists efforts to change its direction or motion. Organizations are the same way. You will find that organizations are not nearly as interested in change as you might think. It's a curious phenomenon, because most people in organizations realize (at least on an intellectual level) that change is needed and the company must continue to grow and evolve, to discover new challenges, and to adapt to the changing times. But on an emotional level, you find that people don't always welcome change quite so readily. Change is risky, uncertain, and sometimes threatening. It can be exciting but can also cause anxiety. People get comfortable doing things certain ways. Change means they have to

work harder to adapt to new methods, policies, and technologies. Organizations develop accepted practices, norms, and "rules of the road" over time and refine them to the point where they are often quite effective and comfortable.

<table>
<tr><td>Fast-Starter Tip</td></tr>
</table>

You can't change the organization until you are accepted into it.

That isn't to say that organizations don't change or that every organization resists change. New hires are usually surprised, though, at the degree to which organizations resist change. You need to be ready for that. One reason you may be surprised is that the college culture in which you have been immersed previously is one that seeks and accepts new ideas from you on a fairly open basis. As was discussed earlier, your professors have encouraged you to challenge existing thoughts and to develop your own ideas and approaches to problems. Organizations are not usually so open. It's not that they are stuck in a rut and totally resist change (although some are and do). But they do tend to be more oriented toward the convince-me-why-I-should-change point of view as opposed to the university, where the view is more "convince me why I should *not* change." Universities are always trying to move knowledge forward, to challenge and destroy (if need be) old ideas. Organizations have a great deal of inertia and reluctance to change that which is working just fine.

The other aspect of this is the source of the new ideas. You might have the greatest ideas in the world, but as a newcomer with no track record it will be very tough to persuade anybody to listen to them at first. "But isn't one reason they hired me because of my creativity and fresh ideas?" you may ask. Well, that's true, but there is an intermediate step, a hurdle you must clear first that is usually overlooked. They want your fresh ideas, but only after you have proved yourself, after they have come to respect you and accept you into the organization.

You see, until then, you are an outsider. And when you suggest a new idea or a new way to do something, it may be seen as a criticism since the implied message is that the old way is not good enough. Your intention may be to support the team, to help the organization reach its goals, but as long as you are seen as an outsider, your new ideas can be seen as an attack rather than a help. This is a very key point because many new hires come in with the presumption that:

- Any new idea is welcome
- The way to shine is to immediately offer as many new ideas as possible
- As long as you have a better way, people will accept it

None of these is necessarily true. In almost all organizations, even those that thrive on change, you have to establish a certain amount of credibility and accrue enough time in the organization to earn the right to suggest changes. "In order to get credibility, you have to be able first to listen and find out more about the group and how it operates, find out what it expects," explained a second-year employee.

Furthermore, you have to remember that the old ideas and ways of doing things were originally created by some person. That person may still be fond of those ideas and may be quite offended by the suggestion that the processes and/or procedures that he or she developed should be changed or discarded. If that person happens to be a peer in your work group, you have lost a valuable ally. If the person happens to be your boss or another person high in the organization, it could be politically disastrous.

Once again, you see the significance of the transition period. Here are some tips to consider:

- Resist your urge to automatically jump in with new ideas
- Take the time to learn what the norms are in your company before jumping in with your suggestions for change
- Don't assume your suggestions for change are immediately welcome
- Find out who "owns" the old way and whether a potential conflict with that person could develop
- Wait until you feel accepted as a team member before suggesting changes
- Look for cues in the organization as to when new hires are "allowed" to make changes
- Be sure your new ideas are presented in a value-neutral way without an implied criticism of the old way. Presenting an "alternative" or "different" way of doing something is much different from calling it a "better" way

WELCOME NEWCOMERS?

One change that every organization deals with regularly is having new people join the ranks. Management depends on a steady supply of new talent, particularly new college graduates, to keep the organization alive and fresh. That is why many organizations will continue to hire at least a few college graduates even in bad times, just to ensure a crop of management and senior-level talent for the future. That is also why they spend money sending people to college campuses to interview new graduates. You have probably seen evidence of their desire for new talent by the manner in which you were recruited. The problem is that you can come away from that process with the mistaken view that everyone in the organization is as anxious as the recruiter to have you join them and just can't wait for you to come to work.

By and large, people will be glad to see you come to work. Most managers can always use new help, and most people are genuinely interested in seeing young people succeed in their first job. But newcomers have disadvantages, too, and the more you understand what they are, the easier you can make the transition process for the organization.

The first reality is that newcomers take lots of time, a commodity that busy people in most organizations don't have a lot of. Newcomers have to be trained, oriented, and indoctrinated in the ways of the organization. Even simple tasks such as getting a memo written or delivering something to a client can take lots of time in giving instructions. It's not that people mind helping you get started, but they often just don't have much extra time. They have tight deadlines to meet, projects to complete,

people pressuring them to do more work, etc., and it can be hard for them to make time to help a newcomer.

That's why you may feel a bit ignored at first. Unless you are entering a formal training program where a group is separated with a staff dedicated to training them, people aren't going to just stop everything they are doing to help you. Don't take it personally, but they may tell you they just don't have time. In a perfect world we would all hope that we could plan it differently, but it doesn't work that way. It can be very disheartening if suddenly people seem to be ignoring you. You have to remember that most of them are able to get things done independently and aren't used to helping you get started.

That leads to another reality, and it is simply that people forget what it's like to be a newcomer. They forget that you don't know even the simple things like where the copy machine is, where to find supplies, or where the bathroom is. They forget you may not know where the good restaurants are, what the boss is sensitive to, how memos are "usually" written, etc. They are just busy people leading active lives and may be many years beyond the newcomer stage.

It's not like when you were in college, where you came in as part of a fairly homogeneous group of freshmen and proceeded through your four years in a fairly orderly way. Your professors and administrators knew that each year hundreds or thousands of students would be at a certain point in their college careers and have certain needs. Thus, the administration and faculty could anticipate these needs and be prepared to meet them.

In most organizations, however, new college grads comprise only a small part of the workforce, and they will be widely scattered throughout the organization. It is quite common for you to be one of only several new hires or even the only one in an entire department. You will be mixed in with a large group of people of many different ages and experience levels, most of whom will have a reasonably good idea of how to go about their work, which you won't. And because there are so few newcomers, those in charge may simply forget what you need.

The network of people you join may be quite accustomed to working with each other. Networks develop unwritten rules about communication and work methods. Members grow accustomed to each other's idiosyncrasies, moods, and habits and grow comfortable in these practices. Then a newcomer rocks the boat. Even if they welcome you, the rules need to be rewritten or adjusted. Your entry into the group upsets what may have been a stable and comfortable system. They have to orient you and get oriented to you.

As a new college graduate, you are fortunate in that you are likely to be truly welcome in the organization. (Other newcomers may not be as welcome.) But be aware of what impact a newcomer has on an organization. Remember:

- Don't expect to be welcomed with open arms by everybody

- Do your homework and take learning initiatives to minimize your burden on others

- Ask for the help you need, as others may be too busy to remember

- Find other new hires with whom to share problems and from whom you can learn

- Help people get to know you, how you work, and how to understand you

- Don't expect immediate acceptance; give the organization and your work group time to adjust to you

- Don't take it personally if you feel ignored

NOBODY'S PERFECT

Organizations are just like people—none is perfect. That sounds like stating the obvious, but you may be surprised to discover how imperfect the company you join really is. When you are looking at it from the outside through the eyes of people recruiting you and the perspective of the glossy recruiting literature, annual reports, etc., all you see is the good side of the organization. Anybody who tries to sell something tends to put the best foot forward. It isn't until you get inside that you see the real truth. No organization or job will be everything you want it to be. All have problems. Every organization has strengths and some glaring weaknesses. All people have things they do very well and things they do very poorly. There are warts, skeletons in the closet, things of which each organization is not proud. All organizations have some real jerks working for them as well as some really great people. Any CEO can quickly tell you many things he or she wishes the company did better. There are always problems to solve and never enough people to solve them.

Fast-Starter Tip

There's no such thing as a perfect employer or job.

As logical as that sounds, this lack of perfection will probably still come as a shock to you when you first encounter it. Part of the reason is that in college, you spend the majority of your time studying and learning the way things "should" be in a perfect, theoretical world. It's easy, then, to develop a very idealistic expectation of the way people behave, the way organizations work, and the way a job "ought" to be.

Very quickly, you discover that this is not the way things work in the real world, which is never as perfect as the theories and textbooks would have you believe. But if that is what you've been taught and come to expect, you are quite likely to be critical of the organization's faults and see it as having something wrong with it. After all, it doesn't measure up to textbook standards, does it?

Most readers, even those who haven't worked professionally, probably have some sense that everything is not quite so perfect or orderly as textbooks might lead one to believe. But experience has shown that most readers also probably don't realize the extent to which they have been conditioned by their training to expect far more perfection than the real world can ever deliver.

That's not to say that there is anything wrong with the theoretical textbook training you have received. Every professional should have a strong theoretical underpinning from which to operate. Without it you have no starting point from which to approach new

problems and no internal navigation system for your professional practice. But one mark of a mature professional is knowing how to adapt theory to the real world, giving up some of the theory to fit reality and initiating change in the real world to approach the ideal more closely.

Only experience and time will teach you the proper balance. Once again, nobody expects you to fully understand all the dimensions of the real world. What almost everyone would like to see is a greatly heightened sensitivity to the fact that things won't follow exactly the way they were outlined in textbooks, and that's okay—it's just the real world. So don't grow frustrated and disenchanted every time the real world isn't as perfect as you would like.

The question, then, is how much imperfection is acceptable to you before you conclude that you've joined the wrong organization? There's no easy answer to this. It's fair to say that you will be prone to judge too harshly in the beginning, so you need to temper your expectations and not jump to hasty conclusions. It's also fair to say though that if the organization has problems or shortcomings that truly bother you, you aren't required to put up with them the rest of your life. The decision you have to make is not whether you have to tolerate shortcomings and a less-than-perfect organization (that's a given) but, rather, which shortcomings and problems are the least troublesome and most acceptable to you. Every organization is different and will have different shortcomings. The one for which you first go to work may have a perfectly acceptable level of shortcomings, but they may be the ones that are most offensive to you.

It's important to have a realistic view of what you can reasonably expect from working life in an organization. Accept that it will likely be less perfect than you expect. Talk to your friends and family about their experiences in other organizations to get a better sample of the real world. Be sure to talk to people who are at the same stage of their career as you so you can get a sense of similar experiences. If your dissatisfaction stems from comparing your organization with a more perfect textbook model, your thinking is probably not valid and your expectations need to be adjusted. If, on the other hand, your experience and your organization are clearly worse when compared with other similar organizations, then you may want to consider a move.

ULTIMATE SURVIVAL TIPS

1. Good task performance is essential, but there's more to being successful. Organizational savvy is essential, too.

2. Work is not fun all the time. Accept the fact that, as a newcomer, you'll have to do a lot of grunt work during your first year.

3. Pay your dues cheerfully. It will help you to earn the respect of your employer and fellow workers. Besides, you can gain useful technical experience in the process.

4. Remember, you're starting at the bottom. If and when you advance in the organization, then you'll be able to delegate some of the less pleasant and routine tasks to others.

5. Organizations resist change. Learn what the norms are in your company before jumping in with suggestions for change. Look for cues in the organization as to when new hires are "allowed" to make changes.

6. Newcomers disrupt an organization as well as help it, so don't expect everyone in the organization to welcome you with open arms. Also, don't feel personally slighted if others in the organization ignore you at times.

7. No job or employer is perfect. The reality is that few organizations measure up to the textbook standards you've learned in school. Adjust your expectations to the realities of organizational life.

9

Your Role As a New Employee

Have you ever wondered how employers view the college-to-work transition? Yes, they worry about it too, although it probably won't surprise you that their concerns are quite different from yours. If you're going to please them, it's important that you understand what their objectives are for your first year, what they're concerned about, and what they like and dislike about new hires. In this chapter, I'm going to give you a chance to sit behind their desk and see new hires through their eyes. You'll be much better able to make a favorable impression if you can understand the employers' perspectives and chart your activities to cater to their agenda. You'll also gain a better understanding of your role as a new employee.

NEW PROFESSIONAL GOALS

As a new professional in a new organization, you have some critical goals to achieve in your first six to twelve months on the job. Some of them are obvious: you already know you need to learn how to do your job. Most new hires don't understand what the rest of the priorities should be and focus on the wrong objectives. Let's look at what your goals should and should not be during the first year, starting with what you should accomplish.

1. **Learn your job.** This sounds obvious but still gets overlooked. You have to prove your competence at the job to which you've

been assigned. "You have to prove yourself all over again—don't go in and expect to just cruise," said one new hire. That means learn your job well and do a great job at it, no matter how unimportant, boring, or trivial you may think it is. Too many new hires look past their first job and spend so much time trying to get promoted that they forget to do the job well. Others just don't focus on it.

2. **Build professional respect and credibility.** Your central tasks during your first year are to gain the respect of your peers, colleagues, and management and to establish yourself as a professional with credibility and integrity. There are many, many elements to accomplishing this (good thing or I'd be out of a job!), but if you do, you will have had a very successful first year on the job. With respect and credibility will then come acceptance into the work groups and acceptance as a valuable part of the team.

3. **Gain acceptance by the organization.** You're an outsider when you start work, and the organization won't automatically fully accept you. You'll be on probation for a while. As you gain the respect of your colleagues, they'll begin to accept you as an insider. In time, you want to be accepted as a member of the team.

4. **Confirm their hiring decision.** Your employers took a chance when they hired you. Based on a limited amount of information, they decided you could be a good performer and make a contribution to the organization. Prove them right.

5. **Show you have potential.** You weren't hired to do the entry-level job but for your potential to advance beyond that level. It doesn't necessarily mean that you will do so at the end of six to twelve months, but you at least need to show you have the raw material to advance.

6. **Make good impressions.** As discussed, impression management is everything. There really isn't time in the first year to do much more than make impressions. But those impressions will help determine your course for the next five years. And everything you do makes an impression. Focus hard on making the right ones.

7. **Become a professional.** For the last sixteen years or so, you've been a student, but now it's time to learn a new role as a professional. That's a bigger transition than you think. The role of a professional is different from other roles in your life and will take some time to learn fully. It's critical that you leave the college student behind and learn to be a professional.

8. **Get to know your organization.** The organization you've chosen to join is a unique one with its own culture, personality, ways of doing things, and people. Even if you think you know it well, you really don't. Your mission in the first year is to get to know your organization, how it works, and what it expects. You can't choose your career strategies and develop a success plan until you do.

You'll notice that this list is as notable for what's not included as for what is. Notice that your goals don't include:

- Making a big splash
- Getting promoted quickly

- Finding a way to impress the big boss
- Trying to make a big contribution or a grand initiative immediately
- Showing everything you know quickly

You'll learn in other sections of this book why these hard-charging kinds of strategies don't work. In fact, they can hurt you badly in your career. Entering an organization is much more complex than it appears and requires a much more thoughtful and restrained strategy. Your time will come to make your big move, but there are some other key tasks to accomplish first. While there may be a few new hires who are capable of making a grand entrance into an organization, almost all who go directly from college to their first professional job will need to take a new view of their own first-year objectives and understand their employer's objectives as well.

IT'S OK TO BE A ROOKIE

You can start your preparation by accepting the fact that you will be a rookie. Nothing in the world can change the fact that you will be new to the organization, have no experience, have lots to learn, and are going to be perceived as a novice. If you're like most new professionals, you are anxious to start your career, to achieve the respect and prestige that being called a professional carries.

What you're probably not so anxious for is to be labeled and treated as a rookie, newcomer, trainee, or the like. You want to be treated like a full-fledged member of the team, with the attendant rights, privileges, and respect. You probably don't like the uncomfortable and scary feeling of not knowing what to do or how to do it—of not being in control. You feel that your inexperience is obvious and that there's a stigma attached to it. You probably don't like the idea of continuing to go to school, whether it's literally in a training program or figuratively in on-the-job training. Most of all, you don't like people treating you like a rookie, not quite trusting or respecting you. All this is perfectly natural and very, very normal. But there's nothing you can do to change any of it, absolutely nothing. You can't wish it away, and no amount of struggling will take it away. It's a phase through which you have to pass.

Fast-Starter Tip

Wear your rookie label proudly.

The fastest way to get beyond the rookie stage is to accept that you are one and do the things that rookies need to do as quickly and as well as you possibly can. That, coupled with a little more time, will move you along more quickly than you might imagine. If you don't accept your rookie status, you're likely to jump past the rookie-level tasks discussed in this book, and, ironically, that will keep you mired in "rookieland" even longer.

One senior executive described the president of his company as an outstanding example of the importance of acknowledging the rookie stage:

He's only 36 years old and running the company. When he graduated from college, he didn't know heads or tails about working for a company, about working in this kind of environment, about doing what is expected

. . . But he told people that he was willing to learn . . . I think he progressed quickly because of his attitude, willingness to learn, and recognition of his rookie status.

Actually, the rookie period has its advantages. It's the only stage in your career when the performance pressure will be lessened to give you time to adapt, learn, and adjust. The expectation level is lower, too; you will be expected to be naive and make mistakes. Moreover, most employers will not expect you to have a high level of productivity at this point in your career. You have license (at least on a small scale) to try things that may not work out, to request interviews with people all over the company, to ask your boss lots of questions, etc. It's OK to be dumb, as long as it's in a smart way.

The challenge is to find the right balance between taking advantage of your rookie license and taking care of impression management. Go too far as a rookie and you'll make the wrong impressions. Your license doesn't allow you to be careless, forgetful, or foolish—just inexperienced. Take advantage of the license just up to the point where it would begin to negatively impact others' perceptions of you. Use this honeymoon period to build the right foundations for future success.

Your employer wants you to spend time working on all the things discussed in this book. You should do them during your first six to twelve months, for you will find it very difficult to do them after you lose your rookie license. Then the productivity expectations go up, leaving little time and energy for other activities, and people expect you to know things and not ask questions. Never again will you have the advantages of your first year and the opportunity to put the building blocks of your career in place. Seize the opportunity, and take full advantage of your rookie license.

YOUR EMPLOYER'S OBJECTIVES FOR YOUR FIRST YEAR

Employers have a very definite agenda for your first year. In most companies, a great deal of thought and effort has gone into designing the first-year experience. It may not always be obvious, but through years of experience and evolution, they have developed a system to meet their objectives. These are the things to which you should pay the most attention. You will have to learn how best to demonstrate that you've met these objectives within your company, but here's what's usually on management's mind.

1. **Build Productivity.** You cost too much to allow yourself to be unproductive. Your employer wants you to attain a basic level of competence in your job as quickly as possible so you are at least earning your keep and making a contribution. How quickly it's expected will vary tremendously. Some new hires are put in positions where they have to be very productive the week they start; others may have months before they are ready to go. Whatever the expected timetable, management wants to see you meet it or beat it if you can.

2. **Build Commitment.** Your employers want you to do more than just perform your job; they want you to build the kind of commitment that will keep you with the organization for a good while and will foster a sense

of ownership and pride in the organization. It's a commitment not only to the job itself but also to the beliefs, values, ideals, and mission of the company, too. It's the kind of commitment that not only keeps you around but also makes you want to go beyond the expected to be a great performer.

3. **Socialize to the Culture.** Socialization can be interpreted a little negatively (like brainwashing), but that's not what's meant here. Socializing means learning the culture of the organization, understanding the people and politics, and getting a "feel" for how the organization gets things done. It's the assimilation of their way instead of just a way. Learning the culture of the organization is just as important to your success as learning your job.

4. **Reduce Turnover.** Simply put, your employers don't want you to leave. If the hiring decision was a bad one or you made a bad job choice, they're willing for turnover to occur, but they hate to see new employees leave quickly. Usually, when a new hire doesn't work out in a particular position, it's not because the job match is bad but because of miscommunications and mistakes that can be avoided. Employers hate to see turnover—it's expensive, so they work hard to avoid it.

5. **Join the Team.** Your employers want you to accept the team and the team to accept you. They want to see you functioning as a team player, working with others to achieve the team's goals. If they'll work with you, that likely means that the team has accepted you, too, and respects your contributions.

6. **Show Growth and Progress.** They know you won't be able to step in and be a star immediately. They know it takes lots of learning and time to become an outstanding employee. What employers want to see from you, though, is significant and steady growth and progress in the first year. That shows that you're a fast learner and capable of continued growth.

7. **Assess Your Potential.** One question foremost in the employer's mind is "What is this person's potential for the future?" They didn't hire you for the job you can do today but rather for your future potential. Even in your first year, they're trying to start assessing how far you can go, how good you are, and how much responsibility you can take on.

8. **Become Important to the Organization.** In some way, they want to see you establish yourself as important to the organization. That could be for the immediate contribution you make or your future potential. Whatever it is, at the end of the first year they don't want to find themselves thinking that it really doesn't matter whether or not you're there. You need to make a difference.

9. **Confirm Hiring Decision.** Basically, they want to be able to say to themselves, "I'm glad he or she is here; we made a good hiring decision."

FINDING OUT WHAT'S EXPECTED

If you are to get on the success spiral, then you are going to need to know exactly what these expectations mean in your specific organization and how to meet them. Unfortunately, for many new hires, it's not until their first performance review that they realize the expectations we're talking about are not just fluff. They are very, very real and are the basis upon which you will be rewarded.

Every organization has different versions of these objectives and different types of expectations. Fortunately, they tend to fall in generic categories across all companies, and that's what is discussed here. But the specifics vary greatly from company to company. Your challenge is to identify within your organization exactly what the expectations are. We know productivity is important, but how much? Exactly how do you show commitment, and how much is expected? How much of a team player do you need to be? So you need to become important to the organization, but how soon? And so on. I'll point you in the right directions and teach you the questions to ask, but you'll have to get the answers.

Finding them won't be as simple as opening a policy book or just asking questions. For one thing, expectations are often unstated. That may not sound fair, but it's true. Some are stated very explicitly, others are so deeply imbedded in the culture that nobody even realizes they are there. Even when they are stated, what's said may not match what's done. It's sort of like if your mother asks you if you study hard, eat right, and go to bed early while you're away at college. Of course, you'll answer yes, because it's the "right" answer, but you really do the opposite. Similarly, your boss may give you the "right" answer, but things really happen differently.

To complicate things even further, you'll rarely find 100 percent agreement across the organization as to what's expected in terms of attitude and performance. The "organization" is not one unified group (unless it's small) but is made up of different divisions, departments, and work groups. Each has a leader who sets the expectations and tone for his or her part of the organization. Some expectations are common throughout the company (you can't be anti-smoking and work for Phillip Morris), but many others vary greatly. So you have to be careful to whom you listen. What works for your friend in department B may not work for you in department A.

You're playing to an audience, and you have to find out what your audience wants. The audience you want to play to is the people who have the power to reward you and advance your career. Unless you happen to work for a real oddball in the organization, your audience is your boss and his or her bosses. If you work for an oddball, you still have to play to that person, but be careful you don't get too distant from the rest of the organization.

Let's look at some strategies for figuring out what's expected:

- Ask yourself why you were hired. What traits did they like in you? That's a pretty good clue to what they want after you start work.

- Look at your peers. What common traits do they have? If you see a pattern, that's an even better clue as to what the organization wants.

- Ask people. Even though many expectations are unstated, you can learn a lot by just asking.

- Talk to your colleagues. Often, bosses have certain things they have to say because of their position. Your colleagues can tell you how it "really is."

- Observe what's done. What people tell you is not nearly as important as what they do. Be a careful observer.

- Find out what's rewarded. That's the most important thing to observe. In organizations, rewards go to those who meet expectations.

ULTIMATE SURVIVAL TIPS

What Your Employer Would Say to You

1. Your first year is one of the most critical periods in your early career. It all starts the minute you walk in the door, so don't underestimate the damage a poor start can cause.

2. Take pride in being a rookie, and be the best one you know how to be.

3. Take the time to find out exactly what we expect of you during the first year.

4. We're really glad to have you, but remember that we have to adjust, too.

5. The personal issues are important to you, but leave them at home.

6. Show us that you are a serious and dedicated professional by focusing your energy on your job.

7. This is not a college campus: leave your college way of life behind.

8. Your expectations need to be adjusted.

9. Understand us before you try to change us.

PART

4

BECOMING EFFECTIVE AT WORK

10

Professional Work Savvy

When I was in college, I was a happy-go-lucky kind of guy. But I realize now that in the business world, you have to control yourself. In school you could just blurt things out and crack all kinds of jokes. When you get into a job, you simply can't do that.

You have now become a professional. Have you stopped to think what that means? It seems like a very natural progression, sort of like going from a junior to a senior in college. Well, it's not. Being a professional is a fundamental change from the role and lifestyle you enjoyed in school. Some pieces of it are familiar to you from the interviewing process, like dressing up in a suit. But many new hires don't realize what professional maturity is, how professional life differs from student life, what new skills are important, and what being a professional really means.

You may or may not feel different, but you will be in a brand-new role that implies much more than putting on a new suit. And this is where some of the problems begin. Try as they might, most of your colleagues will not be able to remember that you are a new professional. They will quickly come to see you as an experienced professional and expect you to act and perform like one. By the time you have been on the job a month or two, it will be hard for them to perceive you any differently than their more seasoned colleagues.

Most new professionals are too slow in making the transition, probably because their change in status can be rather sudden. One week you're a college student, then suddenly—perhaps only a few weeks later—you're a professional. Your colleagues will have higher expectations of you than you are anticipating and will look for you to make the transition to a professional much faster than you may be prepared for.

Your challenge then—and it's a big one—is to walk through the door looking, acting, and thinking like a professional as much as you can. The more quickly you make the transition to the role of a professional, the more quickly you will be accepted and earn respect within the organization. The new hires who are accepted quickly and given responsibility early are those who understand this, know what it means to be a professional, and are willing and ready to make this transition.

This chapter will help you prepare for this transition by outlining the elements that define professionalism, describing the characteristics of successful professionals, and discussing some professional skills you will need to acquire.

WHAT IS A PROFESSIONAL?

"Professional" is one of those terms that is used quite a bit but is not clearly defined and, thus, has different meanings. Since you become a "professional" when you graduate, you need a strong sense of what the word means.

Let's look at some of the important elements of professionalism:

1. **Specialized knowledge and extensive preparation.** Becoming a professional requires many, many hours of study and preparation. As a professional, you are expected to have a high level of knowledge and expertise. You are paid to use the knowledge.

2. **High standards of performance and achievement.** Professionals expect a lot of themselves and others. They are determined to do the right thing and do it well. That is more important than the number of hours they invest in their work. A professional is not satisfied unless his or her work meets these standards.

3. **High standards of ethics and integrity.** Professionals are driven by a code of ethics outside of the rules and procedures of the organization to which they belong. They have a sense of "right and wrong" and judge themselves and their work against it. Their integrity means that they adhere strongly to a set of values about how they do their work.

4. **Strong commitment to work.** Professionals work hard. They believe in the value of work and the rewards to which it leads. They are willing to pay the price to meet their high performance standards.

5. **Collective spirit outside the organization.** Professionals feel they belong not only to their organization but also to a collective body of other professionals with similar training and work. There are many examples of this, such as doctors, lawyers, managers, and engineers. This collective spirit often leads to formal standards of ethics, performance, and training.

6. **Ongoing training and study.** Professionals feel an obligation to stay current in their field. This requires a commitment to continued training and study.

7. **Acceptance of responsibility.** Professionals seek and accept responsibility. They usually can be trusted and are given responsibility for the activities of the company. Because their quality and performance standards are high, they can be entrusted with tasks that, if performed poorly, could have

significant negative impacts on the company, its customers, or the public.

8. **Higher level of compensation.** Professionals are usually among the highest-paid people in the country because of their extensive training and higher performance expectations.

9. **Seeking rewards other than just money.** While monetary rewards are usually very important to professionals, money alone is usually not enough to keep them working. Most work at the profession they chose because it gives them great personal satisfaction and happiness as well as a good salary.

10. **Sense of ownership of their work.** The projects or tasks in which a professional engages are not just jobs to be completed to keep the boss happy. Professionals feel a sense of ownership in what they do, a sense of pride as if they are doing the job for themselves and for their own benefit, regardless of the real reason. A professional doesn't work just to meet the standards of the company: a professional works to meet the standards of his or her own pride. Professionals work for others as if they were working for themselves.

At least in the perfect world, that's the way every professional would be. Clearly, not every professional fits this description exactly, nor does each professional meet these standards equally. It should also be clear that a professional has an attitude and a demeanor quite different from a student's, a clock puncher's, or an unskilled laborer's. These people are important to organizations, too, but they see the world differently, are usually paid less, and have less expected of them.

Most students have worked part-time sometime during their high school or college days. When you did, you weren't expected to perform like a professional, nor were you paid like one. Your attitude and approach were much different from what they will be on your first job. Professional is more than just a word or a label. You can see that it truly means a different attitude, a different personality, and a different set of expectations. You need to be ready for it.

CHARACTERISTICS OF SUCCESSFUL PROFESSIONALS

To be ready for this new role, you must also possess both the characteristics and the skills of a professional. There is a very important distinction between these two requirements. Employers don't mind giving you some time to learn the skills. However, they get very frustrated if you don't have the basic characteristics of a professional—they expect to see them from day one. As you read ahead about professional maturity, integrity, and judgment, remember that being new is not an acceptable excuse to your employer for you not having these essential characteristics.

Professional Maturity

Just about every manager I talked to wants to see new hires demonstrating professional maturity. It's something the managers have difficulty defining, but it's something they know when they see it. Let's take a stab at describing it.

It starts with acting the part. Being a professional is different from being a student, and you're learning that it clearly does require that you look, think, and act a bit differently. The problem is that it takes many new hires the better part of their first year to figure that out. While they're figuring it out, they're still acting like college students, not professionals. That's not maturity. Once you enter the working world, you have to convince yourself that from day one your college days are over, and you will accept your role as a professional.

A large part of maturity is self-responsibility. Professionally mature people clearly demonstrate that they are willing to take responsibility for their lives and their performance. They do so by showing initiative to take charge of themselves and the willingness to be accountable for their actions.

If you want to be responsible for yourself, you will need to anticipate the consequences of your actions. Mature professionals look beyond their immediate actions to see what the eventual results may be; in so doing they are able to eliminate embarrassing and avoidable mistakes. Less mature professionals often act before they think and are surprised by the results.

Fast-Starter Tip

You're paid to think before you act.

Part of learning to anticipate consequences is learning self-control. A large part of self-control is understanding that moderation is important in the professional world and that one's behavior needs to be modified to fit the situation. Your emotions, opinions, behavior, etc., all need to be toned down. Mature professionals realize that extreme behavior is rarely tolerated in professional life. Unlike new hires, who are prone to be overly enthusiastic and to react too strongly to negative situations, mature professionals learn to control these extremes at work. They recognize that extreme behavior, whether good or bad, is viewed as a sign of youth and immaturity in the workplace. You don't have to be boring, but if you are like most new professionals, you may need to tone down your behavior.

Self-control is much easier when one focuses on the big picture. Mature professionals know there's more to a job than just the small piece of the work they see and are involved in on a day-to-day basis. They understand the broader purpose of what they're doing and can locate themselves in it. They work not just for today but for what's going to happen five to ten years from now. They aren't afraid to make sacrifices today for longer-term career satisfaction.

Mature professionals have the ability to manage themselves. By being responsible and exercising self-control, they show others that they don't need someone looking over their shoulder all the time. They take the responsibility and initiative to manage themselves, their behavior, and their work so they can be effective.

Part of managing yourself is the ability to exercise discretion. Mature individuals know when to be serious and when to have fun. They know when they can relax a little and when to work hard. They know when their behavior can have a critical impact on the company and when it can't. Clearly you won't know all of this when you walk in the door, but you should have the maturity to know that you *need* to know it.

If you are managing yourself well, you'll realize from the beginning how important it is to learn what behavior is appropriate in what circumstance. Immature new hires show no awareness of this concept at all.

Fast-Starter Tip

A professional attitude makes the difference.

Mature professionals also avoid insignificant conflict. Because people in organizations are different, there is ample room for petty disagreements. With maturity comes the realization of how important people are in the organization. To maintain good relationships, mature professionals don't let small things escalate into conflicts. They learn to get along, and, if there is any conflict, it is over important things.

Another mark of the mature professional is the desire to go beyond the expected. Until you graduated from college, you got along basically by doing what was expected. Now, the key is to exceed expectations. Mature professionals want to grow professionally and personally; they aren't content to plod along, stuck in the current situation.

These are some of the elements of the somewhat fuzzy idea of professional maturity. It's an attitude and a presence that is easy for management to sense and feel, although hard to articulate. You'll notice that it has little to do with level of experience in a particular organization or field. While it's true that professional maturity does come with experience, it is entirely possible to demonstrate a great deal of maturity without experience. People don't expect you to

have experience and will tolerate mistakes that result from your inexperience. What they do expect is a responsible attitude that identifies you as a mature professional. If you make mistakes out of immaturity and irresponsibility, you'll be criticized for them. Make the same mistakes because of inexperience but demonstrate a mature attitude, and you will be excused.

Integrity

Integrity is one of the most important traits you can develop. It is the thing that leads people to trust you and be willing to rely on you. Without personal and professional integrity, you won't go very far.

The most important thing about integrity is that once you've lost it, it's very hard to get back. Your integrity is a very precious commodity that will take years to develop. It's one of your most valuable assets. You should guard it with the greatest care and nurture it constantly.

So what exactly is integrity? In the business world, integrity is defined more by actions than by anything else. You can show that you have it by:

- Doing what you say you will by the deadline you committed to
- Taking responsibility for the mistakes you make and correcting them
- Not lying to others or giving others the constant "runaround"
- Giving credit to others when it's due, i.e., not stealing others' ideas
- Doing consistent, high-quality work
- Not letting your boss and your colleagues down
- Looking out for others as well as yourself

- Being honest and ethical
- Keeping your mouth closed when asked to

In some ways, this sounds a little like "motherhood and apple pie," but integrity really is a critical professional trait. Your integrity is what enables the people around you to feel comfortable with you, to have confidence in you as a teammate, and to know you won't stab them in the back when they aren't looking. There are enough people in the business world without integrity. You'll quickly spot them, and you don't want to be among them. If colleagues lose faith in you, you've got big problems.

Judgment

Good judgment is another important characteristic that management is expecting you to demonstrate early on. When most people think of good judgment, they think of it as arising only from experience and thus conclude that new hires can't have any. That's wrong! While new hires can't have the judgment of experienced people, they are expected to show good judgment. And you can!

The first kind of good judgment you need to show is understanding when you don't know enough or have enough experience to be able to have good judgment! As discussed in Chapter 1, a key to being a good new professional is knowing what you don't know. It's no disgrace for you to call in more experienced people when you're in a situation you couldn't be expected to handle. Sure, you need to be a fast learner and try to stand on your own two feet as soon as possible, but there are many, many things that you won't be able to handle your first year, even if you are the fastest-rising star in the company. You have to know your limit.

What you can do to compensate for your own inexperience is borrow from other people's experiences. If you're faced with a situation at work that you don't have the experience to handle, don't just turn it over to someone else. Sit down with an experienced person and ask for his or her perspective and judgment. People are flattered when approached because they are considered "expert." Learn from others and borrow from their experience (be sure you tell them you're doing so). While you're learning, you'll also be showing good judgment by knowing you need to ask. There's no need to reinvent the wheel. In most companies, there is a wealth of experienced judgment all around from which you can benefit.

But that's only half the story. There are plenty of people who have been around for a long time but still aren't considered to have good judgment. And that's because they haven't learned how to put their experience to good use. Here are some things you can learn right now to help you show good judgment:

1. **Thinking ahead.** People who have good judgment take the time to think about not only their immediate actions but also the many steps beyond them. They work hard at anticipating likely outcomes and consequences and think about how people might react. They play out alternative scenarios in their mind.

2. **A broad perspective.** Good judgment requires that you have a good understanding of the entire organization and learn how your department and job fit into the broader scheme of things, both within and outside the organization.

3. **The ability to integrate.** You and your job are part of a complex, interrelated system. Everything you do will have an impact somewhere else, too. To have good judgment, you have to see yourself as part of an integral whole.

4. **Knowing your limits.** Knowing what you're not good at is just as important as knowing your strengths. Even the most powerful and successful people in the world have to hire others to do things they can't. People with good judgment understand this and will quickly call in others when necessary.

5. **A sense of "grayness."** Nothing in the world is black and white. People with good judgment understand and accept that we don't live in a perfect world. Professional life is full of compromises, trade-offs, priorities, things that are "80 percent correct," balancing interests, etc.

You won't have good judgment overnight, but you can see from the above list that there is much you can do to cultivate it. Your new employer expects to see a certain amount of good judgment when you start work and then to watch it grow.

PROFESSIONAL SKILLS

You've spent many years in school learning and acquiring new knowledge and skills. Most of what you've learned was information-based or task-related. As a professional, you'll need to acquire some other skills so you can be successful and apply what you've learned in school. Let's take a look at some of these skills.

Getting Results

Everybody knows that you have to get your work done and accomplish what you are asked to do. The problem is that not everybody can.

You'll quickly discover that getting something done is usually not a straightforward matter. Problems arise, other people want to change things, you can't find the information you need, a critical person to talk to is on vacation for two weeks, or the solution won't work as your boss thought it would. Even the simplest projects often proceed like this. In the professional world, accomplishing something is akin to running an obstacle course more than a straight line.

That means there are always plenty of very legitimate excuses for not meeting deadlines or not being able to accomplish what you're asked to do. But that's not what your boss wants to hear. Professionals are hired for their ability to find solutions, not topple before roadblocks. Sure, circumstances may arise that nobody can do anything about, but your job is to get things done. That may mean going over, under, or around the problem or obstacle. It may mean finding a whole new strategy, getting other people to help, etc. Your employer expects you to use your creativity to get things done if at all possible.

This is another cultural shift. In college, excuses and obstacles were often acknowledged. That is, if the resources you needed to finish your project weren't in the library, you could easily ask for an extension on the paper. If you were a part-time student and became very busy at work, you could ask for an incomplete and finish the course later. There is no penalty for asking, and usually you could rearrange the assignments to make it more convenient. Work isn't like that. When a difficulty arises, you don't change the schedule or the assignment; you first do all you can to find some way to get it done. Often, you have to meet the deadline no matter what the obstacles.

Getting things done is a really special skill. If you look across any organization, you'll find some very smart people who never seem to accomplish very much. They have the talent, and their excuses or reasons for not getting results all seem valid when examined individually, so on the surface there's nothing really wrong with those employees—except that they don't get many results. You'll also see other people with no more talent who encounter many similar obstacles but, somehow, get things done. And that's really the bottom line—getting results.

Your challenge in your first year on the job is to show that you're one of those people who can get things done. Show that you're not a whiner or complainer and that you're not looking for excuses. It takes a person who has the tenacity to keep plowing ahead when obstacles do arise and the creativity to find new ways to surmount problems. If you can get a reputation as a person who finds ways to get things done instead of finding reasons not to, you'll gain immediate respect. Then, when you encounter the truly insurmountable problem (there really aren't many), people will respect that, too. The bottom line at performance review time is not just how hard you tried, but how well you delivered what was asked of you.

Interpersonal Communications

A central theme of this book is the importance of people in your career. Becoming an effective professional means you need to learn how to meet people, develop a rapport with them, understand them, develop good working relationships, and make conversation at company events. In short, your interpersonal communication skills are critical to your success as a professional. In your first year, they are essential tools to building the kind of relationships you need and making the kind of impressions you want. Managers, new hires, second-year employees, and executives continually talk about the critical importance of developing interpersonal and communication skills.

The whole business is working with people. You need to know what people are like before you work with them. Find out what makes them click. And what works with them may not work with somebody else.

It's not what you say as much as how you say it . . . What you say is the smallest part of what people take. It's how you say it; the tone and the body language communicate a lot more.

You have to be open to other people's ideas. Even if you don't agree with people, at least listen to them and try to understand from where they are coming. One thing that can really hurt you is shouting down other people's ideas and burning bridges.

Few new hires bring to the workplace the interpersonal skills they need. Your college career has been devoted mostly to task-related knowledge. Even worse though is that few new hires realize how much they need to develop these skills. That means there is a tremendous opportunity for you to rise above your peers by working hard to develop strong interpersonal skills. The following sections highlight some key areas to work on.

Understanding Communications

Communication is so complex that it is difficult to explain it in even an entire book. However, there is a very basic communications model that is easy to remember and will be enormously helpful to you. It says that there are three steps to any communication. First, the speaker must translate his or her thoughts, feelings, and intentions into some sort of message that communicates those thoughts, feelings, and intentions to another person; that is encoding. Then the speaker must actually deliver or transmit the message to the other person, using words, gestures, body language, etc. Finally, the receiver in the communication must interpret these elements and decode them into what he or she thinks is the intended message.

I have always loved this model because it is simple enough for me to use every day. Every time I miscommunicate with someone or am particularly concerned that my communication be effective, I think about this three-step process. Effective communicators pay attention to all three steps, whether they do it consciously or unconsciously. They are usually in touch with their own feelings and thoughts, they develop the skills to translate those into effective messages, and they learn to read and evaluate other people so they can transmit their message in a manner that the other person is most likely to interpret correctly.

When you look at this model carefully, you can see all the places it can break down through nobody's fault. Cultural and regional differences, environmental and situational fac-

tors, moods, and pure mistakes can easily confuse communications. Good communicators work to make sure all three phases of interpersonal communication are in sync before drawing any conclusions about other people's thoughts, feelings, or intentions. To avoid miscommunication, they keep the following considerations in mind. You can become a better communicator by heeding them in your day-to-day communications.

- Just because your intentions are obvious to you doesn't mean they are obvious to the other person.
- Just because the other person doesn't understand your message doesn't mean his or her interpretation is wrong.
- Just because you think you communicate clearly doesn't mean the other person understands.
- Don't assume anything!

Think about this model as you interact with your new colleagues and your boss. Think about the many differences in your backgrounds, your newness to the company, the differences in experience and professional maturity. Your challenge, initially, is to figure out how people transmit their messages in your new organizational culture so you can learn to decode them properly and then to encode your own messages effectively. Remember, the rules have changed now that you're in the work world; therefore, you'll have to work extra hard to meet this initial challenge.

Good Communicators

Over the years, I've watched many people who always seem to communicate well, and I've often asked myself, "What is it that makes them so effective?" I've concluded that it's a set of special characteristics. Let's look at them.

Unconditional positive regard, interest, and empathy are all part of the encoding stage. Unconditional positive regard is a term communications expert Carl Rogers defines as "a warm caring for the person—a caring which is not possessive, which demands no personal gratification." It is an atmosphere which simply demonstrates "I care" and not "I care if you behave thus." It's an attitude of accepting people as they are and respecting them just because they are people. It's a nonjudgmental attitude. When you meet people like this, you don't feel that you have to prove yourself or earn their respect and positive feelings. You still have to prove your professional maturity and competence to earn their professional respect, but there is an underlying personal respect that exists automatically and isn't tied to your professional worth.

Coupled with that should be a sincere interest in people. To be effective, you should be genuinely interested in what other people think and feel. I've had "friends" who pretend to like me, spend time with me, etc., but when we are together, I find that all they do is talk about themselves. If they have no genuine interest in me, I become just someone to stroke their ego, and that's not very pleasant. Similarly, nobody likes colleagues who are interested in what you have to say only when it helps them.

If you are to know how to encode your message, you have to have a certain degree of empathy. Empathy is the ability to see the world through another person's eyes, to remove yourself from your own feelings, and to try to experience the world as another person does.

Good communicators can always imagine how another person might be experiencing the world and encode their message in a way that is sensitive to the other person's perspective.

The second stage of the model requires you to be articulate and expressive. Articulateness is simply the ability to put into words what you are thinking or feeling. The English language is a wonderful collection of words that, if used properly, can convey just the right sentiment or thought. As a professional, you need a good command of the language to express your ideas and thoughts accurately and clearly. Nobody can read your mind.

But articulateness is not enough; you also need to be expressive. As used here, expressiveness means two things: the ability to use your nonverbal as well as your verbal communication tools and your willingness to share your thoughts and feelings. Nonverbal communication consists of all the other elements of communication besides words, e.g., facial expressions, body language, tone of voice, eye contact, and posture. It is estimated that anywhere from 60 to 80 percent of communication is actually nonverbal. It's amazing how much the nonverbal elements add to and affect communication. Smiles, gestures, etc., add so much to your words to make them come alive and convey your true emotions, while poor or inadequate use of nonverbal communication can quickly torpedo even the most articulate statements. You need to pay as much attention to your nonverbal cues as you do to the words that you use.

In addition, you can't possibly be an interesting communicator unless you freely share and express what's on your mind. How friendly do you feel toward people who build walls and protect themselves by not sharing their thoughts, feelings, etc.? Now I am not suggesting that you reveal your life's story and deepest, darkest secrets to every colleague you meet. Moreover, the rules of professional decorum and your organization's culture will place limits on how expressive you may be. But within the limits of what's professionally acceptable, you have to share some of your thoughts and ideas to establish any reasonable degree of rapport. In other words, some degree of openness is necessary for good professional communication.

Finally, stage three consists of listening and paying attention. Listening is so important and so poorly done that I have included a separate section on it. It may sound simple, but many do it wrong. Part of good listening and communicating is paying attention to the other person and what he or she is saying. How can you really listen if you are distracted by other thoughts? How can you decode correctly if you aren't attentive enough to see and hear all that the other person is communicating? Attentiveness means using all your senses to "tune in" to the other person.

All of these need to be wrapped in an environment of honest communication. Too often in today's world, people communicate by game playing—with hidden agendas—and by assuming things about other people. Nobody will deny that there is a certain amount of gamesmanship in the politics of organizations, but nothing destroys relationships more than deception. The best relationships, business or personal, are built on the parties' communicating in an honest fashion. This means expressing anger and displeasure as well as happiness and pleasure. It means asking questions if you aren't sure what the other person thinks or feels. It means stating your thoughts and feelings honestly and assertively. It means that you know everything that is happening between you is "on the table."

Establishing Rapport

The first step in developing a relationship or opening up communication is to develop a rapport with a person. "Rapport" is difficult to define. Think of it as laying the foundation for future communication and opening the door. Rapport is what you experience when you find someone you get along with particularly well and can talk to easily. Throughout your first year, as you meet people in the organization, you'll want to quickly establish a degree of interpersonal comfort. Then later, when you begin to work more closely together, you'll have already set the stage for good communication.

Here are some measures that will make it easier for you to establish rapport:

1. **Smile.** Everybody likes friendly people: smiling warmly projects friendliness and encourages conversation.

2. **Exchange pleasantries.** A period of small talk and pleasantries helps break the ice and relax both parties. Don't expect to get right down to business.

3. **Find a common interest.** Look for some shared interest with the person. Whether it's enjoying the weather, having similar hobbies, or living in the same neighborhood, find something you can share.

4. **Be friendly.** Project a genuine warmth and approachability that is inviting to the other person.

5. **Open your face.** People often tighten their faces when they are nervous or anxious.

The result is a scowling, frowning appearance that discourages rapport. Relax your face. Open your mouth and eyes wide for 15 seconds to release tension; you'll look much more approachable.

6. **Open your body.** Similarly, crossing your arms, putting your hands in your pockets or clasping them tightly in front of you, and turning away from the other person project a stay-away message. Face the other person, free your hands by your side, and use your body language to express your friendliness.

7. **Have an expressive handshake.** Use your handshake to say, "I really am glad to meet you." Don't shake the person's arm off, but do put some feeling into it.

8. **Make eye contact.** You can't warm to someone you won't look at.

Making Good Conversation

One tool to help you build rapport with people is learning to be a good conversationalist. A good conversationalist is a welcome guest at any occasion or in any office. Throughout your career, you will find yourself in situations where you will want to make conversation with people you don't know at all or only superficially. Many people find this difficult. It's easy to converse with people you know well or would like to know well. But how do you make good conversation with those you don't know well, probably never will know well, and have no desire to know well? Well, it's not too difficult. Here are some tips:

1. **Find common ground.** Look for something that you might have in common. The weather, the hotel you are in, the menu in the restaurant, etc., are always good start-

ing places. Stay away from politics and religion; they are often sensitive topics and can lead to heated discussions.

2. **Ask questions.** As long as you don't get too personal, ask other people about themselves. Standard questions like "Where are you from?" "How long have you worked here?" or "Do you have any kids?" can get the ball rolling.

3. **Get people to talk about themselves.** It's an old trick to find something other people really like and get them talking about it. People love to talk about themselves if you just get them to open up. They also feel good about you if you have shown lots of interest in them and their life.

4. **Volunteer yourself.** Offer some information about yourself to give the other person something to talk to you about. For example, mention a hobby or big event in your life or a big piece of news. Don't wait to be asked; just blurt it out.

5. **Don't argue or disagree.** Keep your ego in your pocket. No matter how friendly they seem, disagreements have no place in casual conversation.

You should realize that almost everyone is at least a little uncomfortable making conversation. Anything you do to carry the conversation, no matter how awkward you may feel, will be greatly appreciated by the other person. Remember, if you are feeling uncomfortable about the situation, the odds are the other person is, too. Good conversationalists don't worry much about being embarrassed. They simply talk about events, the weather, other people, and themselves.

Listening

Listening is a learned process requiring a conscious effort on the part of the listener. Most people think of listening as a natural, instinctive behavior, but it is not. Hearing, which is the physical act of responding to sound, is a natural body behavior, but listening, which is to hear and understand, is an acquired skill.

The problem is that it is very easy to hear something without really listening to the sounds we receive. Most of us prefer to talk instead of listen, and we are often guilty of "listening with one ear." Experienced subordinates learn to listen attentively to their boss and are more effective because they are able to respond precisely to questions or requests. They waste little time, provide direct answers, and establish good rapport by doing so. In more casual situations, good listeners make people feel important because they rarely ignore anything that is said.

Here are ten tips for good listening:

1. **Be prepared to listen.** Remind yourself to be an active listener. Decide to follow these methods.

2. **Stop talking.** Close your mouth long enough to give the other person a chance to say the things he or she wants to say. You can't listen and talk at the same time.

3. **Don't rehearse.** Many people rehearse their next statement or answer at the same time they are listening. While doing so, you may tune out some of what is said. Listen to the whole question. Then formulate your answer.

4. **Shut out distractions.** Focus your attention completely on listening. Learn to ignore distracting noises or other interference.

5. **Don't interrupt.** For heaven's sake, never break in as the other person is talking. Always let the other person finish.

6. **Clarify.** Ask for clarification if you are unsure of a statement's exact meaning.

7. **Attend to the entire message.** Listen to the content and the tone. Watch the nonverbals. All the pieces work together to give you the complete message.

8. **Reflect.** Restate the question as you heard it, particularly for critical points or questions. It helps you and the other person be sure you understand.

9. **Don't react emotionally.** Watch for your emotional "hot buttons"—that is, certain words, ideas, or phrases that cause you to react emotionally. Don't become defensive.

10. **Don't form judgments.** Just collect the information while listening. The analysis and judgment can wait until after the interview.

Time Management and Setting Priorities

It's a simple fact of every professional life that there are far more things to do than time in which to do them. If you try to do them all and do them well, you'll end up either burned out or exhausted or ineffective. One manager remembered his boss describing his job as "almost like juggling—see how many things you can get up and keep in the air at one time. And being smart enough to be able to manage that dynamically and get rid of something when new things come your way." Every professional has to learn good time management.

You've heard the expression "Time is money." It's really true. One of the most precious resources you have is your time. It is a limited resource, and you can't create more hours in the day. You can only use the hours there are more effectively. One of the most important decisions you will make on a daily basis is how you choose to spend your time. While in the first year you may not have as much control over your time as in later years, you do have much more control than you think. It's enough that you need to learn how to manage it.

There are many books written on the subject, so I won't attempt to include a complete course here. Rather, I'll just hit some of the elements of good time management that are particularly important to new hires:

1. **Prioritize your work.** The real key to time management is to figure out which tasks are truly important (they may all look important) and devote the majority of your time to them. You've probably heard of the 80/20 rule, and it applies here: 80 percent of the benefit to the organization, and thus to your career, will be derived from about 20 percent of the tasks in front of you. A new hire advised that you consider "Ranking so you don't spin your wheels on junk that doesn't have to be done. It's not first-in, first-out. Don't take from the bottom of your in-box; sort through it." You want your efforts focused as much as possible on the 20 percent of tasks that really make a difference. If you don't know which tasks these are, ask your boss or colleagues.

2. **Decide how much quality.** The 80/20 rule also applies to how thoroughly you do each task. Not all need to be done perfectly. There are some important tasks that need to be completed with the highest possible quality, while many others just need an acceptable level of quality. New hires have a tendency to do everything, even the smallest tasks, to perfection. Again, it's a matter of prioritizing. Ask yourself whether it's going to make a difference to anybody if every detail isn't covered. If you don't know, ask your boss or colleagues.

3. **Avoid wasted time.** There is no shortage of time wasters on the job. Talking to other people at the water cooler or in their office is a common problem. As a professional, you'll have lots of control over your time, which also means you can easily waste it if you're not careful. Some talking to people is necessary to build good rapport, but limit it to that. Also consider whether you're doing your job as efficiently as you can. You'll be amazed at the amount of time you can "create" just by being more efficient.

4. **Don't procrastinate.** Procrastination is a huge time waster. Most professionals have certain parts of their job that they don't enjoy very much. The natural inclination is to put off those parts as long as possible so you can do the more enjoyable parts. Often, you just waste time and energy by constantly thinking about what you should be doing and dreading what you have to do. The solution: simple discipline. Force yourself to do whatever it is you have to do and get it out of the way as quickly as you can. You'll be amazed at how much energy you save. Approaching it one step at a time always helps.

5. **Use to-do lists.** If you're not already familiar with to-do lists, learn how to use them.

In most jobs, it's impossible to keep up with all the tasks, phone calls, memos, meetings, etc., without writing them down. A good to-do list helps you structure and prioritize your day. It also keeps you from embarrassing moments when things slip your memory.

6. **Find your peak time.** We all have different biorhythms that make us more effective at a certain time of the day. Some people do their best work early in the morning, others late in the day. A key to time management is to try to work on your most routine tasks such as opening mail or doing paperwork during your downtime. New hires often can't control their schedule enough to do this all the time, but they should try to do it as much as possible.

Selling

Professionals in every field are always selling something. Conventional thought would lead you to believe that it's only the people in marketing who sell. That's not true. They may be the only ones who sell products, but all professionals have to sell their ideas, performance, potential, and themselves. One new hire commented, "I think the whole thing is sales. You are selling your ideas, you are selling yourself to your boss, and you are selling what you have done to whoever you are providing it to. And you can't mess up on any of these." The world is full of bright, capable people with good ideas who go unnoticed because they don't know how to sell themselves on those great ideas. It's a different form of salesmanship, but it's important that you learn how to do it.

Selling Yourself

The most important thing you have to learn to sell is yourself. You've already done some of that while finding your job. But selling yourself isn't just something you do during a job search; it's something you do every single day. New hires are continually selling themselves during their first year, convincing people to respect and accept them.

How do you sell yourself? By your professionalism, performance, behavior, attitude, and appearance. Selling yourself is a foreign concept at first because most of us grow up hearing the familiar maxim "Don't brag about yourself." We're taught not to be conceited but to be modest and humble. That's good for social situations, but it's too stringent a standard for the professional world. If you don't make people aware of your accomplishments, contributions, and capabilities, they may well go unnoticed. Often it's done subtly by making sure your boss gets copied on the right memos, by asking someone to write a congratulatory memo on your behalf, or through an annual accomplishment report. Other times it may be more direct and open, such as when you're persuading someone to give you a juicy assignment or a promotion.

Selling yourself is not done through boasting and puffery. Nor is it done by denigrating other people. Rather, it's a matter of making sure people know what you're doing by using concrete examples. It may also be showing someone what you're capable of by your past performance. Be sure it's done in a smart, professional way, but don't be afraid to sell yourself by making sure you get full credit for what you've done.

Selling Your Ideas

A difficult adjustment for many new hires is to realize that new ideas and initiatives aren't automatically accepted; they have to be sold. Just because they're good ideas doesn't mean everybody is going to accept them automatically. Even very experienced people have to sell their new ideas. So throughout your entire career you will need to convince your boss, his or her bosses, committees, project teams, colleagues, or your board that an idea is worth pursuing. If you can't do that, you'll be stuck implementing other people's ideas and won't go very far in your career.

Part of effective selling is knowing your customer. That means knowing the person or group to whom you're selling and understanding what their needs and "hot buttons" are. Once you do, you then focus your selling so that it's most effective. Within your organization, that means knowing exactly who needs to be sold on your idea and how to make your idea the most appealing to other people.

You'll quickly find that ideas don't sell unless you can show people how supporting them will benefit their organization. Your idea or concept has to be well thought out and structured to appeal to a variety of people. You have to do your homework so that you know exactly what it is about your idea you can sell.

Dress

I expect you've heard all you want to hear about professional dress by the time you've finished the interview process. Unfortunately, though, dress doesn't get less important; it gets more so. How you dress is a very important factor in creating your professional image. Without ever saying a word or doing anything, you make or break your image just by your dress. As one manager put it, "If you look the part, you get the first 'yes' from others in the organization. The second 'yes' comes when you act the part." If you don't dress the part, you start with a "no" that then must be overcome with your behavior and performance.

"Appropriate" dress varies a great deal, depending on the job you're in, your company, your career path, the region of the country, etc. There is no way I could begin to tell you what to wear, given all these possible variables. What you have to understand though is that for every situation, there are norms and rules, usually unwritten, that govern how you should dress. If you are a consultant, a conservative suit and tie may be the norm. If you are a line supervisor in a manufacturing plant, less formal clothes may be the norm, but supervisors are still expected to wear a tie. As a field engineer, you may need jeans when you're in the field and a suit when you make a presentation at corporate headquarters. The key point is that there are norms and expectations and you need to find out what they are very quickly.

Your goal the first year should be to blend in, to wear the "uniform" that is widely accepted in your environment. You want to dress to clearly broadcast that you are part of the team, a professional just like everyone else, and you want to fit in. That means the first year is no time to make fashion statements, assert your individual style through clothing, or wear suggestive clothing that captures the attention of your colleagues and managers for all the wrong nonprofessional reasons.

Office Skills and Practices

You can't forget that being an effective professional means not only doing big things well but also capably handling the everyday things that make working in the office and with professional colleagues easier. These are the nuts-and-bolts skills with which most new hires have no experience. Yet some play a crucial role in your professional image. Others are part of office etiquette; you'll need to learn what the rules and customs are in your new organization. Here, however, are some tips regarding office skills, which have general application to all types of organizations:

1. **Telephone manners.** Most professionals transact lots of business over the telephone. Even within your own building, you'll find you use the phone extensively instead of walking to other offices. Since people count on it so heavily, you need to use it properly. Make sure you have a friendly but professionally warm telephone voice; return your phone messages promptly, at least within 24 hours; identify yourself when you answer the phone; tell your receptionist where you are and how long you'll be gone when you leave your work area; and don't dodge phone calls.

2. **Memo writing.** Every professional needs to know how to write a good memo. Unfortunately, a good memo is nothing like the things you wrote in college. You have to learn what the organization prescribes for memo etiquette. Generally, memos must be short and concise with little fluff; one page or less is often the norm. Forget the "introduction-body-closing" narrative style. Say what you need to say and stop. Put your main point in the beginning. You don't need to defend everything you say, just the major supporting facts. And don't forget the fine art of determining who gets a "cc" or copy of the memo.

3. **Meeting skills.** Another reality of professional life is meetings. Lots of them. You may not have to run many yourself at first, but eventually you'll need to learn how to chair an effective meeting. The chairperson can make all the difference between a productive and unproductive meeting. More important at first is learning to be a good participant in a meeting. Let the chairperson run the meeting. Follow his or her agenda, and don't challenge his or her authority. Be a good listener. Don't hog the meeting; let everyone participate and have a fair say. Be considerate of everyone's opinion and position on the issues. Particularly when you are new, you'll learn a lot if you listen well.

4. **Group presentation skills.** Since so much emphasis is on teamwork, you'll find yourself making frequent presentations to groups of people. Some may be informal, and others will be quite formal, such as presentations to senior managers. In some organizations, the presentations you make will be the chief means that senior people have of developing impressions of you. Learn how to make an effective presentation. Practice so you're not nervous or uncomfortable, at least in a visible way. Be prepared to think fast on your feet to field questions. Learn how to use audiovisuals to make your points clearly.

5. **Saying "I don't know."** If you are asked a question to which you don't know the answer, don't be afraid to say, "I don't know." Nobody expects you (or anybody) to know everything. In no circumstances should you try to bull or bluff your way through an answer. Even if you should guess the answer, you'll only get in trouble.

6. **Secretary relationship skills.** One of the most important persons in any organization for getting things done is your secretary. Get to know your secretary, how he or she likes to work, and how to communicate and get along with him or her. If you develop a good rapport and your secretary likes you, you can be so much more effective during your first year on the job. Make your secretary an important person. Don't make the mistake of looking down on a secretary, because without secretaries, you'd be sunk.

7. **Saying so if you can't deliver.** Other people need to know they can depend on you to deliver what you promise by the deadline you promise. But things do happen to prevent that sometimes, and people will understand if you warn them ahead of time. Never, never wait until the last minute to tell someone you can't meet your deadline. Even if it's just going to be tight to make it but you think you can, warn them so they can make contingency plans.

8. **Getting organized.** New staff members are often keepers of information for the boss and the department. Learn how to sort, file, and organize your work and information you work with. It's hard to be professional if your office is cluttered and disorganized.

9. **Office machines.** The modern office is a technological wonder. You'll need to learn how to operate copiers, phones, computers, answering machines, and a variety of electronic and mechanical equipment. While a clerical staff person will often do much of it, so will you.

10. **Office gossip.** Gossip is like a poison. What you need here is to learn to stay away from it. Let others do it all they want, but you stay out of it.

It's tempting to dismiss many of these office skills and practices as insignificant and not important to your image and job. Granted, some of them are little things, but they add up and play a role in your effectiveness.

WORK SAVVY CHECKLIST

To check yourself, complete this quick quiz:

1. For each skill listed below, grade yourself A to D on how well you perceive you manage these critical aspects of being a star performer. (BE HONEST!)
2. For those skills rated less than A, arrange a professional development opportunity within the next year to achieve the desired skill level. Ask for feedback from your supervisor on specific areas in question.

GRADE	PROFESSIONAL SKILL
_____	Managing time efficiently
_____	Setting priorities
_____	Juggling multiple projects
_____	Writing memos, letters, and reports
_____	Making oral presentations
_____	Managing work flow
_____	Managing and participating in meetings
_____	Selling ideas
_____	Telephone skills
_____	Working with a secretary
_____	Organizing my work and office
_____	Setting realistic deadlines
_____	Meeting deadlines
_____	Producing the right level and quality
_____	Motivating myself

ULTIMATE SURVIVAL TIPS

1. College gave you lots of knowledge but did not teach you how to be a professional.

2. You're expected to look, act, think, and talk like a professional from day one.

3. A key complaint of employers about new hires is lack of professional maturity. There's no excuse for it.

4. Professional maturity, integrity, and judgment are not just a function of time; they can be learned.

5. The bottom line is getting the job done.

6. Getting the job done means learning how to communicate well with people.

7. Manage your work, or it will manage you and you'll never get anything done. Practice effective time management.

8. Manage yourself, too.

9. Don't let what you wear mark you as an inexperienced rookie.

10. Good office skills will let your true ability shine through.

CHAPTER

11

LEARNING ABOUT YOUR NEW JOB

· ·

This chapter combines the last two steps in the twelve-step plan: learning your work tasks and acquiring new knowledge, skills, and abilities. They are combined because they are usually handled well by new hires and companies, not because they are unimportant. Make no mistake—you must learn how to do the tasks you are assigned to and learn to do them well.

Most companies have some type of orientation and training program, and there are probably as many different types of programs as there are companies to work for. Every company develops an approach to indoctrinating new hires that fits its culture, style, and business needs. While it is impossible to predict the exact nature of the program you'll encounter, it's important that you have realistic expectations about training, know what its purpose and focus are, and understand the common methods used to train new hires.

EXPECTATIONS ABOUT TRAINING

One of the first things you need to realize is that many companies don't do a very good job of orienting and training their employees. Despite all the concerns voiced about how productivity needs to increase, how important employee development is, and how expensive recruiting new employees (and especially losing them) can be, many companies simply forget that the starting point for addressing these concerns is a strong training program for new hires. There are companies that invest a tremendous amount of time and money in new-hire training and do it very well, and there are those that don't do much at all. Many new hires are quite surprised by this, particularly since they've just spent several years in an environment where training and education are everything.

New hires come in to their new jobs expecting everything to be very neatly organized. They think somebody will teach them how to do a task, and then they'll be asked to do it. Then they'll learn something else and do it also. They believe nobody will ask them to do anything before they've been trained to do it. And all this will be planned before they start and be very neatly laid out for them when they arrive. After all, that's the way college was.

Fast-Starter Tip

You won't learn much, if anything, until you realize how much you don't know.

It rarely works that way. To start with, unless you're joining a larger organization with a highly structured training program, orientation is rarely planned so well. Even if the training program is well planned, it may not be directly coordinated with your job. The real world of work just doesn't follow such predictable, neat patterns. Invariably, business reasons will force your boss to ask you to do something for which you haven't been fully trained yet. You can't tell your boss, an important customer, or the president of the company to wait a few weeks until you're trained for the task. You have to learn on your own and find a way to get the task done.

Your training experience can range from disorganized ("we'll work it out and train you as we go along") to well laid out (although well-organized plans can still go awry). Consequently, you need to change your expectations about training. You have to be prepared to work with the company, do the best you can to get the training you need, and help get the job done. The last thing you want to do is start your career by complaining about the company training program, particularly if it's just because the program is not as well structured as a college curriculum.

Most new hires can also expect to be pushed to do more things with much less preparation and training than they had in college. In college, you tend to study, think, and practice things for a long time before having to perform what you've learned on exams or class projects. But even in companies that train their people pretty well, you're likely to be asked to perform after only a fairly brief and intensive training period. New hires are usually disoriented by this, since it is a much more high-pressure kind of learning than they were used to in college. But most organizations can't afford to let you idle for a long period of time, since they continue to pay you while you train. The bottom line is: you have to be ready to learn quickly and move forward with much less certainty than you had in college.

PURPOSE AND FOCUS OF TRAINING

Job training has a very different purpose from the education you received in school. Education has a long-term perspective and focuses on building foundations, teaching you how to learn and think. You were probably frustrated at times in your college career because the material was too theoretical and didn't seem practical enough. Training, on the other hand, has a short-term horizon and focuses on the practical, day-to-day aspects of the job. At first, it will probably be a relief to be doing something you can apply immediately. That's one advantage of training. The disadvantage is that you won't be given the time or be asked to think so deeply about the subject matter and underlying theory as you were in college. You'll also find that job training becomes outdated more quickly and has to be repeated.

Another problem with new-hire training programs is that they tend to be heavily task-related. In one way that's good, because it helps you demonstrate task competence quickly, and that's a big boost to getting started. But, as noted previously, task-related competence is only half the picture. What many training programs fail to provide are discussions about the culture of the organization, its politics and people, success factors, how to build networks, lessons on professionalism, and so on. That's why this book does not dwell on task competence, which most people (students and employers) are already tuned in to, but, rather, on such nontask-related competencies as becoming organizationally savvy.

But it's very difficult to learn from most training programs how to use nontask-related competence successfully within the work environment. Why is that? In part, this occurs because nontask-related matters often aren't discussed in such open forums as training sessions; instead, these things are usually the subject of "inside stories" reserved for off-the-record sessions with employees. Or it may be due to simple oversight. Not realizing the importance of nontask-related competence or believing that it will be covered elsewhere, many companies simply ignore the subject in putting together training programs. Normally, then, it will be up to you to acquire nontask-related competence on your own. Don't expect it to be handed to you in a manual or lectured on during your training. Also, don't assume that it's unimportant because it isn't provided in your training. I guarantee you that nontask-related competence is important, and it is up to you to take the initiative and make sure you get it.

DURATION AND METHODS OF TRAINING

The length of your training will vary enormously, as will the timing of it. In some companies, you will spend months doing nothing but training. In others, it may be only days or a few weeks. It may come as one big span of training time or may be chopped up into alternating periods of work and training. It could be that you spend some months on the job and then go to classes. Many companies are making extensive use of self-paced learning programs, videotaped training sessions, etc., instead of the traditional classroom format.

Most companies will offer at least some type of orientation program. Orientation is not task-related training but rather helps introduce you to the lay of the land and gives you a perspective within which to place your current job. These programs might take days to tell you about the organization's culture, history, goals, strategies, structure, and so on, or orientation might just be a few hours in your boss's office with a quick walk-through of the organizational chart.

On-the-job training (OJT) is still a common approach, especially in smaller organizations that don't have either the staff to develop a formal training program or the number of people to justify it. Even in large companies, though, OJT is a major component of the training. You won't have the luxury of sitting around in a classroom or laboratory practicing forever, unless you're in a high-risk or public safety kind of occupation. "Learning by doing" is a basic philosophy of any program; the only question is whether it will be backed up by classroom-type instruction. The advantage of OJT is that you do get firsthand experience very quickly. And it feels good to jump right into your responsibilities and start making a contribution. The problem is that jumping right in is often like learning to swim by being thrown into a 10-foot-deep pool of water: it's sink or swim. On-the-job training can be very good if done properly, but it can also be a very confusing and frustrating time for new hires. The pressure is immense if you're asked to perform the day you walk in the door.

At the other extreme are organizations that operate company colleges. These firms plan lengthy training programs, often lasting for months. Some of these can be the equivalent of going to graduate school in their intensity, volume of work, and hours spent in the classroom. Some large companies actually own campuses away from their offices that would make many colleges envious. The advantages and disadvantages of this approach are exactly the opposite of those of on-the-job training. Lengthy programs do prepare you well before you go to work, but they delay the start of your "real" job for what can seem like an interminably long time.

Most company training has evolved into a program of alternating class and work. In this format, you typically spend three to four weeks working at an aspect of your job and then go to class for a few weeks. You usually continue this cycle for your first six months or year on the job. By receiving on-the-job and classroom training, new hires get the best of both worlds. You get the classroom training to better prepare you for your tasks, but you also get to contribute quickly. This type of training is particularly effective, because you learn something in class and then get to try it out on the job.

Some companies make extensive use of outside courses in some circumstances. If your job requires specialized training, the company may choose not to have an in-house course. Or if the company is small, it may rely heavily on outside courses. There are many outstanding training programs provided by outside vendors. The only problem is that you learn very little about your own employer and may not get much opportunity to meet fellow new hires from your company. For this reason, many companies avoid extensive use of outside courses for new hires or arrange for the outside trainer to come to the company to provide the training.

MAKING THE MOST OF YOUR TRAINING

Most new hires are hungry to jump right into work. They're excited about starting their career and are tired of waiting. They're enthusiastic about the opportunity to really contribute something professionally after four (or more) long years of college preparation. They may also be a bit scared, and the longer the wait, the more anxious they get. Companies are also anxious to get you to work, in part for selfish reasons but also because studies have shown consistently that the happiest new employees are those who are given the chance to contribute early and are challenged soon (although many employers also have learned that you can throw somebody in too quickly).

I know that many new hires hate training programs. I mean, after four years of college, who needs more school, right? It's wonderful to be excited and anxious to get to work, but don't overlook the importance of your training time.

First, if you don't have the right training, you're going to make nothing but a fool of yourself. And that's going to hurt not only your professional reputation but also your confidence.

Second, training programs serve as a buffer and decompression time. They separate you from the rest of the company for a period of time—usually a week or two right in the beginning of your job—to allow you to begin adjusting. It's during this time that you can make the mental transition from student to professional. You can have some time to look around a little bit, absorb the culture, and observe possible role models. You have a chance to adjust to your new professional role and leave the student role behind. And you can mess up, too, all within the relatively safe confines of a training class. Also, it's a great chance to build a little camaraderie with fellow trainees so you don't feel so isolated when you join the rest of the company.

Third, training programs provide a great opportunity to develop a network of colleagues within the company. In fact, many companies will structure some type of program for this reason alone. What happens is that over and over again as the years go by, you'll use the network of people you met when you were new hires together. Even in your first year, you'll find a good network invaluable in getting your job done and developing a personal support network.

It's up to you, though, to make your training work for you. It's very easy and tempting to take it lightly, particularly if you come directly into a training program without first spending some time on the job. You'll realize once you're on the job how terribly important training is and how tough it is to get more if you've already completed yours. Take it lightly and you just may end up out of a job. The person who studies hard and earns high grades during training may be chided by peers, but the laugh may be on them, since that same person will probably surge ahead of them in job performance. Your employer would not devote the time and money to have you in training if it weren't important.

Training programs can be very intense and demanding. Some of them feed you lots of information faster than you can absorb it. It may make college look like a piece of cake. Or you may be disappointed. Sometimes it doesn't seem as stimulating or intellectually invigorating as college. Be prepared for either.

Fast-Starter Tip

Take your training as seriously as you do your job.

When you are grouped with other new hires, you have opportunities to meet new friends, to party together, and to build lasting relationships. (In fact, most companies try to build this into the training experience.) But it's easy to fall into the trap of oversocializing and viewing training as no more than "fun" time. It's tempting because it feels a lot like being back in college. That college party mentality may creep back in, and you may forget that you're now a professional. And if you think that nobody notices, guess again—what about your training instructors and facilitators?

True, everybody wants to have fun during training, but remember, this isn't college. The training instructors aren't college professors whom you'll never see again, and your fellow trainees aren't college classmates; they're all your colleagues. You really can't let your hair down like you used to do in college. You have to approach training in a more restrained fashion and remember that, while it has its fun moments, it's still work. Don't do anything in training that you wouldn't want your manager to know, because he or she will probably hear about it. Remember that your manager will be talking to your instructors to see how you are doing. And your manager (and others) also will be checking to see who are the top trainees.

Your challenge, then, is to make the training program work for you. Here's how:

1. **Take it seriously.** You may not understand why you need to learn what you're learning, and you may not enjoy more schooling, but your employer considers it important and so should you. Don't view it as something you just have to put up with. Be careful to look interested and enthusiastic, not bored and indifferent. Others are watching.

2. **Learn all you can.** No matter what the material, learn it. You have no idea in the beginning what you will need to know later or even two months from now. You can bet somebody thinks it's important, or it wouldn't be included. It's probably the last time you'll have so much time and so many resources available to you. Remember, only A work counts.

3. **Ask questions (don't skip this).** Sounds like what every teacher you've ever had has told you, right? It really is important. You won't learn unless you ask. What you may not realize is that not knowing and asking questions will not always be accepted in your career. There will come a point when the wrong questions will embarrass you. Take advantage of your "rookie license" to ask all you can while it won't hurt you.

4. **Look beyond what's taught.** Even if the company focuses only on task-related training, you can start learning the rest. Pay close attention to the instructors. They have likely been selected in part because they are success stories and excellent examples of the company culture. Study them as role models. Notice how they act and dress. Even the curriculum itself will tell you something about the company culture. Use the informal parts of the program to learn more about the politics of the company.

5. **Network.** Make it a point to meet and socialize with every one of your classmates. Be sure that you are on friendly terms with all of them when you leave the class. That will get your network started and open channels for future communication.

6. **Be active in designing your training.** Work closely with your boss to design a good training program. Talk to him or her about what you are strong in and where you need some more work. Ask for more resources.

Even if there is a formalized program already planned, you can play a proactive role in supplementing it.

7. **Locate other resources.** No training program can possibly teach you everything you'll need. Perhaps the most important thing you can learn is where to find the training resources to get the rest. Find out the people, materials, and programs you'll need to continue your learning after the program ends, and make sure you know where they're to be found.

ULTIMATE SURVIVAL TIPS

1. Orientation programs are not a waste of time, nor is training.

2. It is natural, but not smart, to be impatient with training programs for new hires.

3. Be dedicated to the orientation and training process; it will pay off.

PART

5

STARTING YOUR NEW JOB

12

HITTING THE GROUND RUNNING

On your first day at work, you are still in the interview mode. You are extremely courteous, well dressed, and attentive to the slightest upset. You probably look like someone who just walked out of an IBM commercial. You speak very clearly and concisely when somebody addresses a question to you. You are scared to death, fearful of making a mistake. All manner of questions are running through your mind: The company is going to teach me about its corporate culture. What culture? Who I am supposed to network with? Am I doing something wrong? Am I asking too many questions? Am I asking too few questions? Am I doing all right, Sir or Madam, Mr. or Ms.? [new hire]

When you accept your job, it's time to start preparing for the transition to work. Whether you report to work in three weeks or three months, it really doesn't matter; once you accept your job, there's work to be done.

STRATEGIES BEFORE YOUR FIRST DAY

What you can't do is wait until the first day of work to get started. As we've discussed, impressions form quickly, and you simply don't have a month or two to get your act together. If you start doing some basic things before you go to work, it can have a major impact on the success of your transition and give you a head start on the other new hires.

A major part of your energy should be devoted to learning your new role as a professional. The day you accept your job, you should start considering yourself a professional. Even if you have another semester of college left, it's not too early to start practicing. It takes time to learn. Start thinking and acting like a professional. How does it feel? Consider everyday situations and try looking at them first as a student and then as a professional. What's different? It's OK to go ahead and enjoy the rest of your student days and lifestyle, but it's important that you start the mental transition to your new role as a professional as soon as you can.

Your other energy should be directed toward learning all you can about your new organization and work group. Your objectives are threefold:

1. To learn what you can about the company, its culture, and its people before you start
2. To get advance orientation to your job
3. To develop a little rapport with the people with whom you'll work

You usually can't do this in great depth before you start, so your approach should be to gain a general "feel" for the organization. That's all it really takes to reduce the confusion when you start work and to be more productive earlier.

Furthermore, if you can get a few people saying good things about you before you even arrive for work, you'll have set a positive expec-

tation in their minds and in the minds of the others they might tell. You'd be amazed how beneficial it is to have people thinking good thoughts about you for weeks or months before you start. Instead of encountering people who have negative stereotypes about new hires or are just wary, you'll be meeting people who already have a positive opinion of you. While it may seem like a small thing, the fact that they expect to like you and expect you to succeed greatly increases the chances of both. Also, just being able to talk comfortably with people and call them by name the day you walk in the door can really help. Consider doing at least some of the following things:

1. **Talk to future colleagues.** Make contact with some key people from the department in which you'll be working. Usually you can obtain their names and phone numbers from the personnel director or your primary contact with the company. Try to have lunch or dinner with someone from the company. Use this opportunity to talk about the company and its history, future, and culture. Find out what you can about the projects your department is working on and the big issues. Use the chance to develop some rapport with future colleagues.

2. **Contact alumni working for your employer.** Alumni from your college who are already working for the company are great sources of information. Since you have a common bond, they'll likely be pleased to help you. That gives them a justification for talking "off the record." They'll tend to be more frank and honest than they would be with a complete stranger and will probably share their own breaking-in experiences with you.

Also, you just might find a mentor or coach among them. Contact your school's placement or alumni office to find them.

3. **Visit the company again.** It's not a bad idea to visit the company again after you've accepted the job. Often, this can be scheduled while you are looking for housing accomodations. It needn't be a lengthy visit—just a chance to meet with some future colleagues and say, "I'm looking forward to starting work." You may have met them already while interviewing, but the relationship had to be more at arm's length then. Now you can talk with them as colleagues, and they can feel freer to welcome you. You can talk about the department, their job, your job, and anything else you can think of to kick off the relationship. Often, colleagues will treat you to dinner or lunch. Remember, they are curious about you just as you are about them.

4. **Meet with your new boss.** The key person to make contact with is your future boss. It won't always be possible for you to do this, but if you can, make a point of doing so. This is the most important relationship to get a head start on. At this time, it would also be appropriate to ask your boss how he or she prefers to work with subordinates.

5. **Start your job training early.** One sure way to make a good impression on your new boss is to ask if there are training materials related to your new job that you can start reading before coming to work. Often, there are policy and procedure manuals, specialized software training, course materials, or something similar you can get a head start on. Then instead of spending

your first week on the job reading, you'll be ready to really do something. An important caveat: If you're given something to read, be absolutely sure you do it. If you aren't sure you'll get through it, don't ask.

6. **Obtain company literature.** At a minimum, you should ask the organization to give you copies of all its public literature, reports, catalogs, etc., if you haven't already done so as a part of making your job decision. When you walk in the door, you should at least have a good general understanding of the organization's business or activity. You'll learn much more after you get there, but it's terribly embarrassing not to know at least the basics.

7. **Do independent research.** Don't rely exclusively on company literature. Spend as much time as you can researching your future employer. Your librarian can direct you to a variety of sources. If you're going to work for a business organization, check the business press, such as the *Wall Street Journal*, *Business Week*, *Fortune*, and *Forbes*. Also check investor publications such as *Standard & Poor's* or *Moody's*. Check trade publications and magazines or newspapers devoted to your industry. Similar publications exist for nonprofit and government organizations. Use this information to get a sense of the history of the company, the issues it's facing currently, and how its stockholders and other constituencies perceive it. (Don't let negative press worry or bias you—it's too late to do anything about your job acceptance anyway.)

A note of caution: don't go overboard with all this. Most companies aren't used to having new hires do these kinds of things, so it will come as a surprise when you do. Too much of it will look like brownnosing and turn off people. Also, most employers will have made plans for your orientation and training along with the other new hires. Grouping you with the others saves time and effort. Thus, if you require lots of special attention in advance, you're causing them extra work. Keep it low-key, and don't press the issue if the organization doesn't want to cooperate with your attempts at advance preparation (quite possible in companies that have extensive training programs). You'll make a positive impression just by showing your interest and enthusiasm. Let them know you'd like to get a head start, and let them guide you as to what will work for them. If you approach things in this manner, most employers will cooperate.

HAVE SOME FUN

Starting your career is serious business, and this is a serious book (for the most part). Because it's serious, you should try to take a trip and have some fun before you start work. "Make sure you have a heck of a lot of fun in between college and the time you actually start working," advised one second-year employee. "Don't start right away. Take time off, and just have a good time."

Your first year and your first few years are demanding. You'll work hard, possibly harder than you're accustomed to. You'll have ten or so holidays per year, and in most organizations it will take you years (usually five) to accrue more than two weeks' vacation. That's not much time off each year, especially when com-

pared to the many weeks of vacation you've had each year while in school. On top of all that, you've just finished four demanding years of college.

Take a break if you can. Visit friends, travel, go to the beach—do whatever it is that feels like play to you. It sounds gloomy to say it, but it's true that it may be many years before you get the chance to be a free-spirited, have-a-good-time person again, as you were in college. There will be many new responsibilities, pressures, and demands on your time. If you're very career oriented, you'll be eager to go to work, and taking time off later may be difficult. Your eagerness is wonderful, but you have forty more years to work. Taking a month off won't hurt you.

As I've said, you should start thinking like a professional before you graduate and take some steps to be ready to go to work. But don't take this so far that you forget to enjoy the last weeks or months of college life, graduation, and a break. Take time to do whatever you need to do so that when you do show up for work, you're rested and ready to apply yourself to the job.

THE UPSIDE OF GOING TO WORK

We shouldn't lose sight of the fact that there are many great things about starting your career. This book focuses on many of the challenges, because you already know how to handle the fun stuff. Let me remind you of what most new hires enjoy.

Getting Paid
We might as well start with the bottom line—the paycheck. After years of living poor, it's

great to get paid well. It may not be all you'd like to have, and it may not go as far as you'd like, but it's still a wonderful feeling. If you manage it well, you can use your salary to have lots of fun and really add to your life.

Independence

One of the things that a paycheck helps to buy is your independence—your own place to live, your own car, paying your own bills (is this really fun?), and doing your own thing. You're on your own, at least for the most part, and that's a great feeling. You can now build your life in your own way.

Professional Respect

After years of being a "lowly student," you're now a professional. People respect you much more, give you responsibility, look to you for opinions and answers. It feels great to have the label and image of a professional. You feel like "somebody" in the world.

Accomplishments

As a professional, you have earned the opportunity to accomplish worthwhile things and make real contributions to important efforts. No more research papers and tests, but projects that really count. The feeling of tackling a tough problem, finding new ways to do things, or coming up with new ideas (especially when they work) is a real high.

Good Work

Compared to all the "grunt" work you've probably done in your part-time jobs, professional work is great. Even at the entry level, the tasks

can be exciting and fun. Sure, they're not all that way, and you're still expected to do some "grunt" work as a rookie, but generally it's much better than other things you've done and better than many other alternatives.

Challenge

One hallmark of professionals is that they thrive on challenge. Your job will give you a chance to use your creative energies. It will challenge you to grow and learn new things. It's fun to be challenged rather than be stuck in boring or routine jobs.

Opportunity

Professionals enjoy higher-than-average career opportunities and upward mobility. It's hard to say how much advancement you can expect, since that depends on your abilities and how you continue to develop, but for the near term you should be able to look forward to a rising income, increasing responsibility, possibly a promotion, and the ability to change jobs if necessary.

Becoming an Insider

It's fun to be an "insider" in a company or organization. You get to know something about its inner workings, hear the gossip, and learn the truth behind the headlines. There's a sense of privilege and pleasure from being inside rather than outside looking in.

Responsibility

It's nice to be trusted with important tasks. Professionals are expected to be able to take on responsibility and are given the independence to do so. After years of learning and preparing, it's fun to be an important part of an organization at last.

THE FIRST FEW DAYS AND WEEKS

I hear new hires talk a lot about their experiences in the first few days and weeks at work. Those first few days are really a critical time for you and the company. It's a time that seems to affect most new hires very deeply, so it's worth taking a close look at what happens, how it affects people, and what you should be doing.

High Emotions

Your big day finally arrives, and you can expect it to be an emotion-packed one. Remember how you felt on other "firsts" (first day of school, first date, going off to college, etc.)? It'll be much the same here. You'll probably try to hide your feelings and appear calm, cool, and collected, but I'm willing to bet you're going to be at your peak of excitement, anticipation, nervousness, anxiety, and (maybe) fear.

It's Not As Big a Deal for Everyone Else

The first thing that strikes most people is that their first day is not nearly as big a deal for other employees as it is for them. It's as though you're throwing a huge party and nobody shows up. The other employees have seen lots of new people show up before; it doesn't affect their jobs as much as other events might, and they've got a thousand other things to do anyway. It's not that they don't care, but for most of them, it's just another workday.

There's No Red Carpet Waiting

After the red-carpet treatment you received while being recruited, you may be surprised to discover that there's no grand welcoming ceremony waiting for you when you arrive at work. It's not uncommon to find that people weren't even expecting you and are not sure where you're to go or what you're to do.

Surprise!

Just about every new hire reports that the first few days are full of surprises. Whether it's a different assignment from the one you thought you'd have, a different welcome from the one you expected, an unexpected change in schedule, or whatever, it's never the way you expected it to be. The safest thing you can do is to expect nothing and go with the flow.

The Start Is Slow and Routine

Part of the surprise at some companies is that you don't walk in the door and jump right into the great, glorious job full of responsibilities you had imagined. Not only will it take time to learn what you need to be productive, but also it will take time for your boss and work group to fit you into the flow of things. Your first few days can range from downright boring to simply routine. That can be very frustrating, because the way most of us picture ourselves on the job is the way it will be months down the road. Most of us aren't prepared for the days and weeks it may take to build up to that point.

It's Sink or Swim

At the opposite extreme are the companies that immediately thrust you into significant responsibility or intensive training programs. It's as though one day you've had nothing more to worry about than getting a paper done, and suddenly you have fifteen people working for you and a shift to run. Or your new work group has a major project under way, and immediately you're going to be working 70 hours per week. If you're in this situation, you can expect to feel very overwhelmed. Hang in there, because that's just their culture and their way of bringing you in. Such experiences can be very disorienting, but things do get better. You just have to take it one day at a time.

You're Overwhelmed

In one fashion or another, most new hires do feel overwhelmed at first. Even if the start is slow and boring, everything is so new and there are so many adjustments to make that it can be too much. Remember, though, there is lots to handle, and it's natural to feel heavily burdened.

You're Tired

Starting work takes lots of energy, and most people get very tired from doing it. You may be surprised at how little energy you have left to go out at night after putting in some hard days at work. Even the hardiest of party-goers will comment on how much energy work takes out of them. If you're exhausted the first few weeks, that's OK. You'll get used to the new routine and its demands and learn how to pace yourself.

Information Overload

There is so much to learn and absorb at first. You may have thought you had to learn lots in school, but the pace of learning on the job will be just as intense at first. That's part of the reason it is so tiring. The trick is to try to figure out what the most important things to learn are and not try to master everything at once. You can't, so don't get frustrated with yourself.

Maximum Impression Management

First impressions are worth far more than you may realize. It's so important that you get started on the right foot. Focus hard on making good impressions on everyone you meet by the way you conduct yourself. Try to accumulate as many "chips" as you can early on so that when you make mistakes (which you will), you have a few to cash in. It's your job to make good first impressions, not theirs.

Tasks and Events

Your initial days will usually consist of the following types of activities:

- Completing lots of forms and paperwork in personnel
- Going on a tour of the facility and your work area
- Getting settled into and setting up your office or work area
- Becoming familiar with the work flow and details such as phones, messages, mail, etc.
- Learning policies and procedures (sometimes whole manuals' worth)
- Meeting people of all types—colleagues, clients, bosses, big wheels, secretaries, clerks—you name it, you'll meet them (of course, everybody will remember your name, but you'll have a tough time remembering theirs)
- Attending orientation and welcome meetings (you'll just have to look interested, even if they are boring)

- Reading, reading, and more reading—not only lists of policies and procedures, but also company literature, product catalogs, training materials, industry reports, files, etc.
- Doing menial tasks (since you won't be able to jump right into the big tasks, you'll probably be called on to do such things as making copies and delivering things; do it cheerfully, as everyone before you has, and consider it motivation to complete your training as quickly as possible)

structured to help you learn important information. If the purpose is not immediately clear, it will become clearer later during your transition to the new work environment.

You will be quite busy during your first weeks and months on the job, so you may have to take the initiative to see that you can find time to complete the exercises. In some cases, you may not be able to get all of the information you are supposed to. That's OK as long as you make every effort you can to get the information.

YOUR CAREER STARTS FROM DAY ONE

Your career starts the day you begin work, not after a few weeks of warm-up or a month or two of getting used to the company. You may meet the president of the company on the first day and not see him or her again for a year or more, so you want to be ready. Too many new hires spend the first few weeks or even months on the job getting ready to get serious about their career, and you wouldn't believe the mistake they make in doing that. The day you walk in the door, you need to be focused on doing the right things. Do your getting ready before you come to work. It's like running a race: First you take some warm-up laps so you'll be in full stride when you start. When it comes to mental preparation, you can do the same thing.

Learning About Your New Organization

The following exercises are designed to be completed during your first six months as a new employee to help you learn about your employer. The questions have been carefully planned and

PART I—GETTING TO KNOW PEOPLE IN THE ORGANIZATION

Meeting, working with, understanding, and communicating with people are vitally important in the workplace. The first set of exercises is designed to get you started in that process by meeting and interviewing some people in your new organization. When interviewing them, feel free to tell them that you are completing an exercise as part of your training. Most will be happy to help you.

Identify four to six people in your new organization that you would like to interview. They should be at different levels in the organization and represent a mixture of job functions. Be sure to include people in both management and nonmanagement positions, and at least one should be fairly new in the organization (five years or less). Identify your interviewees below, including name and title.

Interviewee #1:_____

Interviewee #2:_____

Interviewee #3:_____

Interviewee #4:_____

Interviewee #5:_____

Interviewee #6:_____

Schedule time with each person and discuss the following subjects with them. Be sure to take careful notes on the attached sheets so you can later recall their answers. Discuss anything you want but be sure to cover the subjects on the interview guidelines. Be sure to explain the purpose of the interview similar to the suggested introduction shown below.

INTERVIEWEE_____

TITLE_____

When scheduling an interview with a person, be sure to explain the purpose of the session. You might use an introduction like this:

"I am meeting with four to six people to discuss various aspects of working at_____. The information I am collecting will help me learn more about the organization. None of the questions is intended to be prying, and I hope none of the questions is offensive. If you are uncomfortable answering any of them, please let me know and we will eliminate those questions."

1a. Discuss your general career history, including such things as education, jobs held, career paths, etc.

1b. Discuss in more detail your career at_____. How long have you been here? What have you been doing? Where do you see themselves headed in_____?

1c. What has your tenure at_____ been like?

1d. What do you see as the rewards and challenges of working at_____? What do you see as_____'s mission and basic values?

How would you describe the daily work life at_____?

What professional characteristics do you feel are needed to be successful at_____?

If a new employee wants to make a positive first impression at_____, what should he or she do?

What do new employees do that leaves the most negative impressions?

What should a new employee expect during the first six months at_____?

What problems do you typically have (or see people having) with new employees?

What attitudes are rewarded by the organization?

What is the typical management style at_____?

What tips do you have for getting along well with one's boss at_____?

What are the best ways to really get to know the organization and how it really works?

What are the most important things to know about getting things done in the organization?

What should a new employee expect to be doing in the first few assignments in your division?

What other people should the new employee get to know in the division?

What advice would you give a new employee such as yourself just starting out?

What things did you do when you were new to the organization that helped you get started on the right foot?

PART II—GETTING TO KNOW THE WORK GROUP

It is vitally important that you get to know your new group as well as you possibly can. While it can take some time to get to know it completely, you can speed up the learning process by taking the initiative to seek out the information you need. The following questions will help guide you.

For this second part of the interviews, you are to get to know the specific group to which you will be initially assigned. If the assignment has not been finalized, then select any work group, preferably one to which you think there is a high likelihood you will be assigned.

You are to schedule time to meet with the manager of that group and several people who work in the group. The purpose of the meetings is to learn as much as you can about that group and its work.

1. How does the group's work relate to the overall mission of the division and of _____?

2. Where does the group fit in the organizational structure of the division?

3. Specifically, what is the group set up to do and why does it exist?

4. What is the group's history?

5. Describe the structure of the group and each person in it. What does each person do?

6. What projects are the group currently working on?

7. What are the major challenges the group faces in completing these projects?

8. What are the most rewarding parts of working on this group's projects?

9. What is daily life like in this work group?

10. What is the physical layout and location of the office like?

11. What tasks would you likely be assigned as a new employee in the group?

12. What would be expected of you if you joined this group?

13. How could you be most helpful if you were to join the group?

14. What does it take to receive an excellent evaluation?

15. What skills or expertise should a person have to be successful?

16. How would you describe the management style of the group's direct supervisor?

17. When working with this supervisor, what things should a person do to build a good working relationship?

18. What are the relationships between the group members like? Do people work closely together or individually?

19. How would they feel about having a new employee join their group?

20. What kinds of policies, procedures, and operating rules should you know about in order to work effectively in this group and in this division?

© 1997 Elwood F. Holton III, used by permission.

ULTIMATE SURVIVAL TIPS

1. There is no way to escape the necessary passages a rookie must go through to be accepted into the organization.

2. You can make your first few days more effective by taking time to prepare and learn before you start work.

3. Be prepared for the first few days and weeks to be very different from what you expected.

4. Recognize that your first days and weeks will be full of surprises and put you through a roller coaster of emotions.

13

First-Year Timetable

It usually takes about a year to reach the point at which you're ready to advance your career. Your first year on the job will move through some fairly predictable phases as you progress toward your new role as a fully accepted and respected member of the organization. In this chapter, we'll look at the six phases of the first year, which are:

- Welcome aboard
- Settling in
- Getting serious
- Adaptation and acceptance
- Advancing
- Breaking away

Each organization is so different that it's very hard to set an exact timetable for the start and finish of each phase. The timetable presented here is for the typical company that views one year as the appropriate period for a new hire to become fully integrated into the organization. The timing can vary somewhat, depending on the expectations of the company, the type of training program used, the individuals involved, business conditions, and so forth. The stages themselves don't usually change much. (Ask colleagues if one year is about right, and if it's not, adjust the time for each stage proportionately.) You might want to show this list to your boss and use it to discover what his or her expectations are for the first year.

This timetable contains many of the major tasks you'll face during your initiation year. The pacing is one that holds you back some in the beginning and lets you build to where you're ready to charge ahead late in the year after you've earned the respect and acceptance of your colleagues. For each phase, I have given a list of steps to complete and another of things to begin doing. A list of issues that are likely to arise during that time is also included, as is a list of things to guard against. Be sure to adapt these lists to your own circumstances, as these are only general guidelines.

WELCOME ABOARD (FIRST WEEK)

Your first week on the job is really just for getting acquainted. Both you and the company have much to learn about one another. This isn't a week for professional behavior. Don't be lulled to sleep, though. Remember that first impressions are **very** important.

Things to Complete

- Filling out all necessary paperwork
- Learning company policies and procedures
- Getting overview of work assignment and organization
- Meeting the people in the work group and department

Things to Begin Doing

- Learning how to do the basics of the job
- Getting to know the boss
- Getting to know colleagues in the work group
- Demonstrating professional behavior

Issues and Concerns That Arise

- Handling all the new things to know and do
- Anxiety about ability to perform
- Confusion
- Great excitement

Things to Guard Against

- College student behavior
- Trying to start too fast

SETTLING IN (FIRST MONTH)

The settling-in period is a time to jump into your new responsibilities and routines. Your first real challenge is to come to understand what you're supposed to do and how to go about getting started. By the end of the first month, you should feel like you've settled down after the initial confusion and are ready to get to work.

Things to Complete

- Learning initial task responsibilities
- Developing good rapport with the work group and manager
- Establishing initial work routine
- Learning basic logistics, such as getting to and from work, work hours, lunch schedules, etc.

Things to Begin Doing

- Identifying the boss's agenda and priorities
- Getting initial reading on culture of organization
- Identifying professional skills that will be needed
- Understanding the differences between college and work
- Identifying the boss's expectations of you
- Settling down to work
- Meeting people in other departments

Issues and Concerns That Arise

- Coping with the role of a subordinate
- Coming to terms with the scope of responsibility and complexity of the organization

- Eagerness to make a contribution
- Dealing with rookie role

Things to Guard Against

- Making premature judgments about people and the company
- Trying to play a bigger role than you're capable of
- Taking it easy—there's still lots of ground to cover

GETTING SERIOUS (THREE MONTHS)

For the first month or so, people expect you to be a little like a lost sheep trying to find your way around. But between your first month and third month, they expect you to get serious about learning your job and launching your career. If you haven't made progress at this point, some people will begin to wonder what kind of performer you are. They don't expect great things from you, but they expect to see an attitude that shows you are getting serious.

Things to Complete

- Mastering initial task assignment
- Finishing early training phase
- Developing strong working relationship with boss and work group
- Developing rapport with people in other departments and making other important connections in company

Things to Begin Doing

- Looking for first feedback, at least informally
- Developing a training and development plan for the rest of the year
- Taking a slightly more active role in the work group

Issues and Concerns That Arise

- Examining the gap between expectations and the reality of the job
- Realizing how much you don't know
- Missing college and friends
- Heightened excitement and anxiety in facing first meaty assignments
- Uncertainty about your performance

Things to Guard Against

- Frustration at not advancing fast enough
- Loneliness and isolation from friends
- Too much partying

ADAPTATION AND ACCEPTANCE (SIX MONTHS)

By six months, you should have adapted pretty well to the organization and to your new routine. At this point, most people are over the initial shock and upheaval of the transition and are beginning to establish themselves professionally. You've tackled the new challenges seriously and should have begun to earn acceptance from your colleagues. You also should be earning respect, not necessarily because of your great contributions but for your mature approach to the transition.

Things to Complete

- Developing a good mastery of initial assignments
- Getting used to the demands and routines of the job
- Solidifying your position with the boss so he or she feels it was a good decision to hire you
- Obtaining an overview of where your department fits with the rest of the company

Things to Begin Doing

- Showing your capacity to grow
- Understanding in more depth the culture of the organization
- Looking for ways to show loyalty and commitment to the organization
- Noticing the politics of the organization
- Targeting growth opportunities

Issues and Concerns That Arise

- Questioning whether you are performing as well as you should
- Asking whether you have begun to prove yourself
- Dealing with it not being what you expected

Things to Guard Against

- Making "dumb" mistakes
- Getting overconfident
- Getting impatient
- Complaining

ADVANCING (NINE MONTHS)

After you pass the midpoint in your breaking-in process, you'll find that you're ready to move forward somewhat. The first half-year was mostly devoted to catching up to the job and the organization. By the three-quarters point, you'll find that you're able to move beyond the basic demands of the job. While your transition is far from over, the initial phase certainly is.

Things to Complete

- Mastering the more complex elements of the first job
- Making a real contribution, no matter how small
- Being able to identify key players in the political structure
- Developing good working relationships in your department
- Finishing most of your initial training
- Leaving the college mentality behind
- Fully understanding the organization's culture

Things to Begin Doing

- Developing strong relationships throughout the company
- Looking for ways to make bigger contributions
- Looking for strategies to distinguish yourself from other new hires
- Building a strong finish to the year so that your annual review will be good
- Developing a better understanding of the politics of the organization

- Making recommendations to the boss

Issues and Concerns That Arise

- Asking whether you understand the organization well enough
- Questioning whether you have learned all you needed to
- Questioning whether the organization has accepted you
- Questioning whether you have earned the trust and respect of colleagues

Things to Guard Against

- Thinking you now understand it all—there's another level of politics and culture you haven't fully comprehended yet
- Lying too low—many organizations will now begin to look for you to assert yourself
- Exceeding your limits
- Overconfidence about being accepted—it's still tentative, and you need to spend a few months reinforcing the organization's decision to accept you before dropping your caution

BREAKING AWAY (TWELVE MONTHS)

At this point, you should be a fully functioning part of the work group and should have gained acceptance and respect. You've paid your dues, a new group of new hires is coming in, and you've earned the right to begin to assert yourself professionally. You're ready to show what you can really do, and you probably know the organization well enough to find a smart way to do that.

Things to Complete

- Developing your resource network
- Developing a good basic understanding of the organization's politics and how they affect your job
- Adapting fully to your new role as a professional

Things to Begin Doing

- Making significant contributions
- Preparing for annual review
- Distinguishing yourself

Issues and Concerns That Arise

- Asking where you go from here
- Questioning if this is the right career path for you
- Determining how to begin to position yourself for future advancement
- Considering how you will do on your annual performance review
- Setting your strategy for breaking away
- Asking if it is good enough, even though it's not what you thought it would be
- Questioning whether you should stay or leave

Things to Guard Against

- Letting your unrealistic expectations in the beginning lead you to a hasty and unwise decision about leaving the company
- Continuing to act or perform like a rookie—your license has expired
- Expecting to be promoted immediately—you're just starting to earn your keep

ULTIMATE SURVIVAL TIPS

1. The first year moves through multiple stages, each with its own tasks and issues.

2. A good sense of timing will keep you from getting too far ahead of yourself or too far behind others.

3. With each stage, you move closer to acceptance by the organization and to the time when you can assert yourself and your ideas.

4. You cannot skip stages; the only variable is the pace at which the organization allows you to move through them.

5. It is rare that the organization's timetable matches your preferences exactly.

6. Find the right balance between patience and assertiveness.

C H A P T E R

14

PERSONAL ISSUES

· ·

The earnings picture and its impact on my lifestyle were real eye-openers. I thought I was going to make all of this money. And have plenty of money to do whatever I wanted to do. But your paycheck goes fast on insurance, car payments, and the like. And then, of course, Uncle Sam kills you with all those taxes. And the bills never stop. You think you are done paying one round of bills, and up comes the next round. I would say three quarters of my paycheck is gone the day I get the bills . . . poof, just like that, it's gone as though a magician had played some disappearing trick with my wallet.

So far, we've talked only about the professional and organizational issues that arise during the transition period. Equally as important are the personal issues. For many new professionals, the beginning of a career is also the beginning of life on their own. Perhaps for the first time, they are completely responsible for themselves, their finances, and their lifestyles. Even if you've been out on your own already, starting a career will mean lots of changes in your personal life.

The first year is clearly a time of great change, personal decision, adjustments, and hard work. The result is usually an increased level of stress and strain, in both your personal and your professional life. It's not an unmanageable amount, but it can become a real problem if you don't take some steps to cope with it. There are very real issues, anxieties, concerns, and fears in most people's minds. They're all very normal, but you still need to cope with them.

It is not possible in one book to cover all the personal issues that can come up, but because problems with the personal aspects of your transition can spill over into your professional life, this chapter addresses the key personal issues that are likely to impact your job. Many good books are available to assist you in these and other areas. The appendix at the back of this book provides an annotated bibliography of books and other resources to help you deal with issues related to your personal transition to work.

DAILY LIFE

Many new hires talk about how much their daily lives and routines have changed and the adjustments they were required to make once they started their jobs. Following are some of the most frequently mentioned changes.

Getting Up Early Every Morning

I haven't known too many college students who like getting up for eight o'clock classes; in fact, you probably have seen the long lines of people trying to get out of them at registration. Now you're working and all of a sudden, you have to get up early every day, week after week, year after year. After years of staying up late and sleeping late, it's a real shock. Fortunately, you do get used to it, but not until months of sleepy-eyed mornings have passed.

Working Night Shifts

Not all new professional work is from eight to five. In fact, as part of paying their dues, many new hires start on the second or third shift. Working from midnight to 8 a.m. is a big adjustment. I'm not sure anybody likes it or ever gets fully used to it, but you really won't have much choice. Most new hires spend only a limited period of time (six months to two years) on this schedule before they rotate back to more traditional work hours. Grin and bear it!

Dressing Up Every Day

If you're like most new hires, you'll find yourself wearing dressier clothes to work every day than you wore in school, even in nonoffice jobs. No more jeans and T-shirts at work. One young woman added, "Remember how much pantyhose hurt when you have to wear them every day?" You'll have to adjust to wearing more formal and less comfortable attire. While assembling and maintaining a professional wardrobe can be fun at first, it can soon become an expensive chore.

Commuting

If you work in a large metropolitan area (where so many of the jobs are), you're going to spend more time commuting than you ever imagined. Thirty minutes to an hour each way is quite the norm. When you put that on top of the hours you spend getting ready for work and actually working, it's precious time wasted. And it takes time to get your route figured out. You'll probably spend some long hours stuck in traffic until you discover what the best times and roads are. If you use mass transportation, you have to get your schedule figured out. Before you start work, it's best to make some trial runs during the exact hours you'll normally be commuting. Also, allow extra time in the beginning until you are confident about your commuting schedule. Your office mates may be able to help.

Lunch

You have to eat lunch, and getting it may not be that straightforward. You'll have to find places to go that you can afford. On a new hire's salary, it won't be easy to afford eating lunch out every day, and you'll be amazed at how much your waistline may grow if you do. If you choose to make lunch every morning, that takes time. In some companies brown-bagging is OK, while in others it may be considered unprofessional. If you're used to eating at the college dining hall, all this will be an adjustment.

Cooking for Yourself

While we're on the subject of food, let's not forget the other meals of the day. Some college graduates may never have done much cooking for themselves (beyond popcorn). Not to be sexist, but men in particular have little experience with cooking. If you're on your own for the first time, learning to cook even the most basic meals can take some time. Good nutrition is extremely important to your general health as you get older and specifically to combat the effects of professional stress: Don't overlook it. At least get a cheap microwave so you can heat ready-to-eat frozen foods quickly. And yes, mom was right, don't skip breakfast.

MANAGING YOUR MONEY AND BENEFIT PLANS

Having money to spend is great, but most new graduates find that what seemed like a great big salary really doesn't go very far. Taxes take a huge chunk of your check, and after you pay for utilities, a professional wardrobe, insurance, your car, etc., you probably won't have much left. You'll quickly find you need to manage your money very carefully to do the things you want. "You need to develop some priorities, you need to make some plans," emphasized one new hire. "I wish when I was coming fresh out of school that someone had really discussed money management with me. The fact that you make XYZ dollars doesn't mean you take home XYZ dollars, and you have to learn just how far you can stretch your money."

All the benefits of professional life won't rain down upon you as quickly as you thought. You'll find that you'll have to save money to buy some of the bigger items you want, but worrying about saving money is not something with which many students have had much experience. If you're any good at it, you'll then have to worry about investing it, another new game you probably don't know much about. It can be a confusing world, with CDs, stocks, bonds, mutual funds, IRAs, and so on. And let's not forget taxes—Uncle Sam will want his share, and you'll need to file tax returns. All in all, your financial life won't be nearly as simple as it used to be, and you will need to learn to manage your money well. Fortunately, there are lots of good books on personal money management, some of which are listed in the appendix of this book.

You will have to familiarize yourself with your company's benefit plans and make some choices. Life insurance, medical insurance, vacation pay, sick leave, dental plans, etc., are probably not things you're used to thinking about, but you will have to now. You may also have the opportunity to participate in company-sponsored savings plans, stock purchase plans, and tax-deferred savings programs (401k and 403b). Large companies will often match your savings to provide an extra benefit. These are great programs, and you should take advantage of as many of them as you can; if managed wisely, these programs can save you lots of money!

TRAVEL

Most professionals have to travel to some extent. Some new hires in such fields as accounting do lots of traveling in the early years. Travel can be great fun, especially when you're single. It's a great chance to see new places, and if you plan your trips well, you may be able to tack on a few days' vacation in some pretty nice places. It can be one of the perks of your job.

But you'll also discover rather quickly that traveling is not as easy as you think, nor is it as much fun after you've been doing it a while. Travel is work, make no mistake about it. You have to learn how to be a good traveler, how to pack, how airlines work, which hotels are good, etc. And you'll get caught up in the paperwork involved in getting reimbursed by the company for your travel. Leaving home means someone has to get your mail and newspaper, take care of your pets, and so on. If you travel a lot, you'll find yourself wondering sometimes where home really is. Living out of a suitcase in hotels is a big adjustment and can get old quickly. Enjoy your travels, but be prepared to make some adjustments. And don't cheat on your expense reports! It's not worth losing a job over a few bucks.

RELOCATION

For many new graduates, going to work means moving to a new town or city. That's usually an exciting event, since you'll be exposed to so many new things to do and new places to go. Yet, like other things we've talked about in this book, relocating has its challenges, too. Here are some of the challenges new hires frequently talk about.

A Place to Live

The first challenge you'll encounter is finding a place to live. After you've accepted a job, your new employer usually will pay for you to return to the city for a few days to house hunt. It's a little unnerving to arrive in a new city and be given only a few days to decide where you want to live. Somehow in two or three days you have to figure out where the best locations are, what you can afford, where the easiest commutes are, and so on. Your company may have relocation specialists who can offer some help, but by and large you'll be on your own. Usually the organization will direct you to a real estate agent who will help you make the decision; if you have friends in the area, all the better. You may be working with a real estate agent for the first time. Then there are leases to sign or mortgages to apply for. Once you get used to it, though, it's great fun to find your own place to live.

A word of caution: if you really don't know the area very well, it's a good idea not to make long-term commitments at this point. Don't sign a lease for more than one year. If you want to buy, consider renting for a year so you can find out where the best places to live really are. I know it's a pain to move again, but it's worth it. Also, you don't really know yet if you'll like working at your new job, and the potential for leaving is high. Staying flexible is a good strategy.

Roommates

Many new hires look for a roommate. In some cities (New York, Washington, Los Angeles), sharing a home is often a necessity just to pay the rent. Other people simply prefer to live with someone. Whatever the reason, finding a roommate in a new city or town can be difficult or risky, since you probably won't know the person with whom you'll end up rooming. Some employers who hire a number of new graduates each year will put you in touch with other new hires looking for roommates. Of course, you won't know the person, and roommate disputes do have a way of creeping into the workplace. The best solution is to find someone from your college who is going to work for the same employer.

Some apartment complexes keep roommate lists, but these, too, can be risky. If you can afford it, it might be best to live alone for a few months until you can meet someone with whom you'd like to room. Or you can rent an efficiency apartment on a short-term lease (storing your furniture, if you have to) to give you time to look for a roommate. Remember, living with a roommate is a lot like getting married, since you'll be around that person every day. You had better make sure that you like one another.

Moving

Nobody likes to move. Even if you're taking the greatest job in the world, the process of moving your belongings is a real pain. Many organiza-tions pay a moving allowance so that you can hire professional movers. In fact, the larger employers will arrange the move for you. And, of course, many college graduates don't have a lot of furniture and personal belongings yet. Still, packing up what you do have, loading it up, and moving it hundreds of miles away is no picnic. And if you do have many belongings and have to pack and move them yourself, it's real work.

The Community

Once in the new city, you may feel a little lost. You won't know much about the community, and that will feel strange. The topics in the local newspaper won't be familiar, the names in the news will be unknown to you, the ways of the local government will be different, etc. Everything will be new, and you'll need to make some effort to research what your new community has to offer. Some good sources of newcomer information are county or city government offices, real estate firms, the chamber of commerce, and local guidebooks. Exploring can be a lot of fun.

Shopping and Personal Services

One thing you'll need to do almost immediately is find places to shop and obtain crucial services. You'll need to find grocery stores, department stores, malls, drugstores, and so on. You'll have to find a bank, a place to get your car fixed, perhaps a lawyer, a shoe repair shop, a tailor—in a small town, you'll need to search for these; in a large city, you'll have your choice of many. The best strategy on finding such places is to ask friends, neighbors, and colleagues for recommendations.

Medical Care

Even though you're young, you'll still need to find sources of routine medical care, such as a dentist, general practitioner or internist, gynecologist, eye doctor, etc. This can be one of the most unnerving parts of being in a new city, because you must place tremendous trust in these people. Again, personal referral is the best way. Some hospitals now offer physician referral services, but I still recommend a personal referral if possible. If your company has a doctor, he or she will be a good source of a referral.

Recreation

Knowing where to play is just as important as settling down to work. Local newspapers will give you plenty of information about local events, nightclubs, movies, etc. The city or county parks and recreation office can provide good guides to their activities. Guidebooks are usually available to direct you to museums and other public facilities. Colleagues at work will be able to tell you about things to do in the area and which are the best restaurants.

Getting Around

One of the greatest challenges of relocation is simply learning your way around. A good street map is an absolute must. What it won't show you, though, are which streets are best during rush hour, where the shortcuts are, what are the most direct routes to take, and so on. You'll need to explore and make many wrong turns before you feel completely at home.

A New Lifestyle

Often, a relocation means adjusting to a different way of life. It could be that you're changing from a small town to a big city (or vice versa), from a coastal city to the mountains, from the Northeast to the South, or from the East Coast to the West Coast. The unaccustomed culture or lifestyle will be fun, but you'll also have some adjusting to do. It can be sort of like going to a foreign country but on a smaller scale. Don't fight the changes, but look at them as a new adventure and enjoy yourself.

Even though the newness is fun, making lots of changes and adjustments is always somewhat stressful. In fact, moving to a new city is one of the top stressors in life. Don't be surprised if, amidst all the excitement, you also feel a bit disoriented, anxious about your new surroundings, and maybe even a little homesick. It's normal and will pass.

For some people, it's not an easy adjustment at all. If you have never spent a lot of time away from home, have lived in one area all your life, or have never made a drastic change, you may feel homesick and alone. That's normal, too. Everybody handles relocating a little differently, so don't feel bad if it's rough for you—although it's important that you don't let that set you back. Quickly take steps to become more familiar with the area. Invite new acquaintances or colleagues to do something with you, and let them show you the best places to do it. Stay in touch with close friends and family to reduce homesickness. Reach out to people so you don't become lonely and depressed. Most of all, don't be afraid to say that you could use some help getting to know the area. Other people have been there before, and most will gladly help you.

IS THIS REALLY WHAT I WANT?

Making the job choice that starts your career is not easy, particularly if you tried hard to make a thoughtful decision. There are so many unknowns, and you probably weren't really sure what you wanted to be doing. Also, it's hard to understand a company very well after only a few days of interviews. Most graduates aren't totally sure of their choices when they make them and hope that, after starting the job, they'll find they made the right one. Surprise! It's the rare person who goes the entire first year without asking, "Is this really what I want to do?" There will be days when work isn't much fun, and you'll wonder why you ever took the job. There will be days you'll wish you were doing something different. There may even be days when you hate your job. When you're feeling disappointed or let down, you'll wonder if you're in the right place.

All of which is perfectly normal and to be expected. The biggest problem, in fact, is that you usually *don't* expect it. New hires often expect to love their job 100 percent and feel as if there's something wrong with periodically doubting their decision. That's not realistic. How could you possibly know for sure what you want to be doing when you've just finished college? Can you really expect never to question your decision? Of course not. And you'll have plenty of company, because all new hires do question their job decisions now and then.

In fact, everybody does it, experienced or not. It's actually healthy to quiz yourself periodically to see if you're really doing what you want to do with your life. As you advance in your career, you should be questioning yourself progressively, and the answers will change as you change.

So don't worry if you find yourself wondering about your job choice. It's normal. But I would discourage you from trying to answer that question until the first six months after training and preferably the first year. There's just too much change, learning, reality shock, culture shock, and general disorientation going on in that time to get a reliable answer. Give the job some time. Let yourself adjust and learn the job so you can make some real contributions. Ask all you want, but wait a while for the answer.

WHERE DID ALL MY FREE TIME GO?

It's an unfortunate fact that a professional career takes a lot of time and energy. When you're getting ready for work, commuting, working 8 to 10 hours per day, unwinding from work, and running a household, there isn't a great deal of free time left during the week. Throw in a few social events tied in with your job, some longer hours, and there's even less time. All those hours use up a lot of energy, so in the hours that are left, you don't feel like doing very much.

Most new hires experience some frustration at the loss of free time. It may not have felt like it at the time, but after you've been at work for a while you'll appreciate how much more free time you had while you were in college. Except for times like midterms or final exam week, there was usually time to go to the gym, see friends, go to a party, or just relax in your room. Not so in professional life, as this new hire explained:

THE ULTIMATE NEW EMPLOYEE SURVIVAL GUIDE

You wake up or look up from your desk one day and realize, gosh, I haven't been to the bank in a half a year, haven't seen the light of day, haven't taken a walk by myself. You haven't done anything for yourself, by yourself, because you've worked so hard during the week, especially those 70-hour weeks so common to a lot of projects. You almost kill yourself to have fun on the weekends so you won't feel burned-out on the weekdays. Then your time is gone, and you think, oh gosh, I haven't done anything for myself, I haven't taken care of myself.

Even in highly structured, even-paced jobs with regular hours, the free time just isn't there like it used to be. If you start a career with highly unpredictable hours such as consulting or if you work very long hours, you may feel as if you have no free time at all.

Making time for leisure in your life is critical. If you wait until you have nothing else to do, no other priority to address, and no other deadline to meet before you make time for yourself, it may never happen. You'll quickly discover that you have to work at scheduling free time. That sounds odd, I admit, but it's necessary. It's almost like making a date with yourself. If you don't, you may find yourself becoming a very unhappy person. Most people need at least some leisure time, particularly in the first year of work. Even when work is a high priority, a little free time is a must. And don't underestimate the difficulty of this adjustment.

LIVING FOR THE WEEKEND

Along with the professional reality of less free time comes the awareness that most of the free

time you get comes on the weekend. You'll soon learn why TGIF (Thank God It's Friday) is a popular refrain among working professionals. The pattern for most professionals is a week primarily occupied with work and the other business of professional life; most of their leisure activity takes place on the weekend. And even the most dedicated professionals do look forward to their weekends!

So your life becomes somewhat segmented—the weekend is your time, and the week is primarily for work. That's a very different routine from your college days. There, work and leisure were not so segmented, with both interspersed throughout the week. You might have had time to play tennis in the middle of the day or get together with friends in the late afternoon. But you also would spend weekend time in the library or studying in your room.

Having work separated from leisure time feels good at first because you can leave work at the office or at least set a quitting time. And weekends are often your own. But as you begin to miss the free time you used to have during the week, you find that you can't wait to get to the weekend.

That's a frustrating adjustment for many new hires. Nobody likes to wish his or her life away, but this is a reality of working life. In time you do get used to it and learn to make the most of your weekends. Of course, the other key is to be sure your work during the week is rewarding, so that you enjoy both your weeks and weekends.

WHERE HAVE ALL MY FRIENDS GONE?

You may not realize before you leave school what a great social life you have and how much it will change. Think about it. The whole time you are in school, you are surrounded by hundreds and maybe thousands of people approximately your own age. They are fun people, looking for good times just like you. They're all going through a similar experience and have similar schedules, and it's easy to find groups to do things with. On top of all that, the school is usually nice enough to provide lots of built-in activities, so your social life almost creates itself. There are dances, concerts, parties, clubs, the student center, special weekend events, etc. School is really a great place to have lots of fun. One of the biggest complaints of most new hires is how much their social life changes after entering the workforce. Since most of them are single, this is a really tough adjustment.

Let's look at some of the big changes:

1. **Everybody at work is older than you are.** Gone are those hundreds or thousands of people your own age. Even in the largest companies, you are likely to be one of only a few people your age placed in your department and may even be the only young person. Suddenly you're spending your days with people of many different ages instead of just your age. A great many of them will be much older than you.

2. **And their interests are all different.** Most of the people will be married and many will have children. You won't find them thinking about dates or getting groups together to do things. It's not that they're boring but just that interests change as people get older and have families.

3. **There's not the same "party feel."** While school is more than just a party, a lot of attention is certainly paid to parties, both

in and out of class. At some schools, social life pretty well dominates the thinking. Not so at work. People are busy and spend lots of time at work *working*. They have many other things to think about besides partying.

4. **There's not as much time.** It's funny how 45- to 60-hour weeks plus commuting time can cut the guts right out of a social life. You might have been busy in college, but there was still a lot of free time for your social life. Even when you were busy, you usually had enough control over the hours to make a social life work. The time just doesn't come as easy on the job. It's hard to meet new people.

5. **Meeting new people can be hard.** Many new graduates relocate to towns and cities where they just don't know many people. Meeting people is not the easiest thing for most of us. But if you don't know many people, there aren't many people your age at work, and you don't have much free time, it can be especially tough to make new acquaintances.

All of this means that a social life won't just fall into place now as it did in college. For the first time in four years, you will have to work at it. Months go by, maybe six months or more. Suddenly you realize that your social life's not happening, and you're feeling lonely and isolated. You realize you aren't having the fun you used to, you aren't seeing your friends very often, and you're starting to feel a little depressed about it. It's only then that you fully realize that your social life really does change. Even if you move back to the area where you grew up, you find that the old friendships you had before college just aren't the same anymore. Socializing now requires a new and different approach.

FEAR OF FAILING

Going to work is a challenge. Most people, if they're honest with you, experience some performance anxiety when they start a new job. It's only natural for you to be a bit anxious about whether you can handle the new challenges, whether you'll be accepted, and how you'll stack up against your colleagues. Not only are such feelings natural, they are helpful, too, because they keep you motivated and sharp. If there wasn't a challenge, you'd be bored. If you're a little worried at first and lose a little sleep, don't let it bother you. In time you'll find that you have met the early challenges, and you'll have grown in confidence as a result.

However, for some new hires, that natural anxiety becomes a real fear of failure. That's not good, as it usually interferes with their work performance and their enjoyment of life. If your anxiety begins to paralyze you so that you can't work well or it affects your health, you may need some counseling to help you through it.

It may reassure you to know that it's rare for an employer to hire someone who doesn't have the ability to be at least an average performer. That means the odds of your failing are pretty small. It's hard for a company to predict to what level of success you will rise, but their assessment process is good enough to know that you won't fall flat on your face.

It's also too early in your career to be consumed by anxiety over the level of success you'll attain. You should be more concerned about becoming a professional and doing the best job you can possibly do today, not about climbing the ladder. There's plenty of time to worry about that later. It's human to think about it, but don't be consumed by it. You can succeed if you work at it. Use your anxiety to keep you motivated, but keep it in perspective.

BURNING OUT

Ambitious professionals who enjoy professional work and care about their careers are prone to burn themselves out. While each person's limits may be different, the human mind and body do have their limits. Most of us like to think that we have limitless physical and creative energy, with no bounds to our capacity for work. If you haven't already found out, you'll soon discover that it's not true. Burnout is the point at which you've passed your limit and can no longer work as productively, creatively, or efficiently as you normally do. It's your body's way of telling you to take a break, recharge your batteries, and take a little time for yourself. It's important that you learn what your personal limits are and recognize the cues that tell you you may be approaching burnout.

Burnout comes in long- and short-term varieties. One year is not enough time in which to experience long-term burnout, but you can encounter the short-term variety. What usually happens to new professionals is that they are so charged up and anxious to make a good impression that they do nothing but work for the first few months. Those that do find themselves "hitting a wall" after about six months—they're exhausted, find it hard to get excited about work, and think a lot about taking time off. That's short-term burnout.

You should be ready for this drop in energy. I won't tell you to avoid it, because, frankly, if you're not tired after the first six months, you're probably not working hard enough at learning the job. The breaking-in process takes a lot of energy, so you ought to need rest or at least to slow down a little. The important thing is that you heed the warning signs and take some kind of respite from work. This could be a long weekend, a week off, a trip back to campus, or even just a week of non-thinking work. Talk to your boss if necessary; most will understand. The first few months are a fast sprint, and you'll need to stop and catch your breath.

In the longer term, you need to learn to pace yourself and balance your life to avoid burnout. New professionals, as we've said, tend to work at high energy levels and put a lot into the work. Most new hires whom I've known have experienced some kind of burnout before they realized that professional life is a long-term thing, not a sprint. You can't always work at top speed, nor can you work all the time. With a healthy balance of work and leisure and a pace that allows for some downtime occasionally, you can avoid crippling burnout. Remember that burnout can make you totally ineffective and unproductive. Think about how that would affect your career. Work hard, but save a little for tomorrow, too.

WHEN SHOULD I MOVE ON?

Nowhere is it written that your first job is going to be perfect for you. Throughout this book,

we've been talking about making your expectations more realistic and accepting the realities of professional working life. You've learned that many of the things you might have been unhappy about are really just part of the working world. I've stressed the importance of learning how to adapt to the job and being prepared to accept many things about it that may not be quite as good as you hoped. The reason for this approach is the overwhelming evidence that a great many recent graduates become disenchanted with their new jobs because what they wanted and expected was simply not realistic.

You may now have the impression that if you are not happy, it's because the job is fine but you're not. You may believe mistakenly that my blanket advice to all new hires is to stay in the first job no matter what, changing and adapting until you fit. That's not true. I strongly believe that people should be in a job that gives them plenty of satisfaction. We know that not everyone is good for every job, and vice versa. In *The MBA's Guide to Career Planning* (Peterson's Guides, 1989), I devote quite a bit of attention to finding which career you are best suited for and forging a job match that will satisfy you.

There are a variety of situations in which I would recommend that you quit your first job and move on to another. The most common of these occurs when you simply have picked the wrong job or career because you did not assess yourself and/or the job or career path well. This happens all the time. The telltale sign is when you find yourself not wanting to go to work in the morning and not enjoying yourself, even when you've adjusted your expectations. There is only so much adapting and adjusting people can do before it begins to go against the basic elements of their personality and interests. It could be that the organization's culture is wrong, the job is wrong, or the career path is wrong. Whatever the reason, if you really are in the wrong place, it's time to reconsider.

Fast-Starter Tip

There's no disgrace in admitting a mistake in choosing your first job.

If you think this may be the case, keep in mind that a new hire's basic tendency is to expect too much from the company and expect it too soon. Shock, surprise, and frustration are normal. You'll find warts on every company. That's not a good reason to leave; rather, it calls for appropriate adaptations on your part. After double-checking that this or the other "facts of life" covered in this book are not the cause of your problems, then perhaps you've made a genuine mistake and it's time to leave.

You shouldn't be afraid to quit nor should you feel like a failure if you do. As one insightful second-year professional commented:

Don't be discouraged or feel bad about yourself if you find out that what you were hired to do is not what you want to do. It's better to say, "This isn't for me" than to try and fit yourself as a round peg into a square hole.

Most professionals do change jobs several times throughout their careers. In the final analysis, you have to do the things that will make you happy in the long run.

It's still advisable to stay with the company for at least a year, perhaps two if possible.

At one time, there was a real stigma attached to those who changed jobs too quickly (so-called "job-hoppers"), but even that is changing. There's a line in an old Kenny Rogers song about playing a poker hand, where he says, "You have to know when to hold 'em and know when to fold 'em." I would suggest that there aren't many companies where you couldn't get some benefit and experience out of a year's employment. So it's best to hold on to your hand and stick with the job for a while to see what you might gain from it. But if you get an opportunity for a better fit before a year is up and you know that you've made a mistake where you are, you'd be foolish not to fold your hand and leave while the leaving is good.

There's such a delicate balance between leaving for the right reasons and leaving for the wrong reasons that it's difficult to get it right. After reading this book, you'll have to trust that you can recognize the difference between the dissatisfaction that comes from youthful naivete and having your bubble burst and the other sort that comes from your gut and tells you there is some fundamental mismatch. Talk it over with a trusted confidant who's old enough to have been through it. Don't rely too much on your friends, because they haven't had enough experience. Talk to your parents, your college's alumni placement officer, or perhaps your coach at work. Don't be quick to quit, but when the time is right, don't be afraid to do it either. You owe it to yourself to do what you feel is right. Be sure, though, that the next time, you spend lots of time on your career planning so you can make a better choice.

There's another situation where quitting may be in order. Suppose you've made a real mess of your first year. As a result, you can see that you are being labeled unfavorably by your colleagues and employer and that your fellow new hires are making much better progress than you: In short, you have been detoured off the success spiral. If this is the case, you may be better off quitting and getting a fresh start elsewhere. As one manager advised:

Once you've gotten off to a really bad start, it's very difficult to get back on track within the same organization. It will take several years and maybe working for a new division or new part of the business to prove yourself to somebody else. When you mess up, that reputation follows you. As a matter of fact, you have little choice but to leave and get another job.

It's unlikely that you should want to leave for this reason during your first year, but during your second year, leaving to make a new start in another job is reasonable. You can usually recover fairly quickly from a few bad months (perhaps six), but there does come a point at which it's better to leave than to spend years trying to undo the damage you've done in the first twelve to eighteen months. It's simply easier to start fresh than to undo a bad reputation. Talk candidly to your employer to see if it's possible to get a fresh start within the company, but if it's not, be prepared to leave. And if you do leave for this reason, be sure you learn from your experiences.

It's always good to step back at the end of the first year and assess what's happened. Consider these things:

- Are the job and employer meeting your needs?
- If not, can you see that they will in the near future?

- Is this the right cultural fit for you?
- Is this the type of career you want?
- What have you learned during the year?
- Where can you go from here?
- Do you have any better alternatives?

Your career is a journey. You'll grow and change throughout your life. It's good to reassess and recheck to be sure you're doing what's good for you. In the final analysis, all that really matters in your career is that it's satisfying to you. If it's not or the fit is not right, it's OK to leave.

COPING STRATEGIES

The first year is clearly a time of great change, personal decision, adjustment, and hard work. The result is usually an increased level of stress and strain, in both your personal and your professional life. It's not an unmanageable amount, but it can become a real problem if you don't take some steps to cope with it. There are very real issues, anxieties, concerns, and fears in most people's minds. They're all very normal, but you still need to cope with them. In this chapter, some personal coping strategies will be discussed.

SIGNALS OF PENDING PROBLEMS

Professional life can be very demanding, especially in the first year. The pace is often hectic, the pressure high, and the lifestyle sedentary. The first year is not too early to learn that you have to take active steps to manage the stress and strain or they will eventually hurt you. The damage can be in the form of a physical disorder such as disease or heart attacks, emotional illness such as depression or unhappiness, addictive behaviors such as alcoholism or drug abuse, or relationship problems such as loneliness or failed marriages. That's not to say the stress of professional life *will* lead to severe problems, but it can and often does if you don't learn to manage it. The first step is deciding that it is your responsibility to take charge of it and that it will not take care of itself. Then you need to start learning good habits while you are young.

The next step is to pay attention to yourself and learn to read your personal indicators of physical and mental health. That means you have to believe you deserve to feel good and healthy and deserve to treat yourself well. Men are notoriously bad about not doing this. Pay attention to what your body tells you. Watch for these kinds of signs:

Physical

- Higher rate of illness
- Extreme fatigue
- Stress-related problems such as ulcers, cold sores, or psoriasis
- Higher incidence of injury or "aches and pains"
- Significant change in physical appearance such as weight gain
- Significant change in appetite

Emotional

- Depression or listlessness
- Unhappiness
- Declining motivation

- Volatile temper
- Relationship problems

These are but a few indicators of how your body and mind begin to signal you that something is wrong. Don't wait until the signals are so strong that real damage is done or you can't ignore them. Practice stepping back and taking a check of yourself periodically to see if you need to make changes or find strategies to cope with the stress and strains of work.

STRESS MANAGEMENT

Stress from the job is the biggest problem you'll encounter. Most new hires go through an adjustment period during which the stress is quite high at first. Learning to cope with it may take months. While college had its exams and tests, most new professionals conclude that work is more stressful. In addition, the stresses are different from those to which you've been accustomed. You shouldn't be surprised if managing your job stress becomes a problem and an important priority for you.

Stress usually sneaks up on you. You'll probably go to work and be so excited, work so hard, and focus so much on your new career for the first two to six months that you won't be too aware of it. But then all of a sudden, you begin to notice that you're overstressed. The signs that stress was building up were there all along, but you didn't notice them until the stress had reached the point at which you needed to do something about it quickly. One symptom is the short-term burnout discussed earlier.

Many books have been written on stress management, and a few of them are referenced in the appendix at the back of this book. Here are a few basics for a successful stress management program:

1. **Setting priorities.** Learn to set priorities at work. You can never accomplish everything. The secret is not to continue to work harder but to work smarter. Figure out what tasks are most important to your career and to the organization, and focus on those.

2. **Time management and organization.** Learn to use your time wisely and effectively, and much stress will be reduced. Also, learn to organize your work and workday well.

3. **Finding ways to relax and have fun.** Make sure you pursue activities outside work for pure pleasure and personal enjoyment. Whether it's hobbies, activities, or parties, do something to relax.

4. **Exercise.** It has been widely proved that exercise is an extremely effective stress reducer. Not only does it help you work off the day's stress, but also it promotes general good health. Healthy people can also handle stress better.

5. **Making time for yourself.** Even in your first year when you must focus hard on the job, you need to make some time to take care of yourself, too. That means not only the physical time used in doing things for yourself but the mental space to think about them, also. It doesn't hurt to pamper yourself in this way.

6. **Transition time.** Allow yourself time at the end of your workday to make the transition from your professional style and pace to your personal life. You'll find it's not like turning off a light switch. Most people need some time at the end of the day to decompress. Allowing for that time is important, particularly if you're married.

7. **Sense of humor.** There are moments when you just need to laugh at yourself and the situation a little. Sure, your career is serious business, but there is such a thing as too much sobriety. Retain the ability to laugh, especially when under pressure. You'll feel better for it, and others will like you better, too.

8. **Discarding perfectionism.** You're not perfect nor will you ever be. Trying to be perfect and perform perfectly will drive you to your grave. It's great to set high standards but realize that everybody makes mistakes and has a few weaknesses.

9. **Setting realistic goals.** Goals should make you stretch some, but they should be realistic and attainable. Set them too high, and you only doom yourself to frustration and failure.

10. **Good nutrition.** It's widely known that well-balanced meals and good nutrition are critical to managing stress. Single professionals are especially prone to not pay attention to their diet. Learn what to eat, how to cook, and make time to do it.

Stress is often spoken of in a negative context. But stress is an ever-present fact of life. In and of itself, it's neither good nor bad. It's how you handle it that makes it work for or against you. Sure, it can get to be more than anybody can handle, but most of the stress problems professionals encounter are self-induced, either by their work habits or by their failure to manage stress properly. Some stress is actually good for you, since it motivates you and gets your adrenaline running. As a professional, you'll need to learn to manage your stress for your personal well-being.

THIS TOO SHALL PASS

When your only experience with the professional world is what you are seeing in your first year, it's hard to believe that things will change in the future. Your head may understand it, but your heart says, "No, I don't want to do this the rest of my life," or "This is too much work to master," or whatever the fear is. Emotionally, it's hard to look beyond where you are while it's happening.

But your first year is not forever. It really does get better, and it really is different later on. First of all, you learn and grow and therefore, your job becomes easier. You also adjust and adapt to the new situation. At first it's uncomfortable, perhaps, because it's unfamiliar. That's intimidating. In time you get used to it and adapt.

Nobody goes into an entry-level job wanting to stay in it for a whole career. Entry-level jobs are just starting points, and your first year is not your entire career. As you progress beyond the entry-level job, you'll get more responsibility and do more fun things. You'll be more accepted and feel more at home.

Don't panic. Look beyond the first year and your immediate situation. The odds are that this, too, shall pass.

FINDING THE RIGHT BALANCE

The previous sections have focused on short-term measures for coping with the stress of your transition to professional life. There's a bigger question underlying all this that you'll start to answer in your first year and will continue to answer throughout your life. That is, "What priority will work have in my life?"

Every person has to search for a suitable balance between work and personal activities. The balance you choose will probably be different from what works for me. And that's fine. There is no right formula but only what fits you best and makes you comfortable. It's up to you to choose. What can be said is that most professionals who achieve a reasonably high degree of financial success and advance in their careers to a reasonably high level of authority or stature have placed a high priority on work. Generally, a lower priority on work will decrease your chances for this type of success.

Defining Success

But there are so many other types of success. There's success with people, there's success with family, with helping others, and with a job well done. We often hold up financial success as the only legitimate definition of success, but that's not really the case. There's plenty of room for you to decide what your personal definition will be. Most people soon discover it's hard to have it all, though. You can't be an enormous financial success, devote lots of time to your family, be active in civic organizations, and have time for all your hobbies and golf, too. Life is a series of trade-offs, choices, and priority setting. There's nothing wrong with trying to have all you can, but most people realize they need a balance.

The sentiments that follow are those of senior managers, and they are typical.

We don't want somebody who works 7 a.m. to 10 p.m. every day. There's more to life than that, and you're a happy employee when you're doing other things you need to be doing such as spending time with family, friends, hobbies, and activities. Be willing to work hard when that's what it takes. But don't feel guilty when you don't work hard, especially if you're getting the job done.

Nobody can really work 18 hours a day all the time. So, are you playing any tennis? Are you running at night? Your mind needs to have a break. When you go home at night, after dinner take an hour and just walk around your neighborhood or watch TV or just let your mind go.

Fast-Starter Tip

You are free to choose your own definition of success.

In fact, you can be quite comfortable financially yet still have time for other things. Or you might decide you don't want much money but prefer a lot of free time. Or perhaps career success is most important to you, and you'll sacrifice other things. The choice is very much yours, and it's one you'll make continually and probably change periodically throughout your life. Most people need a balance between their personal and professional lives.

While the overachieving workaholics are legendary, most successful professionals find they need to make room for other parts of life, too. They work hard, probably harder than normal, but they also make time for themselves and their families. Some degree of moderation seems to work best over the long term.

Implications for New Professionals

For the new professional, the implications of this are several. First, most are surprised and frustrated by the many trade-offs they have to make. They're surprised at how much of their life their career consumes and how their personal life is limited. They're used to having more leisure time, so they aren't skilled at making the choices and trade-offs. That's stressful.

They're also thrust into a situation that most professionals know very well—having to make short-term sacrifices for long-term gain. In fact, the quantity of work in one's life balance rarely stays the same. It usually shifts back and forth between too much, just the right amount, and too little. There are times, such as your first year on the job, when your life balance really won't be much of a balance at all but rather heavily weighted toward work. That's normal. New hires are surprised by this. Many are dismayed to find themselves working so hard their first year probably because that's all they know, and they project that lack of balance onto their entire career. The imbalance is usually just short-term, and that's quite appropriate.

It's important that you do several things during your first year. First, you'll need to start thinking about what balance you really want in your life. Do you want to be on the fast track? If so, are you willing to make the sacrifices needed to achieve the successes? What else is important to you in your life? What are your priorities? How do you define success? You'll have to start making choices in your career sooner than you think, so you need to anticipate them and start sorting out your priorities early.

I still say, though, that your priority during your first year should be your job. Even if you really want a more balanced life, your first year at work is so important that it needs your greatest attention. It takes lots of effort and time to launch your career well. After a fast start, you can always choose to slow down, but it's very difficult to speed up after a slow start. By focusing hard early in your career and tolerating what may be an imbalance for you, you give yourself the flexibility to make whatever choice you want later. Early in your career, you're not likely to know what life balance you really want, so why eliminate options? You'll need to work at keeping some degree of balance your first year just to keep your sanity, but don't worry if you're spending a lot of time on work. It's worth it.

Choosing your life balance is a very important decision. I don't know whether people ever know for sure if they have made the right choices, at least not until they have the benefit of hindsight. But there's room in the world for every type of balance, so the choice is yours. Be sure you understand the risks and consequences of each decision you make.

PERSONAL SUPPORT NETWORKS

One of the interesting reactions in the new-hire focus groups I conducted was how much they enjoyed having the chance to talk about the issues related to their transition from student to professional and their frustrations and concerns. Those chances don't usually arise at work. Many of the issues are not ones you want to share over the water cooler with your boss or even your fellow new hires. Yet, if you're struggling, unsure, or worried, you need to talk to people. Otherwise, you'll just carry it bottled up inside you, feeling isolated and alone. Personal support networks are important aids to keep those fears and anxieties from growing and overwhelming you.

Fellow new hires are a natural choice since they are going through the same experience as you and will quickly understand your problems. They're also easily accessible. For the most part, they're a good choice. The sense of shared experience and support is great and can be very helpful. They do understand what you're going through and will often band together to support you. "A lot of times, the new hires don't talk to each other. They are so proud that if they are having problems, they aren't going to tell their peers," observed one manager.

But you do need to be a little careful. Just because fellow new hires are in the same position as you doesn't mean you should trust them too much. Things said in confidence can get out and come back to haunt you. Also, there is a tendency in some organizations for new hires to become quite competitive with each other late in their first year. They have been known to use whatever they can to gain an advantage. You needn't be cynical about them, but a little caution is well advised.

That means you'll still need someone with whom you can really open up. Outside friends are a must. Probably the best choice is other new professionals (or people not very far past that stage) who have no connection with your company. They'll understand your problems and dilemmas but have no conflict of interest. They can see things more objectively, and you don't have to worry that what you say might be used against you or be heard by the wrong person. You should make an effort to find friends of this type and not rely too heavily on your friends at work.

Let's not forget the coach you've found at work. If you've found a good one, you have a great resource when you're in trouble. People who take on this role are usually quite good about keeping what you say in confidence. Since they're well beyond you in tenure and status, they have no need to use what you say against you, and they're probably not interested anyway. Yet being inside your company, they understand the people and situations and thus can give insightful advice. They've probably helped others a few times before, too.

You'll need more than just professional support though. Family and friends are so important at any difficult time. Even if they don't or can't understand the particulars of your situation, they can listen and they probably understand you pretty well. Their messages of "You're OK" and "We love you" can be a big help during rough times when you doubt yourself. Don't get too isolated from them.

There's nothing wrong with turning to a professional counselor either. New-job stress is not insignificant for some people, and reaching for a helping hand from a professional is not silly. An employment or career counselor would be best if the issues are professional ones. A personal counselor might be appropriate if the issues are coping with the anxiety, stress, and uncertainty.

Support groups that deal with the transition to work specifically are hard to find, but there are surrogates. You might take a course in stress management, professional-image management, or time management, for example. There's a certain amount of support that comes from sharing "war stories" with people in a class. These skill-specific types of classes are great if you need help in only one area. When combined, they can give you a surprising amount of support.

Professional groups give you an opportunity to meet with other young professionals in your area. Civic groups (whose members are usually professionals), a professional group in your field, or a young professionals' networking group can be useful. Whatever the type, being among and around other professionals gives you a sense of common experience and lends perspective to your situation. While you will not want to talk in too much detail, you'll probably get some good general advice.

Your personnel office can also be a big help. One of the roles of the personnel office is to be a confidential third party in order to give employees an outlet. Many of the issues you'll deal with are perfectly OK to discuss with your personnel representative. Of course, not all are: for example, don't tell them you're thinking of leaving!

Many firms also offer employee assistance programs with a confidential system to refer you to counseling services, usually outside the company. These programs are designed to help employees deal with personal problems, no questions asked. Don't be afraid to use them.

The bottom line is this—if you need some help, ask for it. There's nothing to be ashamed of if you're struggling with making this transition. Everybody has some concerns and uncertainties, and if they tell you differently, they're lying. Some people truly have a very hard time with it. There's no shame in seeking help, only in not seeking it.

ULTIMATE SURVIVAL TIPS

1. For many new professionals, there are significant personal transitions to make.

2. It is very common for new professionals to have some difficulty adapting to the new way of life.

3. Give yourself time to adjust and learn what the personal side of life as a working professional is all about.

4. Personal time will not be as plentiful as it was in college.

5. While your personal life may get less attention than it used to, you can't ignore it. It is important, too.

6. Your first job does not have to be your last job. Make changes, if necessary, after giving it a fair shot.

EPILOGUE

Many people who reviewed this book or discussed it with me have said, "I only wish I had had someone to tell me these things when I started my career." The book's message has struck a very personal chord, especially in older readers, because all of us made many mistakes during our transition from college to career, and either personally or professionally we suffered for them. I hope the advice offered here can keep you from the same stumbling, uncertain, and frustrating beginning to your career.

It's always a challenge to break new ground, and this book has done just that. Though much has been written on the subject in academic journals, amazingly little has been published for those who need it most: college graduates. I believe this book goes a long way toward meeting that need.

If you have gotten no other message, I hope you have begun to appreciate the importance of treating your first year on the job as a special time requiring special steps. The full significance of this may not yet be clear, but it will be in time.

And so, as you become a professional, my sincere hope is that my book will help you to make a great start in creating the kind of life and the happiness you deserve. Best wishes for a wonderful career!

Ed Holton

Index

PETERSON'S GUIDES AND PETERSON'S ONLINE WORK TOGETHER TO SERVE YOU BETTER!

When you want to make the most out of your career, Peterson's guides and Peterson's online are your partners for success!

Portfolio Power
Learn to create a dynamic portfolio to use to search for a job, change careers, negotiate promotions, or market a business.
ISBN 761-4, $14.95 pb (with CD)/$20.95 CAN

Personal Job Power
Discover strategies to develop and use your personal power to advance, survive, and thrive in today's uncertain business world.
ISBN 599-9, $12.95 pb/$17.95 CAN

Getting It Done
Follow a groundbreaking eight-step model to help you gain focus, improve work habits and creativity, and reduce stress.
ISBN 705-3, $14.95 pb/$20.95 CAN

Compact Guide to Graduate Schools in the U.S. 1998
Find the facts on 767 institutions in the U.S. that have been identified by the Carnegie Foundation for the Advancement of Teaching as meriting a Master's II or higher classification.
ISBN 765-7, $24.95 pb/$34.95 CAN

Guide to Distance Learning Programs 1998
Find the right distance learning program through over 1,000 degree and certificate programs available from nearly 900 accredited colleges in the U.S. and Canada.
ISBN 875-0, $26.95 pb/$37.95 CAN